330
/Beg

D1347027

Foundations of Economics

Second Edition

David Begg
Stanley Fischer
Rudiger Dornbusch

Mc Graw Hill **Education**

London · Boston · Burr Ridge, IL
Dubuque, IA · Madison, WI · New York
San Francisco · St Louis · Bangkok
Bogotá · Caracas · Kuala Lumpur
Lisbon · Madrid · Mexico City
Milan · Montreal · New Delhi
Santiago · Seoul · Singapore
Sydney · Taipei · Toronto

Foundations of Economics, Second Edition
David Begg, Stanley Fischer, Rudiger Dornbusch
ISBN: 0-07-709985-0

Education

Published by McGraw-Hill Education
Shoppenhangers Road
Maidenhead
Berkshire
SL6 2QL
Telephone: 44 (0) 1628 502 500
Fax: 44 (0) 1628 770 224
Website: www.mcgraw-hill.co.uk

British Library Cataloguing in Publication Data
A catalogue record for this book is available from the British Library

Library of Congress Cataloging in Publication Data
The Library of Congress data for this book has been applied for from the Library of Congress

Acquisitions Editor: Julian Partridge
Senior Development Editor: Caroline Howell
Editorial Assistant: Sarah Butler
Senior Marketing Manager: Petra Skytte
Senior Production Manager: Max Elvey
New Media Developer: Douglas Greenwood

Produced for McGraw-Hill by Steven Gardiner Ltd, Cambridge
Text Design by Steven Gardiner Ltd
Cover design by Fielding Design Ltd
Printed and bound in Great Britain by the Bath Press

Brief contents

Contents

Preface

Useful foundations need to be reliably up to the job, help you understand the rest of your life, and fun enough to make you want to bother.

Foundations of Economics is specially designed for students studying introductory economics in a single term or semester. The book streamlines the argument that make its parent text *Economics*, seventh edition the 'student's bible' for economics (BBC Radio 4).

Foundations of Economics covers only the core topics but trains students to think for themselves, using a wide range of data and examples, and offers authoritative commentary on topical issues.

Learning by doing

Few people practise for a driving test just by reading a book. There is no substitute for finding out whether you can actually do a hill start. We give you lots of examples and real-world applications in order to help you master economics for yourself. Try to do the examples at the end of every chapter, and compare your answers with those we give at the end of the book.

Don't read on 'cruise control', highlighting a few sentences and gliding through paragraphs that we worked hard to simplify. Active learning is much more efficient. When the text says 'clearly', ask yourself 'why' it is clear. See if you can construct your own diagrams before you look at ours.

To assist you in working through the text, we have developed a number of distinctive features. To familiarise yourself with these features, please turn to the Guided tour on pages xiv–xv.

Online Learning Centre

A range of supplementary teaching and learning resources has been developed to accompany the new edition and are available on the Online Learning Centre website for the textbook.

For lecturers:
- *Twelve chapter-by-chapter Lecture Presentations* summarise the key concepts from each chapter, for use as presentations in lectures and seminars or as student handouts.
- *Chapter-by-chapter Lecturer Manual* offers a synopsis of each chapter and

teaching suggestions for presenting the material from the book in a one-semester module.

■ **600 Test Questions in a Test Bank platform**, to create tests, assessments and exams based on the textbook.

■ **All figures from the text** available to download, to enable lecturers to manipulate, print and present the graphs and diagrams to students.

For students:

■ **Twelve chapter-by chapter Student Tests** enable students to test their understanding of each chapter online.

■ **Case Studies and Applications** provide contemporary examples demonstrating economics in action.

■ **Web links and further reading resources** allow students to research companies, government, and academic sources and journals online.

■ **Glossary of key terms:** a complete glossary of economics terms and definitions to aid revision of the important ideas and concepts.

To access these resources and further updates, visit the Online Learning Centre website at:
www.mcgraw-hill.co.uk/textbooks/begg

Key changes to the second edition

The second edition has been completely rewritten to meet the needs of today's busy students, on whom the pressures are ever greater.

■ **Slimline text of only 300 pages** With a lot to learn in a short time, students need a short and clear text, and rely on the authors to select material that merits inclusion in a foundations book.

■ **Complete answers to all questions** It is frustrating to attempt problems but then be unable to confirm whether the answers are correct. The second edition provides complete answers to every question.

■ **Online Learning Centre** providing a range of new lecturer and student resources to accompany the book at www.mcgraw-hill.co.uk/textbooks/begg.

■ **New section on globalisation** We continue to make sure that the text deals with topical issues, such as the demise of Railtrack and the launch of the euro. Globalisation is such a big issue we have created an entirely new section, which concludes the book.

Guided tour

Section opening page
sets the scene for each
area of study, providing a
brief introduction to the
topics covered.

Learning outcomes
present the key
concepts that you
should understand
when you have finished
this chapter section.

3

Costs, supply and perfect competition

3-1 How costs affect supply

Learning outcomes

By the end of this section, you should understand:

- Technology and production techniques
- How input prices affect the choice of technique
- Total, average and marginal cost
- Returns to scale and average cost curves
- Fixed and variable factors in the short run
- The law of diminishing returns
- A firm's supply decision, in the short run and long run
- Temporary shutdown and permanent exit

The last chapter introduced the bare
bones of a theory of supply, which
depended on both costs and revenue.
Now we need to put more flesh on this
theory. This chapter and the next deal
with two ideas. First, adjusting production methods takes time. Given time,
firms may be able to reduce costs by
choosing more appropriate methods
of production. Second, the revenue
obtained from selling any particular
output depends on the extent of competition in that market. This chapter
deals with the limiting case of perfect
competition. Chapter 4 examines the
consequences of less competitive
situations.

New companies, such as Orange and
Amazon, lost a lot of money before
eventually starting to make profits. And
existing companies, such as British
Airways and British Telecom, made big
losses in the cyclical downturn of
2001–02, despite previous periods of
healthy profits. Thus, firms don't always
close down when they are losing money.
They may keep going because they
expect demand to rise or costs to fall. We
need to distinguish between the short-
run and the long-run supply decisions of
firms. In the short run, a firm can't fully
adjust to new information. In the long
run, full adjustment is possible. In this
section, we focus on how costs affect

Key terms are highlighted where they first appear in the text, so that you can note the new term and the definition that accompanies it.

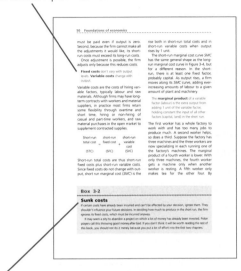

Boxes provide examples, illuminating ideas and theories presented within the chapter and offering an insight into how economics applies to the real world.

Tables and figures are presented in a simple and clear design to help you understand key economic models and to absorb relevant data.

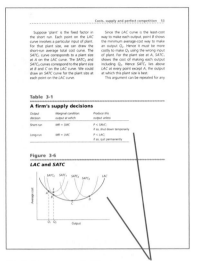

Recaps sum up the ideas that have been discussed in each chapter, reviewing the concepts and topics that you should now comprehend.

Review questions provide questions and problems to test your understanding of the material. Solutions to exercises are available at the end of the text so you can check your progress.

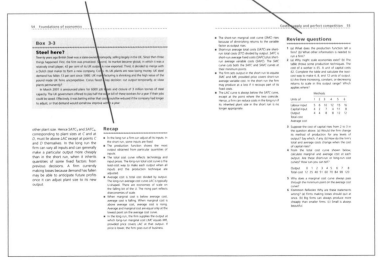

Acknowledgements

The publishers would like to thank the following reviewers who provided their comments and suggestions for developing the new edition of this book:

Bob Arnot, Glasgow Caledonian University

David Barlow, University of Newcastle upon Tyne

Douglas Chalmers, Glasgow Caledonian University

Vince Fitzsimons, University of Huddersfield

Barry Harrison, Nottingham Trent University

Harry Hiller, University of Middlesex

Jesper Jespersen, University of Roskilde, Denmark

Debra Johnson, University of Hull

James Johnston, University of Paisley

Adrian Kay, University of Glamorgan

Nat Levy, University of Middlesex

Margaret O'Quigley, University of East Anglia

Haiyan Song, University of Surrey

We would also like to thank all contributors to the Online Learning Centre website resources, in particular, Richard Godfrey of the University of Wales Institute, Cardiff, for the creation of student and lecturer test questions.

Every effort has been made to to trace and acknowledge ownership of copyright and to clear permission for material reproduced in this book. The publishers will be pleased to make suitable arrangements to clear permission with any copyright holders whom it has not been possible to contact.

What is economics?

1-1 What economists study

Learning outcomes

By the end of this section, you should understand:
- That economics is the study of scarcity
- How opportunity cost reflects scarcity
- How society rations scarce goods and services
- Pros and cons of relying on the market
- Positive and normative economics
- Microeconomics and macroeconomics

Economics is much too interesting to be left to professional economists. It affects almost everything we do, not merely at work or in the shops but in the home and the voting booth. It influences how well we look after our planet, the future we leave for our children, the extent to which we can care for the disadvantaged, and the resources we have for enjoying ourselves.

These issues are discussed daily, in bars and buses as well as cabinet meetings and boardrooms. The formal study of economics is exciting because it introduces a toolkit that allows a better understanding of the problems we face. Everyone knows a smoky engine is a bad sign, but sometimes only a trained mechanic can give the right advice on how to fix it.

This book is designed to teach you the toolkit and give you practice in using it. Nobody carries a huge toolbox very far. Like Swiss army knives, useful toolkits are small enough to be portable but have enough proven tools to deal both with routine problems and nasty surprises. With practice, you will be surprised at how much economic analysis can illuminate daily living.

Every group of people must solve three basic problems: what goods and services to make, how to make them and who gets them.

Economics is the study of how society decides what, how and for whom to produce.

Goods are physical commodities such as steel and strawberries. Services are activities such as massages or live concerts, consumed or enjoyed only at the instant they are produced.

Society has to resolve the conflict between people's limitless desires for goods and services, and the scarcity of resources (labour, machinery, raw materials) with which goods and services are made. Economics is the analysis of these decisions. Its subject matter is human behaviour, and its method is to develop theories and test them against the facts.

You can afford the necessities of life – food, shelter, health, education – and some extras, such as travel and entertainment. You are richer than some people but poorer than others. Income distribution across people is closely linked to the what, how and for whom questions. Table 1-1 shows income per person in different countries. In poor countries, average income per person is only £280 a year. In the rich industrial countries, income per person is £18 340 a year, nearly 70 times larger. For whom does the world economy produce? Mainly, for the 15 per cent of its people in the rich industrial countries. What is produced? What people in those countries want.

Why are there big differences in incomes between groups? This reflects how goods are made. Poor countries have little machinery, and their people have less access to health and education. Workers in poor countries are less productive because they work in less favourable conditions.

Income is unequally distributed within each country as well as between countries. The degree to which income is unequally distributed affects what goods and services are produced. In Brazil, where income is unequally distributed, many people work as domestic servants, chauffeurs and maids. In egalitarian Denmark, few people can afford to hire servants.

Scarcity and opportunity cost

Economics is the study of scarcity. When something is so abundantly available that we get all we want, we do not waste time worrying about what, how and for whom it should be produced. In the Sahara, there is no need to worry about the production of sand.

Table 1-1

World population and income, 2000

	Country group		
	Poor	Middle	Rich
Income per head (£)	280	1310	18 340
% of world population	40	45	15
% of world income	3	18	79

Source: World Bank, World Development Report

Box 1-1

At your service

In developed countries, agriculture is 2 per cent of national output, industry only about 30 per cent and the rest is services. Services include banking, travel, communications, tourism, entertainment; and public services (defence, education, health). Next time you hear complaints about the loss of jobs in manufacturing, remember it is less than a quarter of national output, and still in trend decline. Most output is services, and this sector's share of national output continues to grow.

% of national output	Japan	France	UK
Agriculture	2	2	2
Industry	38	27	30
Services	60	71	68

Source: World Bank, *World Development Report*

Box 1-2

Scarcely a hospital bed

Real, inflation-adjusted, government spending on health rose by one third in the 1990s. So why did people think health services were being cut? First, we are all living longer. Older people need more health care, so the same total spending means lower standards per person. Second, medical advances have led to successful but very expensive treatments. Making these available to some people reduces the resources left for others.

Health spending had risen with national income. However, with an ageing population, health spending must rise *faster* than national income if people are to get the same standard of care as in the past. And to get every new treatment, however expensive, health spending has to rise *much faster* still. Unless taxes rise a lot, people will still feel their health care is inadequate.

The real issue is *scarcity*, on what taxes to spend our limited resources. Do we have fewer teachers and televisions in order to pay taxes and divert more resources to health? If not, we can't avoid rationing health care. This rationing can be done through markets (charging for health care so people choose to have less) or through rules (limiting access to treatment). Society's decision affects what is produced, how it is produced, and, dramatically in this example, for whom it is produced.

For a **scarce resource**, the quantity demanded at a zero price would exceed the available supply.

When resources are scarce, society can get *more* of some things only by having *less* of other things. We must *choose* *between* different outcomes, or make trade offs between them.

The **opportunity cost** of a good is the quantity of *other* goods sacrificed to get another unit of *this* good.

Governments may make these tough

choices, but markets also play a key role.

The role of the market

A **market** uses prices to reconcile decisions about consumption and production.

Markets and prices are one way society can decide what, how and for whom to produce. During the British beef crisis, caused by fears about mad cow disease, pork prices rose 30 per cent while beef prices fell. This provided the incentive to expand pig farming, and stopped too many shoppers switching to pork until the new piglets were ready for market.

How might resources be allocated if markets did not exist?

In a **command economy** government planners decide what, how and for whom goods and services are made. Households, firms and workers are then told what to do.

Central planning is complicated. No country has ever made all decisions by central command. However, in China, Cuba and the former Soviet bloc, there used to be a lot of central direction and planning. The state owned land and factories, and made key decisions about what people should consume, how goods should be made and how much people should work.

Imagine that you had to run the city where you live. Think of the food, clothing and housing allocation decisions you would have to make. How would you decide how things were made, and who got what? These decisions are being made every day in your own city, but chiefly through the mechanism of markets and prices.

The opposite extreme from central planning is a reliance on markets in which prices can freely adjust. In 1776, Adam Smith's *The Wealth of Nations* argued that people pursuing their self-interest would be led 'as by an invisible hand' to do things in the interest of society as a whole.

In a **free market economy**, prices adjust to reconcile desires and scarcity.

Hoping to become a millionaire, you invent the DVD. Although motivated by self-interest, you make society better off by creating new jobs and using existing

Figure 1-1

Market orientation

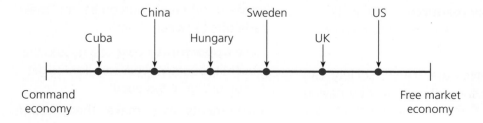

resources more productively. In a free market, people pursue their self-interest without government restrictions. A command economy allows little individual economic freedom, since decisions are taken by the state. Between these extremes is the mixed economy.

In a **mixed economy**, the government and private sector interact in solving economic problems.

The government affects economic activity by taxation, subsidies and the provision of services such as defence and the police force. It also regulates the extent to which individuals may pursue their own self-interest. All countries are mixed economies. Some are close to command economies, others are much nearer the free market economy, as Figure 1-1 shows.

Positive and normative

Positive economics deals with scientific explanation of how the economy works. **Normative economics** offers recommendations based on personal value judgements.

Positive economics aims to explain how the economy works, and thus how it will respond to changes. It formulates and tests propositions of the form: if this is changed then that will happen. In this sense, positive economics is like natural sciences such as physics, geology or astronomy.

When a good is taxed, its price will rise. Many propositions in positive economics command general agreement among professional economists. As in any science, there are some unresolved

Box 1-3

Poor marx for central planners

During 1989–91, the Soviet bloc abandoned Marxist central planning and began transition to a market economy. The Soviet bloc grew rapidly before the 1970s, but then stagnated. Economic failure brought down the Berlin Wall. Key difficulties that emerged were:

■ **Information Overload** Planners could not keep track of all the details of economic activity. Machinery rusted because nobody came to pick it up, crops rotted because storage and distribution were not co-ordinated.

■ **Bad Incentives** Complete job security undermined work incentives. Since planners could monitor quantity more easily than quality, firms met output targets by skimping on quality. Without environmental standards, firms polluted at will. Central planning led to low-quality goods and an environmental disaster.

■ **Insufficient Competition** Planners believed big was beautiful. One tractor factory served the Soviets from the Latvia to Vladivostok. But large scale deprived planners of information from competing firms, making it hard to assess managerial efficiency. Similarly, without electoral competition, it was impossible to sack governments making economic mistakes.

questions where disagreement remains. Research in progress will resolve some of these issues, but new issues will arise, providing scope for further research.

Normative economics is based on subjective value judgements, not on the search for any objective truth. Should resources be switched from health to education? The answer is a subjective value judgement, based on the feelings of the person making the statement. Economics cannot show that health is more or less desirable than education. However, it may be able to answer the positive question of what quantity of extra health could be achieved by giving up a particular quantity of education.

Micro and macro

Economics has many branches. Labour economics deals with employment and wages, urban economics with housing and transport, monetary economics with interest rates and exchange rates. However, a different classification cuts across these branches.

> **Microeconomics** makes a detailed study of individual decisions about particular commodities.

For example, we can study why individual households prefer cars to bicycles and how firms decide whether to make cars or bicycles. Comparing the markets for cars and for bicycles, we can study the relative price of cars and bicycles, and the relative output of these two goods.

However, in studying the *whole* economy, such detailed analysis gets too complicated to keep track of the behaviour in which we were interested.

We need to simplify to keep the analysis manageable, but not distort reality too much. Microeconomics offers a detailed treatment of one aspect of economic behaviour but ignores interactions with the rest of the economy in order to keep the analysis manageable. However, if the indirect effects are too important to be swept under the carpet, another simplification must be found.

> **Macroeconomics** analyses interactions in the economy as a whole.

It deliberately simplifies the individual building blocks of the analysis in order to retain a manageable analysis of the whole economic system. Macroeconomists do not divide consumer goods into cars, bicycles, televisions, and calculators. Rather, they study a single bundle called 'consumer goods' in order to focus on the interaction between household shopping sprees and firms' decisions about building new factories.

Recap

- Economics analyses what, how and for whom society produces. The central economic problem is to reconcile the conflict between people's unlimited wants and society's limited ability to make goods and services to meet these demands.
- Industrial countries rely extensively on markets to allocate resources. The market uses prices to co-ordinate production and consumption decisions.
- In a command economy, central planners decide what, how and for whom things are produced.
- Modern economies are mixed, relying mainly on the market but with a large dose of government intervention. The optimal level of intervention is still debated.
- Positive economics studies how the economy actually behaves. Normative economics makes prescriptions about what should be done.
- Microeconomics gives a detailed analysis of particular activities. To simplify, it may neglect some interactions with the rest of the economy. Macroeconomics focuses on these interactions but simplifies the individual building blocks.

Review questions

1 How are the problems, what, how and for whom, settled within your own family?
2 Which of the following are scarce? (a) Water in the desert. (b) Water in a rainforest. (c) Economics textbooks. (d) Hours a day for work, rest and play.
3 An economy has 5 workers. Each worker can make 4 cakes or 3 shirts. (a) How many cakes can society get if it does without shirts? (b) How many shirts can it get if it does without cakes? (c) What is the opportunity cost of making a shirt?
4 Which of the following statements are positive and which are normative? (a) Taxing cigarettes reduces the quantity sold. (b) Cigarettes should be highly taxed. (c) Brits earn more than Jamaicans. (d) Jamaicans should work harder. (e) All Africans earn high salaries.
6 Society abolishes higher education. Students have to find jobs immediately. If there are no jobs available, how do wages and prices adjust so those who want jobs can find them?
6 *Common fallacies* Why are these statements wrong? (a) Since some economists are Tory but others Labour, economics can justify anything. (b) There is no such thing as a free lunch. To get more of one thing you have to give up something else.

Answers on pages 278–90

1-2 How economists think

Learning outcomes

By the end of this section, you should understand:

- Why theories deliberately simplify reality
- Nominal and real variables
- How to build a simple theoretical model
- How to interpret scatter diagrams
- How 'other things equal' lets key influences be ignored but not forgotten

It is more fun to play tennis if you can serve, and cutting trees is easier with a chain saw. Every activity or academic discipline has a basic set of tools, which may be tangible, like the dentist's drill, or intangible, like the ability to serve in tennis. To analyse economic issues we use both models and data.

A **model** or **theory** makes assumptions from which it deduces how people behave. It deliberately simplifies reality.

Models omit some details of the real world in order to focus on the essentials.

An economist uses a model as a traveller uses a map. A map of London omits traffic lights and roundabouts, but you get a good picture of the best route to take. This simplified picture is easy to follow, yet provides a good guide to actual behaviour.

Data are pieces of evidence about economic behaviour.

The data or facts interact with models in two ways. First, the data help us quantify theoretical relationships. To choose the best route we need some facts about where delays may occur. The model is useful because it tells us which facts to collect. Bridges are more likely to be congested than six-lane motorways.

Second, the data help us to test our models. Like all careful scientists, economists must check that their theories square with the relevant facts. The crucial word is relevant. For several decades the number of Scottish dysentery deaths was closely related to the UK inflation rate. But this was a coincidence, not the key to a theory of inflation. Without any logical underpinning, the empirical connection was bound to break down sooner or later. Paying attention to a freak relationship in the data increases neither our economic understanding nor our ability to predict the future.

Economic data

To gather evidence, we can study changes over time, or changes across groups or regions at the same point in time. Table 1-2 shows a *cross-section* of unemployment rates in different countries in 2001, and Table 1-3 shows a *time-series* of UK house prices between 1960 and 2000.

The average price of a new house rose from £2500 in 1960 to £124 700 in 2000. Are houses really 50 times as expensive as in 1960? Not once we allow for inflation, which also raised incomes and the ability to buy houses.

> **Nominal values** are measured in the prices at the time of measurement. **Real values** adjust nominal values for changes in the general price level.

In the UK, the retail price index (RPI) measures the price of a basket of goods bought by a typical household. Inflation caused a big rise in the RPI during 1960–2000. The third row of Table 1.3 calculates an index of real house prices, expressed in 2000 prices.

> An **index number** expresses data relative to a given base value.

For house prices in 1960, we take the nominal price of £2500 and multiply by [100/(7.4)] to allow for changes in the retail price index during 1960–2000, yielding £33 800. Comparing 1960 and 2000 but allowing for inflation, real house prices quadrupled, from £33 800 to £124 700. Most of the rise in nominal house prices in the top row of Table 1-3 was actually due to inflation.

Table 1-2

Unemployment by country, 2001
(% of labour force)

US	Japan	Germany	France	UK
4.2	4.6	6.9	8.8	5.4

Source: OECD, *Economic Outlook*

Economic models

After a career in business, you become head of the London Underground. The Tube is losing money. You want to change the level of fares to get more revenue. Revenue is $P \times Q$, where P is the Tube fare and Q the number of passengers. You can set the fare,

Table 1-3

UK house prices
(average price of a new house)

	1960	1980	2000
House price (£000s)	2.5	27.2	124.7
RPI (2000 = 100)	7.4	39.3	100.0
Real price of houses (2000 £000s)	33.8	69.2	124.7

Source: ONS, *Economic Trends*

Box 1-4

Millionaires galore

One in every 500 adults in Britain is now a millionaire. The Lottery created only a handful of Britain's 85 000 millionaires. It's mainly just the effect of inflation. The table below shows how much an old-fashioned millionaire would be worth at today's prices. Being a millionaire gets easier all the time.

£1 million in prices of year:	1988	1978	1968	1948	1938
= £ millions at 2000 prices	2	4	11	22	43

Sources: ONS, *Economic Trends*; UN, *Economic Surveys of Europe*

but what determines the number of passengers?

The number of passengers will fall if the Tube fare is higher, but will rise if passengers have more income to spend. You now have a bare-bones model of the demand for Tube journeys. They depend on Tube fares and income.

Higher Tube fares *add* directly to revenue, by raising P and hence revenue per passenger, but also *reduce* revenue by reducing Q as fewer people take the Tube. Theory alone cannot tell you the best fare to maximize $P \times Q$. The answer depends on how much Q falls when you raise P.

Some empirical research may establish the facts. Experimental sciences, including many branches of physics and chemistry, conduct controlled experiments in a laboratory, varying one input at a time while holding constant all the other relevant inputs. However, like astronomy and medicine, economics is primarily a non-experimental science. Astronomers can't suspend planetary motion to study the Earth in isolation, and doctors rarely poison people just to see what happens. Similarly, economists do not create 50 per

cent unemployment to see if wages will then fall.

Most economic data is collected while many of the relevant factors are simultaneously changing. We need to disentangle their separate influences. To make a start, we can pick out two of the variables in which we are interested, pretending the other variables remain constant.

A **scatter diagram** plots pairs of values simultaneously observed for two different variables.

Figure 1-2 measures the Tube fare on the horizontal axis, and Tube revenue on the vertical axis and plots a scatter diagram in which each point represents a different year. It is pretty clear that years of low fares are also years of low revenue.

Through the scatter of points, Figure 1-2 draws a line in the position that best fits the points, showing the *average* relation between fares and revenue during the period. It seems that higher fares *cause* higher revenue, but we should not jump to conclusions. Incomes also rose a lot, and our theory tells us that

Figure 1-2

Tube fares and revenues

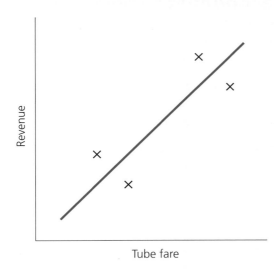

Figure 1-3

How income affects tube passengers

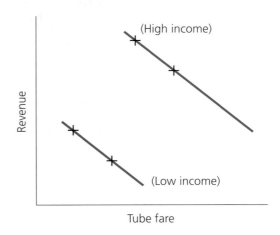

higher incomes let people afford to use the Tube more.

Other things equal

When one 'output' is affected by many 'inputs' we can always draw a two-dimensional diagram relating the output to *one* of the inputs, treating the other inputs as given. Moving along this line shows how the highlighted input affects the output. However, if any *other* input changes, we need to show this as a shift in the relationship between output and our highlighted input.

> **Other things equal** is a device for looking at the relation between two variables, but remembering other variables also matter.

Figure 1-2 can be interpreted as saying that higher Tube fares cause higher revenue only if no other important input to the passenger decision was changing. Since income rose significantly, we need to redraw the diagram.

Figure 1-3 replots Figure 1-2 to take account of changing income, a change in one of the 'other things equal' implicitly assumed when drawing a diagram relating revenue only to tube fares. We now draw one line corresponding to points when income was high, and another line through points when income was low.

In this example, replotting the diagram reverses our previous conclusion. Other things equal, higher tube fares *reduce* revenue. In Figure 1-2 this effect was obscured by the simultaneous effect of rising income.

Box 1-5

Get a Becker view: use an economist's spectacles

Can an economist's tools be applied to other social behaviour? To crime? To marriage? To drug use? Chicago economist Gary Becker won the Nobel Prize for Economics for applying the logic of economic incentives to other facets of human behaviour. Some examples of Becker in action . . .

Divorce: 'We should replace judicial determination with marriage contracts that specify, among other things, the financial and child custodial terms of a divorce. Marriage contracts would become much more common if we set aside the legal tradition that they are not unenforceable.'

Drugs: Prohibition of alcohol gave the US Al Capone but failed to stop drinking. The end of Prohibition 'was a confession that the US experiment in banning drinking had failed dismally. It was not an expression of support for heavy drinking or alcoholism'. Becker's solution for drugs is the same – legalise, boost government tax revenue, protect minors, and cut out organised crime's monopoly on supply.

UK policing has begun to stop arresting people smoking cannabis in public, switching police resources into the combat of hard drugs like cocaine and heroin. UK cannabis seizures in 2000 were only half those of 1997. As supply rose, the price on the street slumped.

In 2002 the UK government began to decriminalise soft drugs. Perhaps they will eventually be legalised. With 1500 tonnes consumed annually in the UK, an excise duty of £3 a gram would raise up to £5 billion a year in tax revenue. It would also reduce the £1.4 billion currently spent enforcing anti-drugs laws, and the £1.5 billion cost of drug-related crime.

Sources: G. S. Becker and G. N. Becker, *The Economics of Life*, McGraw-Hill, 1997; *The Observer*, 8 July 2001

Recap

- A model is a deliberate simplification of reality.
- Data or facts suggest relationships to be explained. Having formulated theories, we use data to test our hypotheses and to quantify the effects implied.
- Index numbers express data relative to a base value. The retail price index is the average price of things bought by households. Inflation is the annual growth rate in the RPI.
- Nominal (current price) variables are valued at the prices when the variable was measured. Real (constant price) variables adjust nominal variables for changes over time in the general level of prices.
- Scatter diagrams plot the relation between two variables. A line through these points shows the average relationship, other things equal. If a relevant 'other thing' changes, we need to plot data separately for the different subperiods.

Review questions

1 The table below shows UK consumer spending and household income in £ billion at 1995 prices. (a) Plot a scatter diagram. (b) Draw a fitted line through these points. (c) Suggest a relation between consumption and household income.

	Income	Consumption
1993	476	434
1994	482	447
1995	495	454
1996	505	471
1997	525	489
1998	539	509
1999	550	530
2000	567	548

2 You are hired as a fancy consultant to advise on whether the level of crime is affected by the fraction of people unemployed. (a) How would you test this idea? What data would you want? (b) What other-things-equal problems would you bear in mind?

3 If economics can't conduct controlled laboratory experiments, can it be a science?

4 Use the data of Table 1-3 to plot a scatter diagram of the relation between nominal house prices and the retail price index. Does this diagram plot time-series data or cross-section data?

5 Suppose the average price of a new house was £30 000 in 1960, £60 000 in 1960, and £150 000 in 2000. (a) Construct an index of nominal house prices, setting the 1960 price equal to 100. (b) Now show an index treating the 2000 price as 100.

6 *Common fallacies* Why are these statements wrong? (a) The purpose of a theory is to let you ignore the facts. (b) People have feelings and act haphazardly. It is misguided to reduce their actions to scientific laws.

Answers on pages 278–90

1-3 How markets work

Learning outcomes

By the end of this section, you should understand:
- How prices reconcile demand and supply
- Equilibrium in a market
- Why demand and supply curves shift
- Price controls
- How markets resolve what, how and for whom things are produced

Some markets (shops, fruit stalls) physically bring together the buyer and seller. Other markets (the Stock Exchange) operate through intermediaries (stockbrokers) who transact business on behalf of clients. E-commerce is conducted on the Internet.

These markets perform the same economic function. Prices adjust to equate the quantity people wish to buy and the quantity people wish to sell. By making the price of a Jaguar ten times the price of a small Ford, the market ensures that output and sales of small Fords greatly exceed the output and sales of Jaguars. Prices guide society in choosing what, how and for whom to produce.

To model a typical market we need demand, the behaviour of buyers, and supply, the behaviour of sellers. Then we can study how a market works in practice.

Demand is the quantity buyers wish to purchase at each conceivable price.

Demand is not a particular quantity but a full description of the quantity buyers would purchase at each and every possible price. The line *DD* in Figure 1-4 shows the demand for chocolate. Even when chocolate is free, only a finite amount is wanted. People get sick from eating too much. As the price of chocolate rises, the quantity demanded falls, other things equal.

Supply is the quantity sellers wish to sell at each conceivable price.

Again, supply is a full description of the quantity that sellers would like to sell at each possible price. The line *SS* in Figure 1-4 shows how much sellers wish to sell at each price. Nobody would supply if they got a zero price. In our example, it takes a price of £0.10 before any

Figure 1-4

The market for chocolate

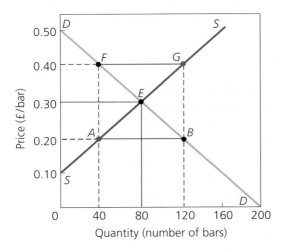

chocolate is supplied. At higher prices, it is more lucrative to supply chocolates. The quantity supplied rises.

> The **equilibrium price** clears the market for chocolate. It is the price at which the quantity supplied equals the quantity demanded.

In Figure 1-4 the equilibrium price is £0.30. At this price, 80 bars is the quantity buyers wish to buy and sellers wish to sell. At prices below £0.30, the quantity demanded exceeds the quantity supplied. There is a shortage, or excess demand, a shorthand for the more accurate statement 'the quantity demanded exceeds the quantity supplied *at this price*'.

Conversely, at any price above £0.30, the quantity supplied exceeds the quantity demanded. Sellers have unsold stock. To describe this surplus, economists use the shorthand excess supply, meaning

'excess quantity supplied at this price'. Only at £0.30, the equilibrium price, are quantity demanded and supplied the same. The market clears. People can buy or sell as much as they want at the equilibrium price.

Is the market automatically in equilibrium? Suppose the price is initially £0.40, above the equilibrium price. Producers wish to sell 120 bars. Sellers have to cut the price to clear their stock. Cutting the price has two effects. It raises the quantity demanded, and reduces the quantity supplied. Both effects reduce the excess supply. Price cutting continues until the equilibrium price of £0.30 is reached and excess supply is eliminated.

If the price is below the equilibrium price, the process works in reverse. At a price of £0.20, the quantity demanded is 120 bars but the quantity supplied is only 40 bars. Sellers run out of stock and charge higher prices. Prices rise until the equilibrium price is reached, excess demand is eliminated and the market clears.

Behind the demand curve

The demand curve shows the relation between price and quantity demanded, other things equal. Three 'other things' are relevant to demand curves: the price of related goods, the income of consumers (buyers) and consumer tastes or preferences.

The price of related goods

Higher bus fares may raise the quantity of Tube travel demanded at each possible price. In everyday language, buses are a substitute for the Tube. However, petrol and cars are not substitutes but complements. You cannot use a car without using fuel. A rise in the price of petrol tends to reduce the demand for cars.

> A rise in the price of one good raises the demand for **substitutes** for this good, but reduces the demand for **complements** to the good.

Most goods are substitutes for each other. Complementarity is usually a more specific feature (CD players and CDs, coffee and milk, shoes and shoelaces).

Consumer incomes

A second 'other thing equal' for a particular demand curve is consumer income. When incomes rise, the demand for most goods rises. Typically, consumers buy more of everything. However, there are exceptions.

> For a **normal good** demand rises when incomes rise. For an **inferior good** demand falls when incomes rise.

Most goods are normal goods. Inferior goods are cheap, low-quality goods that people would prefer not to buy if they could afford to spend a little more. Students buy cheap cuts of meat but move up to steaks when they get a good job.

Tastes

The third thing held constant along a particular demand curve is consumer tastes or preferences. In part, these are shaped by convenience, custom and social attitudes. The fashion for the mini-skirt reduced the demand for textile material. The emphasis on health and fitness has increased the demand for jogging equipment, health foods and sports facilities but reduced the demand for cream cakes, butter and cigarettes.

Shifts in the demand curve

Figure 1-4 drew the demand curve for chocolate bars for a given level of three other things: the price of related goods, incomes and tastes. Movements *along* the demand curve isolate the effects of chocolate prices on the quantity of chocolate demanded, other things equal. Changes in these other things *shift* the demand for chocolate. Figure 1-5 shows a shift in the demand curve from *DD* to *D'D'*. The entire demand curve shifts to the right. This changes the equilibrium in the chocolate market from *E* to *E'*. The

Figure 1-5

Ice cream prices and chocolate demand

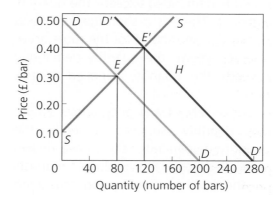

new equilibrium price is £0.40 and the new equilibrium quantity 120 bars.

When the demand curve shifts from *DD* to *D'D'*, there is initially an excess demand *EH*. This bids up prices until the new equilibrium at £0.40 is reached.

To sum up, the quantity demanded reflects four things: its own price, prices of related goods, incomes, and tastes. We could draw a two-dimensional diagram relating quantity demanded to any one of these four things. The other three would be the 'other things equal' for that diagram. In drawing demand curves, we choose the price of the commodity itself to put in the diagram with quantity demanded. The other three things become the 'other things equal' for a demand curve.

Why single out the price of the commodity itself to plot against quantity demanded? Because it shows the self-correcting mechanism by which a market reacts to excess demand or excess supply, by changing the price to restore equilibrium.

Behind the supply curve

There are also three 'other things equal' along a supply curve. These are technology available to producers, the cost of inputs (labour, machines, fuel and raw materials), and government regulation. Holding these three things constant, movements *along* a particular supply curve show the effect of prices on quantity supplied. A change in any of these 'other things equal' shifts the supply curve, changing the amount producers want to supply at each price.

Technology

Better technology shifts the supply curve to the right since producers supply more than before at each price. Better cocoa refining makes it possible to produce more chocolate for any given total cost. Faster shipping and better refrigeration lead to less wastage in spoiled cocoa beans. Technological advance enables firms to supply more at each price. As a determinant of supply, technology must be interpreted broadly. A technological advance is any idea that allows more output from the same inputs as before.

Input prices

A particular supply curve is also drawn for a given level of input prices. Lower input prices (lower wages, lower fuel costs) induce firms to supply more at each price, shifting the supply curve to the right. Higher input prices make production less attractive and shift the supply curve to the left.

Government regulation

Given a free choice, suppliers choose the lowest-cost production method from their viewpoint. If regulations make suppliers use a different production method, this must be more costly for suppliers. It shifts the supply curve to the left, reducing quantity supplied at each price. More stringent safety regulations prevent chocolate producers using the most productive process because it is dangerous to workers. Anti-pollution devices raise the cost of making cars. When regulation prevents producers

Box 1-6

Green piece

Our planet is running out of rain forests and fish stocks. Why do we manage the environment so badly? An economist's response is 'because we don't price it like other commodities'. The market 'solved' the problem of scarcity when OPEC restricted oil supplies. High prices induced more supply and less demand. Why not price the environment, encouraging people to look after it?

Until now, the reason has been technology. Anyone can walk in a field, dump rubbish after dark, pump chemicals into a river, or drive down a public street. Gradually, however, electronic monitoring of usage is getting easier and cheaper. It will then be possible to treat the environment as another commodity to be marketed. This will give rise to a vigorous debate about the 'what, how and for whom' questions.

We know how to charge cars for using a particular street at a particular time. A smart card in the car could pick up signals as it passed various charge points. The driver would get a monthly bill like an itemised phone bill. Rush-hour traffic would pay more when congestion was severe. The 'for whom' question could also be addressed. Residents could get a flat-rate annual payment, in exchange for supporting road pricing. Pricing the environment has a big advantage. It introduces a feedback mechanism, however crude, so that when society makes mistakes an alarm bell rings *automatically*. The price of scarce things rises.

from selecting the cheapest production method, regulation shifts the supply curve to the left.

Shifts in the supply curve

Along a given supply curve we hold constant technology, the prices of inputs and the extent of government regulation. An adverse change in any of these makes production more expensive. Figure 1-6 shows this as a shift to the left in the supply curve from *SS* to *S'S'*. Equilibrium shifts from *E* to *E'*. The equilibrium price *rises* but equilibrium quantity *falls*.

Conversely, a supply-curve shift to the right can be viewed as a shift from *S'S'* to *SS*. Equilibrium shifts from *E'* to *E*.

An increase in supply leads to a higher equilibrium quantity and lower equilibrium price.

Supply curve shifts make equilibrium price and equilibrium quantity move in *opposite* directions. Earlier we saw that demand-curve shifts make equilibrium price and equilibrium quantity move in the *same* direction. By noting what happens to equilibrium price and equilibrium quantity we can thus deduce whether it was the supply curve or the demand curve that shifted.

Price controls

Government actions may shift demand and supply curves. For example, tougher safety regulations raise producer costs

Figure 1-6

A reduction in supply

Quantity of chocolate

Figure 1-7

The effect of a price ceiling

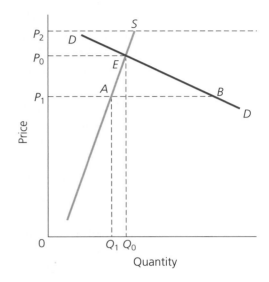

Quantity

and shift the supply curve to the left, affecting prices even though prices can adjust freely. Sometimes, the government also controls the price itself. Price controls may be floor prices (minimum prices) or ceiling prices (maximum prices).

> A **price control** is a government regulation to fix the price.

Price ceilings may be introduced when there is a sharp fall in supply. Wartime scarcity of food would mean high prices and hardship for the poor. Faced with a national food shortage, a government may impose a price ceiling on food so that poor people can afford some food.

Figure 1-7 shows this market. The supply curve is far to the left. The free market equilibrium price P_0 is very high. Instead of free market equilibrium at E, the government imposes a price ceiling at P_1. The

quantity sold is Q_1 and excess demand is AB.[1]

The ceiling price P_1 lets the poor buy food they could not otherwise have afforded, but reduces total food supplied from Q_0 to Q_1. With excess demand AB at the ceiling price, some form of rationing is needed to decide which potential buyers get supplied.

Rationing may be highly arbitrary. Food suppliers may reserve supplies for their friends, not necessarily the poor, or take bribes from those who can afford to pay to jump the queue: a 'black market'. Ceiling prices may be accompanied by government-organised rationing, to ensure that available supply is shared out fairly, independently of ability to pay.

1 A price ceiling at P_2 above the equilibrium price is irrelevant. Free market equilibrium at E can still be attained.

A ceiling price aims to reduce the price for consumers. Conversely, a floor price aims to raise the price for suppliers. A national minimum wage is a floor price for labour. Figure 1-8 shows the demand curve and supply curve for labour. The free market equilibrium is at E, at a wage W_0. A minimum wage below W_0 is irrelevant since the free market equilibrium can still be attained.

At a minimum wage W_1, firms demand Q_1 hours of work. There is excess supply AB. Any workers who can sell as much labour as they want are better off than before – their wage is higher – but some workers are worse off, since total hours worked fall from Q_0 to Q_1.

Many governments also set floor prices for agricultural products, and then buy up the excess supply unwanted by the private sector. European butter prices are set above the free-market equilibrium price as part of the Common Agricultural Policy. European governments have bought massive stocks of butter that otherwise would have been unsold at the control price. Hence the famous 'butter mountain'.

Figure 1-8

A minimum wage

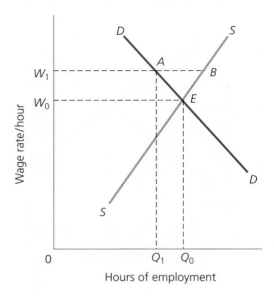

Recap

- Demand is the quantity that buyers wish to buy at each price. Other things equal, the lower the price, the higher the quantity demanded. Demand curves slope down.
- Supply is the quantity that sellers wish to sell at each price. Other things equal, the higher the price, the higher the quantity. Supply curves slope up.
- The market clears, or is in equilibrium, when the price equates the quantity supplied and the quantity demanded. At this point, supply and demand curves intersect. At prices below the equilibrium price, there is excess demand (shortage), which raises the price. At prices above the equilibrium price, there is excess supply (surplus), which reduces the price. In a free market, deviations from the equilibrium price are self-correcting.
- Along a given demand curve, the other things assumed equal are the prices of related goods, consumer incomes, and tastes or habits. Changes in these shift demand curves.
- Along a given supply curve, the other things assumed constant are technology, the price of inputs, and the degree of government regulation. Better technology, lower input prices, or less regulation increase the quantity supplied at each price.
- Any change inducing a rise in demand shifts the demand curve to the right, raising both equilibrium price and equilibrium quantity. Any change inducing higher supply shifts the supply curve to the right, raising equilibrium quantity but reducing equilibrium price.
- An effective price ceiling must lie below the free-market equilibrium price. It then reduces the quantity supplied, raises the quantity demanded and creates excess demand. An effective price floor must lie above the free-market equilibrium price. It then reduces the quantity demanded and raises the quantity supplied, creating excess supply. The government may buy up this excess supply.

Review questions

1 Given the data for toasters shown below, plot the supply curve and demand curve, and find the equilibrium price and quantity.

Price	10	12	14	16	18	20
Quantity demanded	10	9	8	7	6	5
supplied	3	4	5	6	7	8

2 What is the excess supply or demand when price is (a) £12? (b) £20?

3 What happens to the demand curve for toasters when the price of bread rises? Show in a supply–demand diagram how the equilibrium price and quantity of toasters change.

4 Cold weather makes it harder to catch fish. What happens to the supply curve for fish? What happens to equilibrium price and quantity?

5 You are a sheep farmer. Give three examples of a change that would reduce your supply of wool. Is a fall in the price of wool a valid example?

6 *Common fallacies* Why are these statements wrong? (a) Manchester United, being a more famous football club than Wrexham, will always find it easier to fill their stadium. (b) The European 'butter mountain' shows how productivity can be improved when farmers are inspired by the European ideal.

Answers on pages 278–90

2

Demand and supply decisions

2-1 Measuring demand responses

Learning outcomes

By the end of this section, you should understand:
- The price elasticity of demand
- The revenue effect of a price change
- Why bad harvests help farmers
- The cross-price elasticity of demand
- The income elasticity of demand
- Inferior, normal and luxury goods

Having examined what economics is and how markets work, we now study demand and supply in more detail. This helps us understand problems such as how sales managers decide what prices to charge, how governments decide what tax rates to set and how farmers respond to changes in weather conditions.

The price responsiveness of demand

A lower price P tends to raise the quantity demanded Q_D. The price elasticity of demand measures the *responsiveness* of quantity to price.

> **Price elasticity of demand** = **(% change in Q_D)/(% change in P)**

If a 1 per cent price rise reduces the quantity demanded by 2 per cent, the demand elasticity is $(-2)/(+1) = -2$. The minus sign tells us price and quantity change in *opposite* directions. Similarly, if a price fall of 4 per cent raises the quantity demanded by 2 per cent, the demand elasticity is $-1/2$, a quantity change of $+2$ per cent divided by the price change of -4 per cent.

Box 2-1

What determines demand elasticities?

The elasticity of demand depends on consumer taste. If everyone must have a mobile phone, higher phone prices have little effect on quantity demanded. If mobile phones are thought a frivolous luxury, the demand elasticity is much higher. Psychology and sociology explain why tastes are as they are. Taking these tastes as given, the easier it is to find a substitute that fulfils the same need, the higher is the demand elasticity.

If the price of *all* cigarettes rises, addicted smokers buy cigarettes anyway. However, if the price of a single brand of cigarettes rises, smokers switch to other brands to meet their nicotine habit. Thus, for a particular cigarette brand the demand elasticity is quite high, but for cigarettes as a whole it is low. The table confirms that narrowly defined commodities have a larger range of price elasticities of demand.

UK price elasticities of demand

Good (broad type)	Demand elasticity	Good (narrow type)	Demand elasticity
Fuel and light	−0.5	Dairy produce	−0.1
Food	−0.5	Bread and cereals	−0.2
Alcohol	−0.8	Entertainment	−1.4
Durables	−0.9	Expenditure abroad	−1.6
Services	−1.0	Catering	−2.6

Sources: J. Muellbauer, 'Testing the Barten Model of Household Composition Effects and the Cost of Children', *Economic Journal*, 1977; A. Deaton, 'The Measurement of Income and Price Elasticities', *European Economic Review*, 1975

Demand is **elastic** if the price elasticity is more negative than −1. Demand is **inelastic** if the price elasticity lies between −1 and 0. If the demand elasticity is exactly −1, demand is **unit-elastic**.

When demand is elastic, price changes have a big effect on quantity demanded. When demand is inelastic, price changes have a small effect on quantity demanded. But why do we care whether demand is elastic or inelastic? We look first at an example about farmers. Suppose a harvest failure reduces the crop supplied to market. Since the demand elasticity for food is low, harvest failures induce big rises in food prices. Conversely, bumper crops induce big falls in food prices.

Figure 2-1(a) shows the supply curve SS after a harvest failure, and the supply curve $S'S'$ after a bumper crop. The equilibrium price fluctuates between P_1 (harvest failure) and P_2 (bumper crop) with little fluctuation in quantities. Figure 2-1(b) shows the effect of similar supply shifts in a market with very elastic demand. Price fluctuations are smaller, but quantity fluctuations are larger. The demand elasticity tells us why some markets have volatile quantities but

Figure 2-1

The effect of demand elasticity on equilibrium price and quantity fluctuations

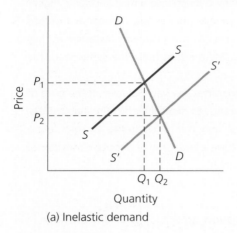

(a) Inelastic demand

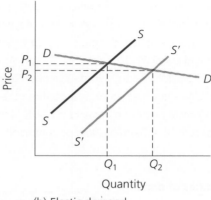

(b) Elastic demand

stable prices, while other markets have volatile prices but stable quantities.

Similarly, when Mercedes has 10 000 cars for sale but 20 000 customers eager to buy at the current price, knowing the price elasticity of demand for Mercedes cars lets its executives in Stuttgart work out how much they can raise the price while still selling all the cars that they have produced.

Price, quantity and revenue

Reducing the price P boosts the quantity demanded Q. The effect on sales revenue $P \times Q$ depends on how quantity responds to price cuts. When demand is elastic, quantity rises by more than the price falls, so revenue rises. When demand is inelastic, price cuts lower P

Table 2-1

Price changes, spending and revenue

Price	Stella			All beer	
P	Q	$P \times Q$		Q	$P \times Q$
2	2	10		30	60
1.5	10	15		32	48
1	20	20		34	34

more than they boost Q. Hence revenue falls.

In Table 2.1, demand for Stella Artois is elastic but demand for beer as a whole is inelastic. Falls in the price of Stella alone raise spending on Stella by increasing its sales a lot, whereas falls in the price of all beer reduce spending on beer.

Table 2-2 relates these results to demand elasticities.

By collectively restricting oil supplies, the oil-producers' organization OPEC made oil prices soar from $13/barrel in 1998 to $28/barrel in 2000. This raised oil producers' revenue since oil demand was *very* inelastic. Oil users had few alternatives to oil in the short run. Cuts in oil supply caused a big price rise and vast revenue gains for OPEC members.

Box 2-2 illustrates a general result. If demand is inelastic, farmers earn more revenue from a bad harvest than from a good one. The demand elasticity is low for many components of our staple diet, such as coffee, milk, bread, tea, and meat.

When demand is inelastic, suppliers *taken together* are better off if supply falls. However, if a fire destroys the crop of a single farmer, that farmer's revenue falls. Lower output from a single farm has almost no effect on supply. The market price is unaffected. The unlucky farm sells less output at the same price as before.

Table 2-2

Demand elasticities and spending changes

Change in total spending caused by	Price elasticity of demand		
	Elastic (e.g. −3)	Unit-elastic (−1)	Inelastic (e.g. −0.3)
Price rise	Fall	Unchanged	Rise
Price cut	Rise	Unchanged	Fall

Box 2-2

Why a bad harvest may be good news!

There's an awful lot of coffee in Brazil, which supplies a big share of the world market. In 1994 a frost in Brazil wrecked the 1995 harvest. Table 2-4 shows the effect on Brazilian exports. Coffee prices more than doubled in US dollars, because of the sharp drop in Brazilian exports supplying coffee to the world economy. What happened to Brazilian export revenue from coffee? It *increased* despite the 'bad' harvest and lower export quantities. The demand for coffee is inelastic.

Brazilian coffee exports 1993–95

		1993	1995
P:	Price (US cents/lb, 1995 prices)	90	210
Q:	Export quantity (1990 = 100)	113	85
P × *Q*:	Export revenue (*P* × *Q*)	10 200	17 900

Source: IMF, *International Financial Statistics*

The individual producer faces an elastic demand – consumers can switch to the output of similar farmers – even if the demand for the crop as a whole is very inelastic.

Short run and long run

In the *short run*, customers may be unable to adjust much to changes in prices. For example, when fuel prices rise, people still need to drive their cars and heat their houses, so there is little immediate change in the quantity of fuel demanded. However, as time passes, smaller cars can be designed and built, and people can move back into city centres to save commuting costs. In the *long run*, the demand for fuel is more elastic.

This result is very general. Even if addicted smokers can't quit when cigarette prices soar, fewer young people start smoking. In response to a price increase, quantity demanded gradually falls as time elapses.

The cross-price elasticity of demand

The price elasticity of demand tells us about movements along a given demand curve. It measures the response to a change in the price of the good itself. We can also ask how Q_A, the quantity demanded of good A, responds to changes in P_B, the price of *another* good.

> The **cross-price elasticity** of good A with respect to the price of good B is the percentage change in Q_A divided by the percentage change in P_B.

The cross price elasticity may be positive or negative. Suppose good A is tea and good B is coffee. A higher price of coffee makes people switch to tea. The cross price elasticity of tea with respect to coffee is positive. Cross price elasticities tend to be positive when two goods are substitutes, and negative when two goods are complements. A rise in the price of petrol reduces the demand for cars because petrol and cars are complements.

The effect of income on demand

Having studied changes in prices, we now study changes in income. For the moment we neglect saving, and assume higher income is all spent. This tends to raise the quantity demanded of most individual goods. However, quantities demanded do not all change by the same amount, so budget shares change with income.

> The **budget share** of a good is the spending on that good as a fraction of total consumer spending.

Table 2-3 shows the UK budget shares of food and services (personal and leisure activities such as eating out and going to the theatre) between 1991 and 2001. Real consumer spending rose over the period. The budget share of food fell, but budget share of services rose.

If the prices of all goods do not change, spending on a good changes only because quantity demanded changes. To show how sensitive quantity demand is to changes in income, we calculate the income elasticity of demand.

$$\text{Income elasticity of demand} = \frac{\text{percentage change in quantity demanded}}{\text{percentage change in income}}$$

The income elasticity of demand measures the effect on quantity demanded when incomes change but the prices of all goods are held constant.

The income elasticity of demand is positive for a **normal good**, but negative for an **inferior good**.

Thus, when income rises, the quantity demand rises for all normal goods. For the few exceptions called inferior goods, quantity demanded actually falls when income rises. Inferior goods are low-quality goods. Poor people buy fish fingers and polyester shirts. With more income, they buy seafood and comfortable cotton shirts. Higher income reduces the demand for fish fingers and polyester shirts.

We also distinguish luxury goods and necessities.

A **luxury good** has an income elasticity above 1. A **necessity** has an income elasticity below 1.

All inferior goods are necessities, since their income elasticities of demand are negative, and hence below 1. However, necessities also include normal goods whose income elasticity of demand lies between 0 and 1.

As income rises, the budget share of inferior goods falls: income rises but quantity demanded, and spending on the good, fall. Conversely, the budget share of luxuries rises when income rises. A 1 per cent rise in income raises quantity demanded (and hence spending on luxury goods) by over 1 per cent. Finally, higher income *reduces* the budget share of normal goods that are necessities. A 1 per cent rise in income raises quantity demanded by less than 1 per cent, so the budget share falls.

Luxury goods are high-quality goods for which there are lower-quality, but adequate, substitutes: Mercedes cars not small Fords, foreign not domestic holidays. Inferior goods are low-quality goods that people readily abandon as they get richer. Necessities that are normal goods lie between these two extremes. As incomes rise, the quantity of food demanded rises, but only a little.

Table 2-3 showed that services are luxuries whose budget share rose with

Table 2-3

Budget shares 1991–2001

| | Real consumer spending (2001 £bn) | % budget share | |
		Food	Services
1991	358	12	44
2001	589	10	49

Source: ONS, *UK National Accounts*

Table 2-4

Demand response to a 1 per cent rise in income

Good	Income elasticity	Quantity demanded	Budget share	Example
Normal	Positive	Rises		
Luxury	Above 1	Rises more than 1%	Rises	BMW
Necessity	Between 0 and 1	Rises less than 1%	Falls	Food
Inferior	Negative	Falls	Falls	Bread

UK income after 1991. Food is not a luxury; its budget share fell as income rose. Nor is it an inferior good. At constant prices that adjust for inflation, it happens that real food spending *rose* from £43 billion in 1991 to £59 billion in 2001.

Table 2-4 summarises the demand responses to higher income, holding constant the prices of all goods. Lower income has the opposite effect.

Income elasticities are vital to business and government in forecasting the changing pattern of consumer demand as the economy grows and people get richer. Suppose incomes grow at 3 per cent a year for the next five years. The demand for luxuries, such as restaurants, will rise strongly. In contrast, the demand for some necessities such as bread may hardly rise at all. The growth prospects of the two industries are very different.

Inflation and demand

Chapter 1 distinguished *nominal* variables, measured in prices at the time, and *real* variables, measured in constant prices to adjust for inflation. If all nominal variables double, every good costs twice as much, but all incomes are twice as high. Nothing has really changed. Quantities demanded are unaltered.

This does not contradict our analysis of price and income elasticities of demand. The former shows the effect of changing one price, holding constant other prices and nominal income. This is not relevant when all prices and incomes rise at the same rate. The latter shows the effect of higher real income. But real income does not change under pure inflation.

Recap

- The price elasticity of demand is the percentage change in quantity demanded divided by the percentage change in the price of that good. These elasticities are negative, since price rises cause quantity falls. Sometimes we omit the minus sign for brevity.

- Demand is elastic (inelastic) when the price elasticity is more (less) negative than −1.

- Price cuts raise (lower) total spending and producer revenue when demand is elastic (inelastic). Spending and revenue are unchanged if demand is unit-elastic.

- The income elasticity of demand shows the percentage change in quantity induced by a 1 per cent rise in income and total spending.

- Inferior goods have negative income elasticities; demand for them falls as income rises. Goods that are not inferior are normal goods, with positive income elasticities of demand.

- Luxury goods have an income elasticity above 1. Higher income increases their budget share, since demand for them rises strongly. Goods that are not luxuries are necessities, with income elasticities below 1. All inferior goods are necessities. Normal goods are necessities only if they are not luxuries.

- Doubling all nominal variables has no effect on demand since the real value of incomes and the real price of goods are unaltered.

Review questions

1 Your fruit stall has 100 ripe peaches that must be sold at once. Your supply curve of peaches is vertical. From past experience, 100 peaches are demanded if the price is £1. (a) Draw a supply and demand diagram, showing market equilibrium. (b) The demand elasticity is −0.5. You discover 10 of your peaches are rotten and can't be sold. Draw the new supply curve. What is the new equilibrium price?

2 Consider the following: (a) milk, dentistry, beer; (b) chocolate, chickens, train journeys; (c) theatre trips, tennis clubs, films. Rank (a), (b) and (c) from most elastic to least elastic demand. Then rank elasticities within each category. Explain your answer.

3 The table shows price and income elasticities. Identify each commodity as a luxury or necessity, and as having elastic or inelastic demand.

	Price elasticity	Income elasticity
Vegetables	−0.17	0.87
Catering	−2.61	1.64

4 Bread is an inferior good. Yet during 1975–2001 UK households' spending on bread and cereals rose from £1.5 million to over £5 million. How do you account for this?

5 Why is demand more elastic in the long run than in the short run?

6 *Common fallacies* Why are these statements wrong? (a) Because cigarettes are a necessity, tax revenue on cigarettes must rise when the tax rate is raised. (b) Farmers should insure against bad weather that might destroy half their crops. (c) Higher consumer incomes always benefit producers.

Answers on pages 278–90

2-2 Demand and consumer choice

Learning outcomes

By the end of this section, you should understand:
- Substitution and income effects
- Effects of real income changes
- Tastes and marginal utility
- Diminishing marginal utility
- The market demand curve

Measuring past behaviour is a good guide to the future when nothing dramatic changes. Sometimes, however, we need to think about what people might do in a future situation completely different from the past. To predict demand behaviour, we need a *theory* of how consumers make choices. A successful theory is consistent with past behaviour but also helps predict responses in new situations.

Effects of a price change: substitution and income effects

As the price of a good falls, people buy more of it. Demand curves slope down. Unfortunately, things are not this simple. Suppose the price of bread falls. For the rest of your life, you need to remember this has two quite different effects.

The **substitution effect** says that, when the relative price of a good falls, quantity demanded rises.

Your intuition will always discover the substitution effect, the bit that is obvious. You have to train yourself to look for, and find, the second effect.

The **income effect** says, for a given nominal income, a fall in the price of a good raises real income, affecting the demand for all goods.

If bread is a normal good, the demand for bread will rise when real income (spending power) rises. Both the income effect and the substitution effect raise the quantity of bread demanded when the price of bread falls. Bread is relatively cheaper so people buy more. Moreover, cheaper bread raises the purchasing power of the given nominal income; this also raises the demand for bread.

Hence, for normal goods, our theory says the demand curve must slope down. Price cuts lead to a higher quantity demanded. However, if bread were an inferior good, higher real income would lead to a *fall* in the quantity demanded. Now the income effect of a price cut would go in the opposite direction from the substitution effect. A fall in the price of bread makes it relatively cheaper, but also raises spending power. For inferior goods, theoretical reasoning alone cannot deduce which of the two effects is larger. We need empirical evidence to resolve the issue. In practice, demand curves for goods and services usually slope down. Inferior goods and services are rare.

In other markets, the 'perverse income effect' that outweighs the 'obvious substitution effect' is more common. Here is a quick taster of things to come. Higher interest rates increase incentives to save, don't they?

> **Saving** means not spending all today's income, reducing consumption today to raise consumption later.

Think of the interest rate as the price of time, the cost of consuming today instead of later. When the cost of consuming today rises, you choose less of it. Surely?

Your intuition has found the substitution effect. Consuming today has got relatively more costly, and you consume less, thus saving more. Where is the income effect lurking? To afford that foreign holiday next year, you do not have to save so much if interest rates are higher and your assets cumulate more quickly! This makes you save less. Empirically, it is very hard to find much

effect of interest rates on total saving. Politicians think higher interest rates boost saving, and are always devising schemes like PEPs and ISAs to provide tax breaks, hoping that higher after-tax interest rates will boost national saving. Economists are pessimistic that this will work. Much of it is just a subsidy to the rich, something to remember if you become Chancellor of the Exchequer!

Effects of income changes

Real income can rise either because nominal income increases while prices are constant, or because the price of a commodity falls while nominal income is constant. The former leads to a pure income effect, the latter must be decomposed into separate income and substitution effects.

Successive rises in real income lead to large increases in the quantity demanded if the good (or service) is a luxury with a large income elasticity of demand. Quantity demanded increases less quickly for normal goods or services with smaller, but still positive, income elasticities. For inferior goods with negative income elasticities, higher income reduces quantities demanded. Poor students give up beans on toast once they become rich bankers.

Tastes and demand

Different people may have different tastes, making different choices even when facing the same prices and enjoying the same income.

> **Tastes** describe the utility a consumer gets from the goods consumed. Utility is happiness or satisfaction.

Tastes depend on culture, history, familiarity, relationships with others, advertising, and so on. Explaining these influences is the role of other social sciences, like psychology and sociology. Economists treat them as an 'other things equal' assumption behind a particular demand curve.

However, tastes can change, with important effects. In the last few decades there have been big changes in social attitudes to organic food and the formality of dress. The demand curve for organic food shifted outwards, but the demand curve for top hats shifted inwards. We shift demand curves when there are changes in the 'other things equal'.

Marginal utility and demand

Fred goes clubbing and drinks lager. Initially, he goes to one club but has no lager. Fred is thirsty and can't enjoy himself. With a lager, he'd be a lot happier.

> The **marginal utility** of a good is the *extra* utility from consuming one more unit of the good, holding constant the quantity of other goods consumed.

Fred's first lager gives him high marginal utility. A second lager gives him extra utility, but not as much extra utility as the first one did. A third and fourth lager add less and less extra utility.

> Tastes display **diminishing marginal utility** from a good if each extra unit adds successively less to total utility when consumption of other goods remains constant.

Figure 2-2

Marginal utility and lager demand

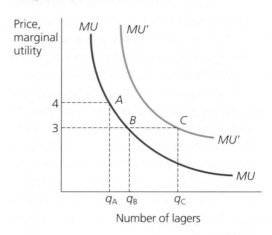

Number of lagers

Figure 2-2 shows Fred's marginal utility, which falls the more he drinks. It also shows the price of each lager. If a lager costs £4, and Fred gets £6 of marginal utility from it, he should buy another one. If he only gets £2 of marginal utility from his last lager, he has bought too many. He should buy lager up to the point the marginal cost (£4 for the last lager) equals the marginal benefit or marginal utility. Figure 2-2 shows Fred choosing point A when lagers cost £4 each.

Figure 2-2 suggests that if the price of lager falls from £4 to £3 Fred will definitely buy more lager because of diminishing marginal utility. But the figure only shows the substitution effect! The marginal utility curve assumes quantities of other goods remains constant. However, as the price of lager falls, Fred can afford more club nights too. Whether this shifts Fred's marginal

Box 2-3

To die for

Anna Kournikova's £7 million a year fees from advertising dwarf the Wimbledon prize money. Ruby Wax advertises the Vauxhall Corsa, Kim Basinger the Peugeot 406, and Thierry Henri the Renault Clio. Why do the manufacturers pay superfees to superstars to promote their wares? They are trying to change your tastes. There are lots of small cars, but only one has va-va-voom. It's the one to die for. No other will do.

    You could buy a car magazine and find out whether the Clio's suspension geometry really is different. But that's not the point. This advertising is about *style*. Not what you think is nice, but what *other people* think is nice. Renault is assuring you that other people, stylish people, think it's cool to drive a Clio. Do so and you can be cool too. This *interdependence* of tastes is what opens the door for so much advertising and PR.

Box 2-4

The water–diamond paradox

Here's a riddle for your friends who don't study economics. Why is the price of water, essential for survival, so much lower than the price of decorative diamonds? Diamonds are scarcer than water. Yet consumers clearly get more total utility from water, without which they die.

    Marginal utility solves the puzzle. The marginal benefit of the first unit of water is enormous. But we each consume lots of water. Since water is relatively abundant, the supply curve for water lies well to the right and the equilibrium price is low. Consumers have moved a long way down their marginal utility of water curve.

    If water is supplied free, consumers should use water up to the point where its marginal utility is zero. May as well wash the car again. Even a small rise in price may lead to a large cutback in usage – demand is very elastic in this region of the demand curve.

utility curve up or down depends on whether lager is a normal or an inferior good, which is the income effect at work.

If lager is a normal good, the income effect shifts the marginal utility curve outwards to MU' in Figure 2-2. This also makes Fred consume more lager (point C). Income and substitution effects go the same way. The demand curve for lager, drawn through A and C, slopes down. If lager was an inferior good, the MU curve might have shifted *inwards* enough to make Fred consume less lager when its price fell.

So far, marginal utility analysis merely reinforces our earlier and simpler discussion of income and substitution effects. However, it was worth learning, as Box 2-4 confirms.

From individual to market demand curve

How do we aggregate individual demand curves to get the total demand in a particular market?

> The **market demand curve** is the horizontal sum of individual demand curves in that market.

We always plot price on the vertical axis. All consumers in a market face the same price P. Suppose at a price of £2 the first consumer demands a quantity of A and the second consumer a quantity of B, the market demand is a quantity of $C = A+B$ when the price is £2. Repeating this procedure at each and every possible price we trace out the market demand curve. Figure 2-3 shows how two individual demand curves D_1 and D_2 are horizontally aggregated to get the market demand curve D.

The market demand curve is important because, together with the market supply curve, it determines the price that clears the market in equilibrium. Having seen how the individual demand decisions can be aggregated to derive the market demand curve, we turn next to a more detailed analysis of supply decisions.

Figure 2-3

The market demand curve

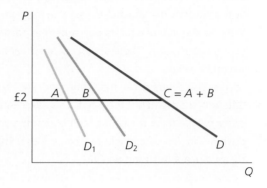

Recap

- A price change has a substitution (relative price) effect and an income (purchasing power) effect. Intuition usually locates the substitution effect. You must also find the income effect.
- Demand curves slope down for normal goods. A sufficiently inferior good could have an upward-sloping demand curve.
- Because of the income effect, higher interest rates need not encourage more saving.
- Higher incomes increase demand for normal goods and reduce demand for inferior goods.
- Marginal utility is the extra benefit of consuming the last unit of a good, holding constant consumption of other goods. Tastes display diminishing marginal utility. This explains both the water–diamond paradox.
- At each price, the market demand curve is the sum of the quantities demand by different people facing that price.

Review questions

1 Are these statements true? (a) A luxury good means demand is elastic. (b) An inferior good has a negative income elasticity. (c) Spending on inferior goods falls if the price rises.

2 'A higher wage raises labour supply by making work more attractive than leisure.' 'A higher wage makes people better off, raising the quantity of leisure demanded.' Which is the income effect and which is the substitution effect?

3 Suppose Glaswegians have a given income, and like weekend trips to the Highlands, a three-hour drive. (a) If the price of petrol doubles, what is the effect on the demand for trips to the Highlands? Discuss both income and substitution effects. (b) In a demand and supply diagram, what happens to the price of Highland hotel rooms?

4 Give three examples where your own utility depends only on the quantity of the good that you consume, and three cases in which your utility depends on the quantities someone else consumes.

5 Name a good for which your marginal utility falls so much that it not only reaches zero but becomes negative when you consume too much of this good.

6 *Common fallacies* Why are these statements wrong? (a) Inflation reduces demand since prices are higher and goods are more expensive. (b) Lower tax rates must increase the hours people choose to work, since take-home pay is higher.

Answers on pages 278–90

2-3 The supply decision

Learning outcomes

By the end of this section, you should understand:
■ Revenue, economic cost and economic profit
■ Stocks and flows
■ Whether profit maximisation is plausible
■ How a firm chooses the output to supply

We now turn to the theory of supply. How much do firms decide to make and offer for sale? For each possible output level, a firm compares what this output costs to make and what revenue it earned from sales. Profits are the excess of revenue over costs. Our theory of supply assumes each firm chooses output to maximise its profit.

A firm's accounts

Firms report two sets of accounts, one for stocks and one for flows.

> **Stocks** are measured at a point in time, **flows** are corresponding measures over a period of time.

The water flowing out of a tap is different per second and per minute. The measurement requires a time interval to make sense. The stock of water in the basin at any instant is a number of litres, and requires no time dimension. A firm reports profit-and-loss accounts per year (flow accounts) and a balance sheet showing assets and liabilities at a point in time (stock accounts). The two are related, as they are for the basin of water. The inflow from the tap is what changes the stock of water over time, even though the latter is only measured in litres at each point in time.

Flow accounts (profit and loss)

> A firm's **revenue** is income from sales during the period, its **costs** are expenses incurred in production and sales during the period, and its **profits** are the excess of revenue over costs.

This sounds very easy, but there are a few tricky complications. Economists and accountants adopt different definitions because they are interested in different things. Accountants have to certify that nobody is stealing cash from the business. They care about cash flow.

> **Cash flow** is the net amount of money received by a firm during a given period.

Economists care about what, how and for whom goods are produced. Accountants keep track of actual cash spent. Economists focus on opportunity cost.

Opportunity cost is the amount lost by not using resources in their best alternative use.

You quit a job as a teacher of IT and start an internet business, paying out £5000 in the first year as you camp in an internet café, whose facilities are used as your office. An accountant treats your costs as £5000. An economist stresses that your time was not free – you could have earned £20 000 a year teaching IT. It only makes sense to switch your labour resources into the internet job if you can earn at least £25 000. For an economist, interested in incentives to allocate resources, a revenue of £25 000 is merely break even; for an accountant it is £20 000 profit after paying the internet café.

Normal profit is the accounting profit to break even after all economic costs are paid. **Economic (supernormal) profits** in excess of normal profit are a signal to switch resources into the industry. **Economic losses** mean that the resources could earn more elsewhere.

Here is a second case in which economists and accounting definitions are different. The internet start-up also requires the IT teacher to use £2000 of her savings to cover everyday expenses. The accountant treats this personal financial injection by the owner as free, but an economist recognises the opportunity cost. If the money could have earned £100 in interest during the year, that is another economic cost to deduct in calculating economic profit.

Suppose the internet company does so well that it buys its own office.

Physical capital is any input to production not used up within the production period. Examples include machinery, equipment and buildings. *Investment* is additions to physical capital.

This capital is a stock and not a flow, but we cannot exclude it entirely from the firm's flow accounts. The capital becomes less valuable during the period for which flow accounts are drawn up. This depreciation is a proper charge on the flow accounts.

Depreciation is the cost of using capital during the period.

It reflects both wear and tear, and gradual obsolescence. Capital has a second economic cost in flow accounts: the money tied up when the capital was bought. The interest this could have earned is an economic cost in the flow accounts of the firm.

Stock accounts (balance sheet)

The balance sheet shows at a point in time the assets and liabilities that the firm has built up as a result of flows in all preceding periods.

Assets are what the firm owns.
Liabilities are what it owes.
Net worth is assets minus liabilities.

Assets include cash in the bank, money owed by customers, inventories, and physical capital such as plant and machinery. Liabilities are debts the firm still has to repay to suppliers and its

Box 2-5

The value of a good name

Goodwill affects the ability of the firm to make money in the future, just as valuable an asset as physical assets accumulated from past behaviour. The consultancy Interbrand tries to calculate goodwill by comparing the stock market value of companies with the identifiable physical and financial assets they own. US giants such as Coca Cola top the worldwide list. Microsoft, Nokia and Yahoo! are well up the list. So are Nike and Adidas. Interestingly, the big banks perform poorly in this rating.

Rank	Company	Industry	Brand value ($bn)
1	Coca-Cola	Drinks	73
2	Microsoft	Software	70
3	IBM	Computers	44
4	Intel	Computers	39
5	Nokia	Mobile phones	38
8	Disney	Entertainment	34
12	Mercedes	Cars	21
18	Sony	Electronics	16
27	Xerox	Copiers	10
30	Nike	Sports goods	8
40	Ikea	Furniture	6
53	Adidas	Sports goods	4

Source: Financial Times, 14 June 2001

bankers. Net worth includes not just these tangible assets minus liabilities, but should also include an estimate for the value of its reputation, customer loyalty and a host of intangible assets that economists call goodwill.

You are considering switching resources between uses. Should you study the flow accounts for the year, or the stock accounts at the time of your decision? The former shows recent behaviour, the latter shows the long-run position. If you can afford to take a long-run view, you may be more interested in the stock accounts. If you have to worry about short-term considerations, the flow accounts may be more informative.

Do firms really maximise profits?

Economists assume that firms make supply decisions to maximise profits. Some business executives, and even some economists, question this assumption. A sole owner is accountable only to herself and may have other aims (nice location, popularity with the local community, doing good). However, most business is done by large companies.

Companies are not run directly by their owners. Company directors have day-to-day discretion and only account formally to shareholders at the annual share-holders meeting. In practice, shareholders rarely dismiss the directors, who have inside information about the true prospects of the firm. It is hard for share-holders to be sure that new directors could do better.

Given this separation of ownership and control, shareholders want maximum profits but directors have some scope to pursue their own agenda. This may include executive perks, such as nice cars and a company jet. If status depends on size, directors may pursue size rather than profits, advertising too much or holding prices lower than is ideal for profits and shareholders' interests.

Even so, profit maximisation is a good place to start in developing a theory of supply. First, even if shareholders are kept partly in the dark, other firms in the industry are better informed. Companies not pursuing profits have low profits, and hence low share prices. A takeover raider can buy the company cheaply, change the policy, make extra profits, and cash up as the share price soars. Fear of takeovers may force the directors to pursue profit maximisation.

Second, shareholders provide incentive for managers to do what shareholders want. They offer directors profit-related bonuses and share options. The total value of these is small relative to company profits but big relative to what directors earn in salary alone. Directors then maximise profits, as the shareholders want.

Box 2-6

Fat cat bosses

Many empire-building managers now indulge in takeovers in spite of, rather than because of, pressure from shareholders.

The Economist, 5 May 2001

The article cited considerable empirical evidence that shareholders in the company doing the taking over usually lose out in the process, and concluded:

The takeover threat has become like a nuclear option: so disruptive that it can be used only as a last resort.

Company bosses have used this greater security to vote themselves fat cat pay rises and ensure huge golden handshakes even if they are leaving the company because it is doing poorly. How can share-holders fight back?

Big institutional shareholders – the pension funds and insurance companies whose assets are shares held in other companies – are being more active in monitoring the companies in which they invest, using a louder voice at companies' annual general meetings. Sackings of unsuccessful bosses are at an all-time high.

An overview of the supply decision

We begin with production costs. Each output level can be made in several ways. A field of wheat can be farmed by lots of workers with few tools, or by one worker with a lot of machinery.

Given the price of each input and the different production techniques available, the firm calculates the lowest-cost way to make each possible output level. This may entail different techniques at different outputs.

The **total cost curve** shows the lowest-cost way to make each output level. Total cost rises as output rises.

Table 2-5 shows different outputs and the corresponding total cost. At any output, the firm has a fixed cost of 10, perhaps the cost of paying interest on old debts. As output rises from 1 to 4, total cost rises from 18 to 54. Extra output incurs extra costs. The third column shows marginal cost.

Marginal cost is the change in total cost as a result of producing the last unit.

The marginal cost of the first unit of production is 8, the rise in total cost from 10 to 18. Similarly, the marginal cost of producing the fourth unit of output is 14, the rise in total cost from 40 to 54.

Having considered cost, now think about revenue. Column 4 shows total revenue from selling the output produced. With no output the firm gets no revenue. One unit of output can be sold at a price of 20, giving a total revenue of 20. This is also the marginal revenue of going from zero to 1 unit of output sold.

Total revenue is the output price times the quantity made and sold. **Marginal revenue** is the change in total revenue as a result of making and selling the last unit.

As output and sales rise, column 4 shows that revenue rises for a bit but eventually gets smaller as sales increase. To sell more and more output, the firm has to cut prices to induce buyers to demand this output. Since all output is sold for the same price, cutting the price to sell new units reduces the revenue earned on previous units. This second effect eventually outweighs the first. Beyond 3 units,

Table 2-5

The supply decision

Output Q	Total cost TC	Marginal cost MC	Total revenue TR	Marginal revenue MR	Economic profits	MR − MC
0	10	–	0	–	−10	–
1	18	8	20	20	2	12
2	28	10	31	11	3	1
3	40	12	36	5	−4	−7
4	54	14	35	−1	−19	−15

extra sales actually cut revenue. Column 5 does the sums for you, showing the marginal revenue from the last unit sold, which takes into account the effect on total revenue of bidding down the price that previous units have been sold for. By the bottom row of Table 2-5, marginal revenue is actually negative.

Armed with the first five columns of Table 2-5, you advise the firm what output to make and sell. One method is simply to subtract total cost from total revenue to obtain economic or super-normal profits. Column 6 shows that that profit maximising output is 2, at which profits are 3. This is similar to the method used by a mountaineer who checks the top has been reached by making sure he can look down on all surrounding sides.

There is another way to check you are at the top. Work out the slope you are standing on. If it is not flat, take the upwards direction. At the very top, the slope is zero. There is no direction you can move in order to get any higher. This is the marginal principle.

> The **marginal principle** says that, if the slope is not zero, moving in one direction must make things better, moving the other way makes things worse. Only at a maximum (or a minimum) is the slope temporarily zero.

Economists use the marginal principle a lot. Profit is maximised at the output at which marginal profit is zero. Otherwise, a different output can add to profit. Marginal profit is simply marginal revenue minus marginal cost. Column 7 uses this decision rule. If marginal revenue exceeds marginal cost, the firm made a marginal profit on the last unit, and should make even more. If marginal

revenue is less than marginal cost, the firm made a marginal loss on the last unit, and already made too much. With a marginal profit of 1 it was a good idea to make as much as 2 units. However, with a marginal loss of 7 from making a third unit, it is best to stop at 2 units. This, of course, is the same answer we got by calculating total profit from total revenue and total cost. Sometimes, it is an easier method to implement.

Plotting **MC** *and* **MR** *curves*

Table 2-5 is an artificial example. Output does not have to be an integer. Dairies can make 1284.8 litres of milk if this is the best output level. Figure 2-4 plots continuous curves for marginal cost *MC* and marginal revenue *MR*. The *MR* curve steadily falls as output rises: price cuts are needed to get customers to buy more. For most of its range, the *MC* curve rises: making the last unit gets harder and harder. For example, a coal mine has to go ever deeper to find more coal.

Figure 2-4

A firm's supply decision

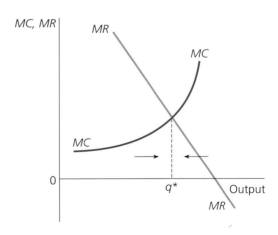

A profit-maximising firm chooses to supply the output q^*, at which marginal profit is zero. Marginal revenue exactly equals marginal cost. At any lower output, *MR* exceeds *MC* and the firm adds to profits by expanding. At any output above q^*, *MC* exceeds *MR* and the firm adds to profits by contracting output.

We can also use Figure 2-4 to examine changes in costs or revenue curves. Anything that shifts the *MC* curve up (such as wage increase, or tougher pollution controls) means that *MC* crosses *MR* at a lower output. The firm supplies less. Conversely, a change in demand behaviour that shifts the *MR* curve up increases the output that the firm supplies

Do firms know their MC *and* MR *curves?*

There are two ways in which to maximise profits. The first is by having a highly professional management with access to excellent management information. Marginal cost and marginal revenue are what they are trying to discover. But a firm may simply be run by an intuitive genius who gets things right without going through all the laborious steps above.

Competition means that most surviving bosses are good at such decisions. If they get things right, they are maximising profit, which ensures that *MC* must equal *MR* whether anyone in the firm knows it or not. Using the marginal principle is how mere mortals keep track of what proven business leaders do instinctively.

So we've mastered the supply decision?

We have found the principle from which all else follows. There are still some details to fill in. First, both revenue and costs may differ in the short run and in the longer run. A firm may have to react to a marginal revenue schedule that changes over time. Even more important, a firm's cost curves change over time. The next chapter highlights key differences between short run and long run.

We also have to add individual supplies to get the market supply curve. This depends on how many suppliers there are and how they react to one another. Chapter 3 explains different forms of market structure and what this means for the supply decision.

Recap

- Flows are measured over time, stocks at a point in time. Profit is the difference between the flow of revenue and cost.
- Economic costs include all opportunity costs. Normal profit is the accounting profit that just covers all economic costs. Supernormal profits are any profits above this level.
- Firms are assumed to maximise profits even if shareholders cannot directly observe the behaviour of directors. Maximising profits automatically entails marginal cost equals marginal revenue.
- An upward shift in the MR (MC) schedule raises (reduces) the output supplied.

Review questions

1 Why might firms, such as accountants and lawyers, where the trust of the customer is important, choose to be partnerships with unlimited liability?

2 You are drawing up a new set of 'Green accounts' for the UK. You decide to deduct environmental depreciation from the flow of UK net output each year. Give three examples of what you might deduct. Could they be measured?

3 A region has many hills. At the very top of each hill, what is the slope? Does having a zero slope guarantee you have found the highest hill? What else might you check? How could a business use this insight?

4 Is there a difference between maximising profits in the short run and in the long run? Could long-run profit maximisation justify any practices that look wasteful in the short run? Are any business practices hard to square even with long-run profit maximisation?

5 Which of the following are flows and which are stocks: (a) income; (b) output; (c) a factory; (d) labour input?

6 *Common fallacies* Why are these statements wrong? (a) Firms with an accounting profit must be thriving. (b) Firms don't know their marginal costs. A theory of supply can't assume that firms set marginal revenue equal to marginal cost. (c) The biggest profit comes from the largest sales.

Answers on pages 278–90

3

Costs, supply and perfect competition

3-1 How costs affect supply

Learning outcomes

By the end of this section, you should understand:
■ Technology and production techniques
■ How input prices affect the choice of technique
■ Total, average and marginal cost
■ Returns to scale and average cost curves
■ Fixed and variable factors in the short run
■ The law of diminishing returns
■ A firm's supply decision, in the short run and long run
■ Temporary shutdown and permanent exit

The last chapter introduced the bare bones of a theory of supply, which depended on both costs and revenue. Now we need to put more flesh on this theory. This chapter and the next deal with two ideas. First, adjusting production methods takes time. Given time, firms may be able to reduce costs by choosing more appropriate methods of production. Second, the revenue obtained from selling any particular output depends on the extent of competition in that market. This chapter deals with the limiting case of perfect competition. Chapter 4 examines the consequences of less competitive situations.

New companies, such as Orange and Amazon, lost a lot of money before eventually starting to make profits. And existing companies, such as British Airways and British Telecom, made big losses in the cyclical downturn of 2001–02, despite previous periods of healthy profits. Thus, firms don't always close down when they are losing money. They may keep going because they expect demand to rise or costs to fall. We need to distinguish between the *short-run* and the *long-run* supply decisions of firms. In the short run, a firm can't fully adjust to new information. In the long run, full adjustment is possible. In this section, we focus on how costs affect the supply decision. We then turn to the influence of demand and revenue on supply decisions.

Inputs are labour, machinery, buildings, raw materials, and energy. An *input* (or *factor of production*) is any good or service used to make output. A technique is a particular way of using inputs to make output.

> **Technical efficiency** means no other technique could make the same output with fewer inputs. **Technology** is all the techniques known today. **Technical progress** is the discovery of a new technique that makes a given output with fewer inputs than before.

Technology relates volume of inputs to volume of output. But costs are values. To deduce the cheapest way to make a particular output, the firm needs to know the price of inputs as well as what technology is available. At each output level, the firm identifies the lowest-cost technique. When labour is cheap, firms will choose labour-intensive techniques. If labour is expensive, the firm will switch to more capital-intensive techniques that use less labour.

Figure 3-1 shows a firm's total cost curve, the least-cost way to make each possible output level. More output always entails a higher cost. The curve slopes up. Note that the firm may switch between different techniques as output changes. Mass production techniques make little sense at low output levels.

Long-run costs

Faced with higher demand, the firm will want to expand output, but adjustment takes time. In the long run, the firm can adjust all input quantities and the choice of technique. In the short run, the firm cannot change all inputs, and may also be unable to change technique. It may be years before a new factory is designed, built and operational.

> **Long-run total cost *LTC*** is the lowest cost of making each output level when a firm can adjust fully. **Long-run marginal cost *LMC*** is the rise in *LTC* if output permanently rises by 1 unit. **Long-run average cost *LAC*** is *LTC* divided by the level of output.

In Figure 3-1 the height of the curve *LTC* is the long-run total cost at each output. Long-run *marginal* cost is simply the slope of the curve, how total cost rises when output increases a little bit.

Long-run average cost is long-run total cost divided by the output level. Thus, whereas the tangent to the curve at point *A* would show long-run marginal cost,

Figure 3-1

The long-run total cost curve

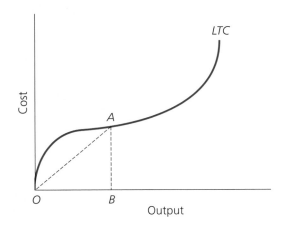

long-run average cost is the vertical distance *AB* divided by the horizontal distance *OB*. The *slope* of the line *OA* shows long-run average costs. The steeper this line, the higher are average costs per unit output.

As output changes, we can look at different points such as *A* on the total cost curve. Drawing a straight line from the point *O* to such a point, we can see how long-run average cost varies with output. For the total cost curve shown in Figure 3-1, this leads to the U-shaped average cost curve in Figure 3-2. As output rises, long-run average cost *LAC* initially falls but then rises again. This is a common pattern of average costs.

There are **economies of scale** (or increasing returns to scale) if long-run average cost *LAC* falls as output rises, **constant returns to scale** if *LAC* is constant as output rises, and **diseconomies of scale** (or decreasing returns to scale) if *LAC* rises as output rises.

The U-shaped average cost curve in Figure 3-2 has scale economies up to point *A*, where average cost is lowest. At output levels above *Q**, there are decreasing returns to scale. Since *LAC* is horizontal at the point *A*, there are constant returns to scale when output is close to *Q**.

Other shapes of cost curves are possible. Later, we shall see that in some industries with large-scale economies, *LAC* may fall over the entire output range. Conversely, the output *Q** may be so tiny that the *LAC* curve slopes up over most normal output ranges.

Scale economies

There are three reasons for economies of scale. Production may entail some *fixed costs* that do not vary with the output level. A firm requires a manager, a telephone, an accountant, a market research survey. It cannot have half a manager and half a telephone if output is low. From low initial output, rises in output allow overheads to be spread over more units of output, reducing average cost. Beyond some output level, the firm needs more managers and telephones. Scale economies end. The average cost curve stops falling.

A second reason for economies of scale is *specialisation*. At higher output, each worker can focus on a single task and handle it more efficiently. The third reason for economies of scale is that large scale is often needed to take advantage of better machinery. Sophisticated but expensive machinery also has an element of indivisibility.

Figure 3-2

The U-shaped *LAC* curve

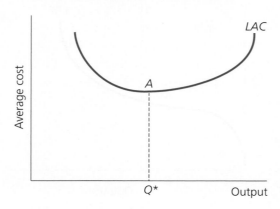

Diseconomies of scale

The main reason for diseconomies of scale is that management is hard once the firm is large: there are *managerial diseconomies of scale*. Large firms need many layers of management, which themselves have to be managed. Co-ordination problems arise, and average costs begin to rise. Geography may also explain diseconomies of scale. If the first factory is sited in the best place, a second factory has to be built in a less advantageous place.

The shape of the average cost curve thus depends on two things: how long the economies of scale persist, and how quickly the diseconomies of scale occur as output rises.

The lowest output at which all scale economies are achieved is called **minimum efficient scale**.

In heavy manufacturing industries economies of scale are substantial. At low outputs, average costs are much higher than at minimum efficient scale. High fixed costs of research and development need to be spread over large output to reduce average costs. Hence, large markets are needed to allow low costs to be attained.

High transport costs used to mean that markets were small. For industries with large fixed costs, this meant that average costs were high. Globalisation is partly a response to a dramatic fall in transport costs. By selling in larger markets, some

Box 3-1

Big is once more beautiful

Suddenly, scale matters in the high-tech world. . . . Customers, saturated with reports of dotcom deaths, are turning back to established companies such as SAP, as well to Oracle and IBM.

The Economist, 21 July 2001

By the first quarter of 2001, investment in venture capital firms was 40 per cent lower than a year before. As technology matures, leadership is shifting back to large companies. In personal computer hardware, established firms such as Dell have cut prices to gain market share and take advantage of scale economies. In business applications, mainframe computers are making a comeback. Companies are cutting costs by scrapping servers and running applications more efficiently on mainframes.

Similarly, makers of telecom equipment are consolidating market share by offering bargains that make life hard for smaller competitors. Even on the internet, by March 2001 users spent 60 per cent of online time at only 14 websites, compared with 110 two years earlier. Online music newcomers Emusic, MP3.com and Napster were supposed to displace the big record labels. Instead, the established giants gobbled up the ailing newcomers.

Information technology has made it easier to run large companies, reducing managerial diseconomies of scale. Cisco, Microsoft and eBay have over 80 per cent market shares in their respective industries, namely enterprise networks, PC operating systems and online auctions.

firms can enjoy big scale economies and lower average costs.

In other industries, minimum efficient scale occurs at a low output. Any higher output raises average cost again. There is a limit to a hairdresser's daily output. A larger market makes little difference. Globalisation has not had a big impact on hairdressing.

We begin by discussing the output decision of a firm with a U-shaped average cost curve. Then we show how this analysis must be amended when firms face significant economies of scale.

Average cost and marginal cost

As output rises, average cost falls whenever marginal cost is below average cost; average cost rises whenever marginal cost is above average cost. Hence average cost is lowest at the output $Q*$ at which LAC and LMC cross. Figure 3-3 illustrates.

This relation between average and marginal is a matter of arithmetic, as relevant to football as to production. A footballer with 3 goals in 3 games averages 1 goal a game. Two goals in the next game, implying 5 goals from 4 games, raises the average to 1.25 goals a game. In the fourth game the marginal score of 2 goals exceeded the average score in previous games, raising the average.

Similarly, when the marginal cost of the next unit exceeds the average cost of the existing units, making another unit must raise average cost. Conversely, if the marginal cost of the next unit is below the average cost of existing units, another unit reduces average cost. When marginal and average cost are equal, making another unit leaves average cost unchanged.

Hence in Figure 3-3 average and marginal cost curves cross at minimum average cost. At outputs below $Q*$, LMC is below LAC, so average cost is falling. Above $Q*$, LMC is above LAC so average cost is rising. At output $Q*$ average costs are at a minimum. As in the football example, this relation rests purely on arithmetic.

Figure 3-3

Marginal and average cost

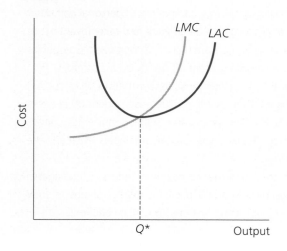

The firm's long-run output decision

Figure 3-4 shows marginal and average cost, but also marginal revenue MR. The marginal condition tells us that the best output for maximising profit is at B, at which marginal revenue equals marginal cost.

Figure 3-4

The firm's long-run output decision

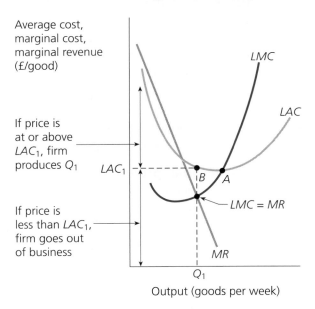

Output (goods per week)

Average profit is average revenue minus average cost per unit. Average revenue per unit is just the price for which each output unit is sold. Hence *if long-run average cost at B exceeds the price for which the output Q_1 is sold*, the firm makes losses even in the long run and should close down. If, at output Q_1, price equals *LAC*, the firm just breaks even. And if price exceeds *LAC* at this output, the firm makes long-run profits and happily remains in business.

Notice the two-stage argument. First we use the *marginal condition* (LMC = MR) to find the best output, *then* we use the *average condition* (comparing *LAC* at this output with the price or average revenue) to determine whether the best output is good enough for the firm to stay in business in the long run. If the

firm's output yields losses, it should close down.

Short-run costs and diminishing returns

In the short run, the firm has some fixed inputs.

A **fixed input** cannot be varied in the short run. A **variable input** can be adjusted, even in the short run.

The short run varies from industry to industry. It may take ten years to build a new power station, but only weeks to open new restaurant premises. The existence of fixed inputs in the short run has two implications. First, in the short run the firm has some fixed costs, which must be paid even if output is zero. Second, because the firm cannot make all the adjustments it would like, its short-run costs must exceed its long-run costs.

Once adjustment is possible, the firm adjusts only because this reduces costs.

> **Fixed costs** do not vary with output levels. **Variable costs** change with output.

Variable costs are the costs of hiring variable factors, typically labour and raw materials. Although firms may have long-term contracts with workers and material suppliers, in practice most firms retain some flexibility through overtime and short time, hiring or non-hiring of casual and part-time workers, and raw material purchases in the open market to supplement contracted supplies.

$$\begin{array}{ccc} \text{Short-run} & \text{short-run} & \text{short-run} \\ \text{total cost} = & \text{fixed cost} + & \text{variable} \\ (STC) & (SFC) & \text{cost} \\ & & (SVC) \end{array}$$

Short-run total costs are thus short-run fixed costs plus short-run variable costs. Since fixed costs do not change with output, short-run marginal cost (SMC) is the rise both in short-run total costs and in short-run variable costs when output rises by 1 unit.

The short-run marginal cost curve SMC has the same general shape as the long-run marginal cost curve in Figure 3-4, but for a different reason. In the short run, there is at least one fixed factor, probably capital. As output rises, a firm moves along its SMC curve, adding ever-increasing amounts of labour to a given amount of plant and machinery.

> The **marginal product** of a variable factor (labour) is the extra output from adding 1 unit of the variable factor, holding constant the input of all other factors (capital, land) in the short run.

The first worker has a whole factory to work with and has too many jobs to produce much. A second worker helps, so does a third. Suppose the factory has three machines and the three workers are now specialising in each running one of the factory's machines. The marginal product of a fourth worker is lower. With only three machines, the fourth worker gets a machine only when another worker is resting. A fifth worker only makes tea for the other four. By

Box 3-2

Sunk costs

If certain costs have *already* been incurred and can't be affected by your decision, ignore them. They shouldn't influence your future decisions. In deciding how much to produce in the short run, the firm ignores its fixed costs, which must be incurred anyway.

It may seem a pity to abandon a project on which a lot of money has already been invested. Poker players call this throwing good money after bad. If you don't think it will be worth reading the rest of this book, you should not do it merely because you put a lot of effort into the first two chapters.

now there are diminishing returns to labour.

Holding all factors constant except one, the **law of diminishing returns** says that, beyond some level of the variable input, further rises in the variable input steadily reduce the marginal product of that input.

Diminishing returns refer to adding a variable factor to fixed factors in the short run. *Decreasing* returns refer to diseconomies of scale when *all* factors are varied together in the long run.

Output is varied by using more labour input. Changes in the marginal product of labour affect the marginal cost of making output. Figure 3-5 shows that, as output rises, short-run marginal costs first fall then rise. While the marginal product of labour is rising, each worker adds more to output than the previous workers, and marginal cost is falling.

Short-run marginal cost *SMC* is the extra cost of making one more unit of output in the short-run while some inputs are fixed.

Once diminishing returns to labour set in, the marginal product of labour falls and *SMC* starts to rise again. It takes successively more workers to make each extra unit of output.

Short-run average costs

Short-run average fixed cost is short-run fixed cost divided by output. **Short-run average variable cost** is short-run variable cost divided by output. **Short-run average total cost** is short-run total cost divided by output.

Figure 3-5

The firm's short-run output decision

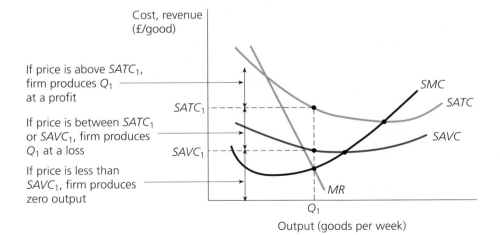

$$\begin{array}{ccc} \text{Short-run} & \text{Short-run} & \text{Short-run} \\ \text{average} = & \text{average} + & \text{average} \\ \text{total cost} & \text{fixed cost} & \text{variable} \\ (SATC) & (SAFC) & \text{cost} \\ & & (SAVC) \end{array}$$

In Figure 3-5 the shape of the SMC curve reflects the behaviour of marginal labour productivity: diminishing marginal productivity makes marginal cost rise as output rises. The usual arithmetic relating marginal and average explains why SMC passes through the lowest point on the short-run average total cost curve. To the left of this point, SMC is below $SATC$, dragging it down as output expands. To the right of A the converse holds.

Variable costs are total costs minus fixed costs. Fixed costs do not change with output, so marginal costs also show how much total *variable* costs are changing. The usual reasoning implies that SMC goes through the lowest point on $SAVC$. To the left of this point, SMC is below $SAVC$, so $SAVC$ is falling. To the right, $SAVC$ is rising. Total costs exceed variable costs, so $SAVC$ is below $SATC$.

A firm's supply decision in the short run

Figure 3-5 shows a firm's output choice in the short run. Profits are maximised by equating short-run marginal cost and marginal revenue at the output Q_1.

Next, the firm decides whether or not to stay in business in the short run. Profits are positive at the output Q_1 if the price p for this output is sold covers

average total costs. If p exceeds $SATC_1$, the firm makes profits in the short run and produces Q_1.

Suppose p is less than $SATC_1$. The firm loses money because p does not cover costs. In the long run a firm closes down if it keeps losing money. However, even at zero output the firm must pay the fixed costs in the short run. The firm calculates whether losses are bigger at an output of Q_1 or at zero output. If revenue exceeds *variable* cost, the firm earns something towards its overheads. The firm then makes Q_1 even though this may involve losses. If p is less than $SAVC_1$, the firm does not even recoup variables costs. It is then better to make zero.

> A firm's **short-run supply decision** is to make Q_1, the output at which $MR = SMC$, provided the price covers short-run average variable cost $SAVC_1$ at this output. If the price is less than $SAVC_1$ the firm produces zero.

Table 3-1 summarises the short-run and long-run output decisions of a firm.

Short-run and long-run costs

Even if it is losing money in the short run, a firm will stay in business if it covers its variable costs. In the long run it must cover all its costs to stay in business. A firm may reduce its costs in the long run, converting a short-run loss into a long-term profit. Figure 3-6 shows a U-shaped LAC curve. Each point on the curve shows the least-cost way to make that output once all factors of production can be varied.

Suppose 'plant' is the fixed factor in the short run. Each point on the *LAC* curve involves a particular input of plant. For that plant size, we can draw the short-run average total cost curve. The $SATC_1$ curve corresponds to a plant size at *A* on the *LAC* curve. The $SATC_2$ and $SATC_3$ curves correspond to the plant size at *B* and *C* on the *LAC* curve. We could draw an *SATC* curve for the plant size at each point on the *LAC* curve.

Since the *LAC* curve is the least-cost way to make each output, point *B* shows the minimum average-cost way to make an output Q_2. Hence it *must* be more costly to make Q_2 using the wrong input of plant. For the plant size at *A*, $SATC_1$ shows the cost of making each output including Q_2. Hence $SATC_1$ lies above *LAC* at every point except *A*, the output at which this plant size is best.

This argument can be repeated for any

Table 3-1

A firm's supply decisions

Output decision	Marginal condition: output at which	Produce this output unless
Short-run	$MR = SMC$	$P < SAVC$; if so, shut down temporarily
Long-run	$MR = LMC$	$P < LAC$; if so, quit permanently

Figure 3-6

LAC and *SATC*

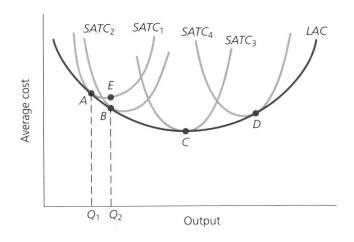

Box 3-3

Steel here?

Twenty years ago British Steel was a state-owned monopoly, selling largely in the UK. Since then three things have happened. First, the firm was privatised. Second, its market became global, in which it was a relatively small player: 43 per cent of its UK output is now exported. Third, it decided to merge with a Dutch steel maker to form a new company, Corus. Its UK plants are now losing money. UK steel demand has fallen 13 per cent since 1990. UK manufacturing is shrinking and the high value of the pound has made UK firms uncompetitive. Corus faced a key decision: cut output temporarily, or close plants permanently?

In March 2001 it announced plans for 6000 job losses and closure of 3 million tonnes of steel capacity. The UK government offered to pay half the wage bill of these workers for a year if their jobs could be saved. Effectively, it was betting either that costs could be reduced if the company had longer to adjust, or that demand would somehow improve within a year.

other plant size. Hence $SATC_3$ and $SATC_4$, corresponding to plant sizes at C and at D, must lie above LAC except at points C and D themselves. In the long run the firm can vary all inputs and can generally make a particular output more cheaply than in the short run, when it inherits quantities of some fixed factors from previous decisions. A firm currently making losses because demand has fallen may be able to anticipate future profits once it can adjust plant size to its new output.

Recap

- In the long run a firm can adjust all its inputs. In the short run, some inputs are fixed.
- The production function shows the most output obtained from particular quantities of inputs.
- The total cost curve reflects technology and input prices. The long-run total cost curve is the least-cost way to make each output when all inputs and the production technique are adjusted.
- Average cost is total cost divided by output. The long-run average cost curve LAC is typically U-shaped. There are economies of scale on the falling bit of the U. The rising part reflects diseconomies of scale.
- When marginal cost is below average cost, average cost is falling. When marginal cost is above average cost, average cost is rising. Average and marginal cost are equal only at the lowest point on the average cost curve.
- In the long run, the firm supplies the output at which long-run marginal cost LMC equals MR, provided price covers LAC at that output. If price is lower, the firm goes out of business.

- The short-run marginal cost curve (*SMC*) rises because of diminishing returns to the variable factor as output rises.
- Short-run average total costs (*SATC*) are short-run total costs (*STC*) divided by output. *SATC* is short-run average fixed costs (*SAFC*) plus short-run average variable costs (*SAVC*). The *SMC* curve cuts both the *SATC* and *SAVC* curves at their minimum points.
- The firm sets output in the short run to equate *SMC* and *MR*, provided price covers short-run average variable cost. In the short run the firm may produce at a loss if it recoups part of its fixed costs.
- The *LAC* curve is always below the *SATC* curve, except at the point where the two coincide. Hence, a firm can reduce costs in the long run if its inherited plant size in the short run is no longer appropriate.

Review questions

1 (a) What does the production function tell a firm? (b) What other information is needed to run a firm?

2 (a) Why might scale economies exist? (b) The table shows some production techniques. The cost of a worker is £5. A unit of capital costs £2. Complete the table and calculate the least-cost way to make 4, 8 and 12 units of output. (c) Are there increasing, constant or decreasing returns to scale in this output range? Which applies where?

Units of	Methods					
	1	2	3	4	5	6
Labour input	5	6	10	12	15	16
Capital input	4	2	7	4	11	8
Output	4	4	8	8	12	12
Total cost						
Average cost						

3 Suppose the cost of capital rises from 2 to 3 in the question above. (a) Would the firm change its method of production for any levels of output? Say which, if any. (b) How do the firm's total and average costs change when the cost of capital rises?

4 From the total cost curve shown below, calculate marginal and average cost at each output. Are these short-run or long-run cost curves? How can you can tell?

Output	0	1	2	3	4	5	6	7	8
Total cost	12	25	40	51	60	70	84	98	120

5 Why does a marginal cost curve always pass through the minimum point on the average cost curve?

6 *Common fallacies* Why are these statements wrong? (a) Firms making losses should quit at once. (b) Big firms can always produce more cheaply than smaller firms. (c) Small is always beautiful.

Answers on pages 278–90

3-2 Perfect competition

Learning outcomes

By the end of this section, you should understand:
- The concept of perfect competition
- Why a perfectly competitive firm's output equates price and marginal cost
- Incentives for entry and exit
- The supply curve of a perfectly competitive industry
- The effect of shifts in demand or costs

We now switch our attention from costs to revenue and demand, for which we need to know about the structure of the industry in which the firm operates. An industry is the set of all firms making the same product. The output of an industry is the sum of the outputs of its firms. Yet different industries have very different numbers of firms. We begin with perfect competition, a hypothetical benchmark against which to assess other market structures.

> In **perfect competition**, actions of individual buyers and sellers have no effect on the market price.

This industry has many buyers and many sellers. Each firm in a perfectly competitive industry faces a horizontal demand curve, shown in Figure 3-7. Whatever output q the firm sells, it gets exactly the market price P_0, and the tiny firm can sell as much as it wants at this price. If it charges more than P_0 the firm loses all its customers. If it charges less than P_0, it attracts all the customers of other firms. This horizontal demand curve is the crucial feature of a perfectly competitive firm.

For each firm to face a horizontal demand curve, the industry must have

Figure 3-7

A horizontal demand curve

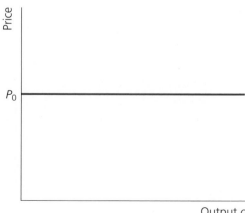

four characteristics. First, there must be many firms, each trivial relative to the industry as a whole. Second, the firms must make a standardised product, so that buyers immediately switch from one firm to another if there is any difference in the prices of different firms. Thus, all firms make essentially the same product, *for which they all charge the same price*.

Why don't all the firms in the industry do what OPEC does, collectively restricting supply to raise the market price of their output? A crucial characteristic of a competitive[1] industry is *free entry and exit*. Even if existing firms could organise themselves to restrict total supply and drive up the market price, the consequent rise in revenues and profits would attract new firms into the industry, raising total supply and driving the price back down. Conversely, when firms in a competitive industry are losing money, some firms close down. This reduces total supply and drives the price up, allowing the remaining firms to survive.

The firm's supply decision

Section 2-3 developed a general theory of the supply decision of a firm. First, the firm uses the marginal condition ($MC = MR$) to find the best positive level of output; then it uses the average condition to check whether the price for which this output is sold covers average cost. *The special feature of perfect competition is the relationship between marginal*

---

1 For brevity, we refer to competitive firms and competitive industry, it being understood that these refer to perfect competition.

revenue and price. Facing a horizontal demand curve, a competitive firm does *not* bid down the price as it sells more units of output. Since there is no effect on the revenue from existing output, the marginal revenue from an additional unit of output *is* its price. Thus, $MR = P$.

The firm's short-run supply curve

Firms in any industry choose the output at which short-run marginal cost SMC equals marginal revenue MR. In addition, perfect competition makes marginal revenue equal to price. Hence, a competitive firm produces the output at which price equals marginal cost, then checks whether zero output is better.

Figure 3-8 illustrates the firm's supply decision in the short run. P_1 is the shutdown price below which the firm fails to cover variable costs in the short run. At all prices above P_1, the firm chooses output to make $P = SMC$.

> A competitive firm's **short-run supply curve** is that part of its short-run marginal cost curve above its shutdown price.

This shows how much the firm wants to make at each price it might be offered. For example, at a price P_4, the firm chooses to supply Q_4.

The firm's long-run supply curve

Figure 3-9 shows the firm's average and marginal costs in the long run. Facing a price P_4, equating price and long-run marginal cost, the firm chooses the long-run output Q_4 at the point D. In the long

Figure 3-8

Short-run supply by perfectly competitive firm

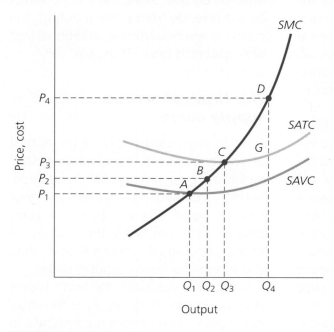

Figure 3-9

Long-run supply by perfectly competitive firm

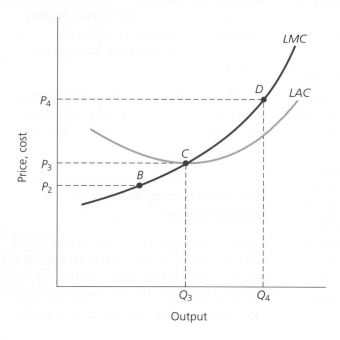

run, the firm exits from the industry only if, at its best positive output, price fails to cover long-run average cost *LAC*. At the price P_2 the marginal condition leads to the point *B* in Figure 3-9, but the firm is losing money and leaves the industry in the long run.

> A competitive firm's **long-run supply curve** is that part of its long-run marginal cost above minimum average cost. At any price below P_3 the firm leaves the industry. At the price P_3 the firm makes Q_3 and just breaks even after paying all its economic costs.

Entry and exit

The price P_3 corresponding to the minimum point on the *LAC* curve is called the *entry or exit price*. There is no incentive to enter or leave the industry. The resources tied up in the firm are earning just as much as their opportunity costs, what they could earn elsewhere. Any price less than P_3 will induce the firm to exit from the industry in the long run.

> **Entry** is when new firms join an industry. **Exit** is when existing firms leave.

We can also interpret Figure 3-9 as the decision facing a potential entrant to the industry. At a price P_3, an entrant could just cover its average cost if it produced an output Q_3. Any price above P_3 yields economic profits and induces entry in the long run.

Industry supply curves

A competitive industry comprises many firms. In the short run two things are fixed: the quantity of fixed factors used by each firm, and the number of firms in the industry. In the long run, each firm can vary all its factors of production, but the number of firms can also change through entry and exit.

The short-run industry supply curve

Just as we can add individual demand curves of buyers to get the market demand curve, we can add the individual supply curves of firms to get the industry supply curve. In Figure 3-10, at each price we add together the quantities supplied by each firm to get the total quantity supplied at that price. In the short run the number of firms in the industry is given. Suppose there are two firms, A and B. Each firm's short-run supply curve is the part of its *SMC* curve above its shutdown price. Firm A has a lower shutdown price than firm B, perhaps because it has modern machinery. Each firm's supply curve is horizontal up to its shutdown price. At a lower price, no output is supplied.

The industry supply curve is the horizontal sum of the separate supply curves. Between P_1 and P_2 only the lower-cost firm A is producing. At P_2 firm B starts to produce too. When there are many firms, each with a different shutdown price, there are many small discontinuities as we move up the industry supply curve. Since each firm in a competitive industry is trivial relative to the total, the industry supply curve is effectively smooth.

The long-run industry supply curve

As the market price rises, the total industry supply rises in the long run for

Figure 3-10

Deriving the industry supply curve

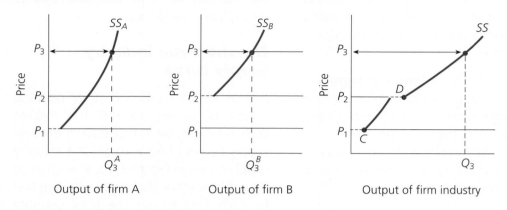

Output of firm A   Output of firm B   Output of firm industry

Figure 3-11

A horizontal industry supply curve

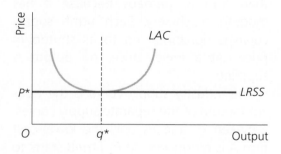

Hence, the long-run supply curve is flatter than the short-run supply curve for two reasons: each firm can vary its factors more appropriately in the long run; and higher prices attract *extra* firms into the industry. Both raise the output response to a price increase.

For each firm, the height of the minimum point on its *LAC* curve shows the critical price at which it can just survive in the industry. If different firms have *LAC* curves of different heights, they face different exit prices. At any price, there is a marginal firm only just able to survive in the industry, and a marginal potential entrant just waiting to enter if only the price rises a little.

two distinct reasons: each existing firm moves up its long-run supply curve, and new firms find it profitable to enter the industry. Conversely, at lower prices, all firms move down their long-run supply curves, and some firms may leave the industry. The industry supply curve is the horizontal sum of the outputs produced by the number of firms in the industry at that price.

The long-run industry supply curve normally slopes up, but in one special case it is horizontal, as shown in Figure 3-11. This occurs when all existing firms and potential entrants have *identical cost* curves.

Suppose P^* is the entry and exit price for all existing firms and potential entrants. Below P^* no firm will wish to supply. At a price P^* each individual firm makes an output q^*. However, industry output can be expanded indefinitely along the long-run supply curve $LRSS$ by the entry of more and more small firms, each making q^*.

Usually, however, the long-run industry supply curve slopes up. First, it is unlikely that every firm and potential firm in the industry has identical cost curves. Second, even if all firms face the same cost curves, we draw a cost curve for given technology *and* given input prices. The collective expansion of output by all firms may bid up input prices. If so, it needs a higher output price to induce the industry to expand output.

Equilibrium in a competitive industry

Although each individual firm faces a horizontal demand curve for its output, the industry as a whole faces a downward-sloping demand curve for its total output. People will only buy a larger quantity if the price is lower. Having now also discussed the industry supply curve, we can now examine how supply and demand determine equilibrium price in the short run and the long run.

In short-run equilibrium, the market price equates the quantity demanded to the total quantity supplied by the given number of firms in the industry when each firm produces on its short-run supply curve. In long-run equilibrium, the market price equates the quantity demanded to the total quantity supplied

by the number of firms in the industry when each firm produces on its long-run supply curve. Since firms can freely enter or exit the industry, the marginal firm must make only normal profits so that there is no further incentive for entry or exit.

Figure 3-12 shows long-run equilibrium for the industry. Demand is DD and supply is SS. At the equilibrium price P^*, the industry as a whole produces Q^*. This is the sum of the output of each tiny producer. At the price P^*, the marginal firm is making q^* at minimum LAC and just breaks even. There is no incentive to enter or exit.

A rise in costs

Beginning from the long-run equilibrium shown in Figure 3-12, suppose a rise in the price of raw materials raises costs for all firms in the industry. The average cost curve of every firm shifts up. The marginal firm is now losing money at the old price P^*.

Figure 3-12

Long-run equilibrium

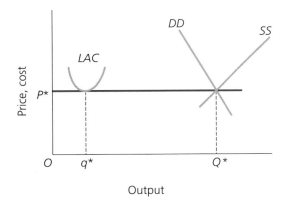

Some firms eventually leave the industry. With fewer firms left, the industry supply curve *SS* shifts to the left. With less supply, the equilibrium price rises. When enough firms have left, and industry output falls enough, higher prices allow the new marginal firm to break even, despite an upward shift in *LAC*. Further incentives for entry or exit disappear.

Notice two points about the change in the long-run equilibrium that higher costs induce. First, the rise in average costs is eventually passed on to the consumer in higher prices. Second, since higher prices reduce the total quantity demanded, industry output must fall.

A rise in industry demand

The previous example discussed only long-term effects. We can of course discuss short-run effects as well. And we can examine changes in demand as well as changes in cost and supply. Figure 3-13 illustrates the effect of a shift up in the industry's demand curve from *DD* to *D'D'*.

The industry begins in long-run equilibrium at *A*. Overnight, each firm has some fixed inputs, and the number of firms is fixed. Horizontally adding their short-run supply curves, we get the industry supply curve *SRSS*. The new short-run

Box 3-4

EMI quits making CDs

In response to internet-induced changes to the music industry, in November 1999 the EMI music company announced its intention to stop making and distributing compact discs. Having decided CDs had been made obsolete by the ability to download tracks direct from the internet, EMI decided to concentrate on developing and producing music, rather than the business of distributing it. The table below shows how the economics of music distribution are expected to change, with the artist and record label grabbing revenue formerly going to distributors.

This example shows how changes in technology can make some products obsolete by making possible new products with lower cost curves.

Costs and profits on a $15 CD

$ spent on	Traditional CD	Internet CD
Promotion	2.50	2.50
Manufacturing	1.00	1.00
Web promotion		1.00
Shipping		1.00
Distribution	3.50	
Retail store	2.00	
Royalty and label profit	6.00	9.50

Source: Financial Times, 3 March 1999

Figure 3-13

A shift in demand in a competitive industry

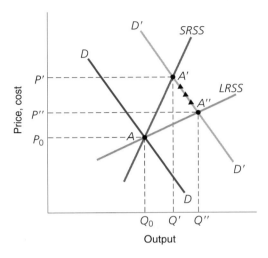

Recap

- In a competitive industry, each buyer and seller is a price-taker, and can't affect the market price. Competitive supply is most plausible when a large number of firms make a standard product, there is free entry and exit to the industry, and customers can easily verify that the products of different firms really are the same.

- For a competitive firm, marginal revenue and price coincide. Output is chosen to equate price to marginal cost. The firm's supply curve is its *SMC* curve above *SAVC*. At any lower price the firm temporarily shuts down. In the long run, the firm's supply curve is its *LMC* curve above its *LAC* curve. At any lower price the firm exits the industry.

- Adding at each price the quantities supplied by each firm, we get the industry supply curve. It is flatter in the long run both because each firm can fully adjust all factors and because the number of firms in the industry can vary.

- A rise in demand leads to a large price increase, but only a small rise in quantity. Existing firms move up their steep *SMC* curves. Price exceeds average costs. Profits attract new entrants. In the long run, output rises further but the price falls back a bit. In the long-run equilibrium, the marginal firm breaks even and there is no further change in the number of firms in the industry.

- A rise in costs for all firms reduces the industry's output and raises the price. In the long run, a higher price is needed to allow the firm that is now the marginal firm to break even. The price rise is achieved by exit from the industry, and a reduction in industry supply.

equilibrium is at *A'*. When demand first rises, it needs a big price rise to induce individual firms to move up their steep short-run supply curves, along which some inputs are fixed.

In the long run, firms adjust all factors and move on to their flatter long-run supply curves. In addition, economic profits attract extra firms into the industry. The new long-run equilibrium is at *A''*. Relative to *A'* there is a further expansion of total output, but, with a more appropriate choice of inputs and the entry of new firms, extra supply reduces the market-clearing price.

Review questions

1 The domestic economy has only one firm, but faces a flood of imports from abroad if it tries to charge more than the world price. Is this firm perfectly competitive?

2 Suppose an industry of identical competitive firms has a technical breakthrough that cuts costs for all firms. What happens in the short run and the long run? Explain for both the firm and the industry.

3 If every firm is a price taker, who changes the price when a shift in demand causes initial disequilibrium?

4 Which industry has a more elastic long-run supply curve: coal mining or hairdressing? Why?

5 Since Ford and Vauxhall are very competitive with one another, should we view them as perfectly competitive firms?

6 *Common fallacies* Why are these statements wrong? (a) Since competitive firms break even in the long run, there is no incentive to be a competitive firm. (b) Competition prevents firms passing on cost increases, whatever their source.

Answers on pages 278–90

4

Market structure and imperfect competition

4-1 Pure monopoly

Learning outcomes

By the end of this section, you should understand:
■ How a monopolist chooses output
■ How this output compares with that in a competitive industry
■ How a monopolist's ability to price discriminate affects output and profits

Having discussed perfect competition, we turn next to the opposite extreme, pure monopoly. Then we discuss other forms of imperfect competition. These are all different types of market structure. As you will see, the extent of competition between firms has a big effect on how firms behave and the decisions that they make.

The perfectly competitive firm is too small to worry about the effect of its own decisions on industry output. In contrast, a pure monopoly *is* the entire industry.

A **monopolist** is the sole supplier or potential supplier of the industry's output.

A sole national supplier need not be a monopoly. If it raises prices, it may face competition from imports or from domestic entrants to the industry. In contrast, a pure monopoly does not need to worry about potential competition.

Profit-maximising output

To maximise profits, a monopolist chooses the output at which marginal revenue MR equals marginal cost MC, then checks that it is covering average costs. Figure 4-1 shows the average cost curve AC with its usual U-shape. Marginal revenue MR lies below the down-sloping demand curve DD. The monopolist recognizes that, to sell extra units, it has to lower the price, even for existing customers.

Setting $MR = MC$, the monopolist chooses the output Q_1. The demand

Figure 4-1

The monopolist's decision

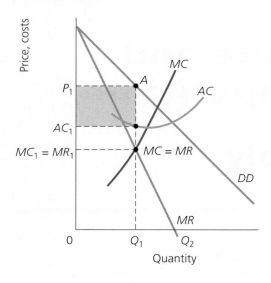

When demand is elastic, lower prices increase revenue by raising quantity demanded a lot. When revenue rises, the marginal revenue from the extra output is positive. Conversely, when demand is inelastic, marginal revenue is negative. To raise quantity demanded, prices must be cut so much that total revenue falls.

To maximise profits, a monopolist sets $MC = MR$. Since MC is always positive, MR must be positive. But this means that demand is elastic at this output. Hence, in Figure 4-1, the chosen output must lie to the left of Q_2. *A monopolist will never produce on the inelastic part of the demand curve where MR is negative.*

Monopoly power

At any output, price exceeds a monopolist's marginal revenue since the demand curve slopes down. In setting $MR = MC$, the monopolist sets a price above marginal cost. In contrast, a competitive firm equates price and marginal cost, since its price is also its marginal revenue. A competitive firm cannot raise price above marginal cost. It has no monopoly power.

> **Monopoly power** is measured by price *minus* marginal cost.

curve DD implies that the monopolist sells Q_1 at a price P_1 per unit. Profit per unit is thus $(P_1 = AC_1)$, price minus average cost at the output Q_1. Total profit is the area $(P_1 = AC_1) \times Q_1$.

Even in the long run, the monopolist *continues* to make these monopoly profits. By ruling out the possibility of entry, we remove the mechanism by which profits are competed away in the long run by additional supply.

Price-setting

A competitive firm is a *price-taker*, taking as given the price determined by supply and demand at the industry level. In contrast, the monopolist is a *price-setter*. Having decided to make Q_1, the monopolist quotes a price P_1 knowing the output Q_1 will be bought at this price.

Changes in profit-maximising output

Figure 4-1 may also be used to analyse the effect of changes in costs or demand. Suppose higher input prices shift the MC and AC curves up. The higher MC curve must cross the MR curve at a lower output. The cost increase must reduce output. Since the demand curve slopes down, lower output induces a higher equilibrium price.

Similarly, with the original cost curves, an upward shift in demand and marginal revenue curves means that *MR* now crosses *MC* at a higher output. The monopolist raises output.

Monopoly versus competition

We now compare a perfectly competitive industry with a monopoly. Facing the same demand and cost conditions, how would the *same* industry behave if it organised as a competitive industry or as a monopoly? Cost differences are often the reason why some industries become competitive while others become monopolies. Only in special circumstances could the same industry be either perfectly competitive or a monopolist.

One case in which the comparison makes sense is when an industry has lots of *identical* firms. From Section 3-2 we know that, as a competitive industry, its long-run supply curve *LRSS* is horizontal. It can always expand or contract output by changing the number of firms. If run as a competitive industry, long-run equilibrium occurs where this horizontal supply curve crosses the industry demand curve. In Figure 4-2 this occurs at *A* where output is Q_C and the price P_C.

Now suppose two things happen. The different firms come under a single co-ordinated decision maker, and all future entry is prohibited. Perhaps the industry is nationalised (but told to keep maximising profits). Long-run costs, both marginal and average, are unaffected,

but now the industry supremo recognises that higher output bids down prices for everyone.

In the special example, *LRSS* is also the marginal cost of output expansion by the multi-plant monopolist. In the long run, the cheapest way to raise output is to build more of the identical plants, each operated at minimum average cost. Hence, equating marginal cost and marginal revenue, the multi-plant monopoly produces at *B*. Output Q_M is lower under monopoly than competition, and the price P_M is higher than the competitive price P_C.

The monopolist cuts output in order to create scarcity and raise the equilibrium price. In Figure 4-2, average cost and marginal cost are equal, since each plant is at the bottom of its *LAC* curve, where it crosses *LMC*. Hence, the monopolist's profits are the rectangle $P_M P_C BF$.

Without fear of entry, the consequent profits last for ever. Notice the crucial role of blocking competition from entrants. Without this, the attempt to restrict

Figure 4-2

Comparing monopoly and perfect competition

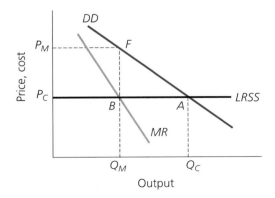

Box 4-1

Telecoms pact ends monopolies

Before 1997 many countries' domestic markets for telecommunications were heavily regulated. Previous editions of our book used the national phone company as an example of a monopoly. Britain and the US had been deregulating telecoms for some time, but the 1997 deal, embracing 68 countries, went much further. The European Union committed itself to complete liberalisation of basic telecoms, including satellite networks and mobile phones, by 2003. The World Trade Organisation (www.wto.org) forecast additional trade worth 4 per cent of the world's output.

The table below confirms that national monopolies were eroded by international competition. The cost (in pence) of an off-peak three-minute long-distance call came tumbling down during 1995–99. This example makes two points. First, many monopolies are the result of government policy to license only one supplier; such policies can change. Second, firm size must always be considered in relation to the relevant market. When technical breakthroughs in telecom technology made the relevant market much larger – satellites are no respecters of national boundaries – the national phone company was suddenly playing in a much larger game. Sooner or later policy-makers had to recognise such realities.

	France	Germany	Italy	Portugal	Spain	UK
1995	25	35	48	56	48	14
1999	18	11	24	25	38	12

output to raise prices is thwarted by a flood of output from new entrants.

Discriminating monopoly

Thus far, all consumers were charged the same price. Unlike a competitive industry, where competition prevents any individual firm charging more than its competitors, a monopolist may be able to charge different prices to different customers.

A **discriminating monopoly** charges different prices to different buyers.

Consider an airline monopolising flights between London and Rome. It has business customers whose demand curve is very inelastic. They have to fly. Their demand and marginal revenue curves are very steep. The airline also carries tourists whose demand curve is much more elastic. If flights to Rome are too dear, tourists can visit Athens instead. Tourists have much flatter demand and marginal revenue curves.

The airline will charge the two groups *different* prices. Since tourist demand is elastic the airline wants to charge tourists a low fare to increase tourist revenue. Since business demand is inelastic the airline wants to charge business travellers a high fare to increase business revenue.

Profit-maximising output will satisfy two separate conditions. First, business travellers with inelastic demand will pay a fare sufficiently higher than tourists with elastic demand that the marginal revenue from the two separate groups is equated. Then there is no incentive to rearrange the mix by altering the price differential between the two groups. Second, the general level of prices and the total number of passengers are chosen to equate marginal cost to both these marginal revenues. This ensures that the airline operates on the most profitable scale as well as with the most profitable mix.

When a producer charges different customers different prices we say it *price discriminates*. There are many examples in the real world. Rail operators charge rush-hour commuters a higher fare than mid-day shoppers whose demand for trips to the city is much more elastic.

Price discrimination often applies to services, which must be consumed on the spot, rather than to goods, which can be resold. Price discrimination in standardised goods will not work. The group buying at the lower price resells to the group paying the higher price, under-cutting the price differences. Effective price discrimination requires that the submarkets can be isolated from one another to prevent resale.

Figure 4-3 illustrates *perfect price discrimination* where it is possible to charge every customer a different price for the same good. If the monopolist charges every customer the same price, the profit-maximising output is Q_1, where MR equals MC, and the corresponding price is P_1.

If the monopolist can perfectly price discriminate, the very first unit can be sold for a price E. Having sold this unit to the highest bidder, the customer most desperate for the good, the next unit is sold to the next highest bidder, and so on. In reducing the price to sell that extra unit, the monopolist no longer reduces revenue from previously sold units. The demand curve *is* the marginal revenue curve under perfect price discrimination. The marginal revenue of the last unit is simply the price for which it is sold.

A perfectly price discriminating monopolist produces at C where $MC = DD$ which is now marginal revenue. Price discrimination, if possible, is always profitable. In moving from the uniform pricing point A to the price discriminating point C, the monopolist adds the area ABC to profits. This is the excess of additional revenue over additional cost when output is higher.

The monopolist makes a second gain from price discrimination. Even the

Figure 4-3

Perfect price discrimination

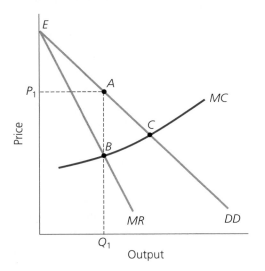

output Q_1 now brings in more revenue than under uniform pricing. The monopolist also gains the area EP_1A by charging different prices, rather than the single price P_1, on the first Q_1 units. Economic consultants often earn their fees by teaching firms new ways in which to price discriminate.

Notice too that whether or not the firm can price discriminate affects its chosen output by affecting its marginal revenue. In the extreme case, perfect price discrimination leads to the same price and output as under perfect competition, since in both cases the firm then sets $MC = MR = P$.

Monopoly and technical change

Joseph Schumpeter (1883–1950) argued that, even with uniform pricing, a monopoly may not produce a lower output and at a higher price than a competitive industry, because the monopolist has more incentive to shift its cost curves down.

Technical advances reduce costs, and allow lower prices higher output. A monopoly has more incentive to undertake research and development (R&D), necessary for cost-saving breakthroughs.

In a competitive industry, a firm with a technical advantage has only a temporary opportunity to earn high profits to recoup its research expenses. Imitation by existing firms and new entrants soon compete away its profits. In contrast, by shifting down all its cost curves, a monopoly can enjoy higher profits for ever. Schumpeter argued that monopolies are more innovative than competitive industries. Taking a dynamic long-run view, rather than a snapshot static picture, monopolists may enjoy lower cost curves that lead them to charge lower prices, thereby raising the quantity demanded.

Box 4-2

Online piracy

Widespread and illegal downloading of copyright recordings from the internet has fuelled a boom in the pirate music market, costing copyright owners £3 billion in lost sales in 2000.

Financial Times, 13 June 2001

New legitimate online distribution services, run by music companies and with proper charges, should help limit music piracy. So should successful court cases against the pirates. The music industry trade body IPFI estimated that 36 per cent of CDs and cassettes were pirated in 2000. IPFI managed to close down 15 000 illegal websites containing 300 000 music files. Downloads from Napster fell from 2.8 billion in February 2001 to a mere 400 000 after a US court case.

Free music is too good to be true. If suppliers cannot rely on payment, eventually they decide not to supply. Then everyone is worse off. The tricky question for society is to get the balance right. With too much copyright and patent protection, music producers make huge profits and we get priced out of music consumption. With too little protection, the industry dries up.

This argument has some substance, but may overstate the case. Most Western economies operate a *patent* system. Inventors of new processes acquire a *temporary* legal monopoly for a fixed period. By temporarily excluding entry and imitation, the patent laws increase the incentive to conduct R&D without establishing a monopoly in the long run. Over the patent life the inventor gets a higher price and makes handsome profits. Eventually the patent expires and competition from other firms leads to higher output and lower prices. The real price of copiers and micro computers fell significantly when the original patents of Xerox and IBM expired.

Recap

- A pure monopoly is the only seller or potential seller in an industry.
- To maximise profits, it chooses the output at which $MC = MR$. The relation of price to MR depends on the elasticity of the demand curve.
- A monopolist cuts back output to force up the price. The gap between price and marginal cost is a measure of monopoly power.
- A discriminating monopoly charges higher prices to customers whose demand is more inelastic.
- Monopolies have more ability and incentive to innovate. In the long run, this is a force for cost reduction. Temporary patents achieve some of the same effect even in competitive industries.

Review questions

1 A monopolist produces at constant marginal cost of £5 and faces the following demand curve:

Price (£)	9	8	7	6	5	4	3	2	1	0
Quantity	0	1	2	3	4	5	6	7	8	9

Calculate the *MR* curve. What is the equilibrium output? Equilibrium price? What would be the equilibrium price and output for a competitive industry? Why does the monopolist make less output and charge a higher price?

2 In addition to the data above, the monopolist also has a fixed cost of £2. What difference does this make to the monopolist's output, price and profits? Why?

3 Now suppose the government levies a monopoly tax, taking half the monopolist's profit. (a) What effect does this have on the monopolist's output? (b) What was the marginal profit on the last unit of output before the tax was levied? (c) Does this help you answer (a)?

4 Why do golf clubs have offpeak membership at reduced fees?

5 Why might a monopoly have more incentive to innovate than a competitive firm? Could a monopoly have less incentive to innovate?

6 **Common fallacies** Why are these statements wrong? (a) By breaking up monopolies we always get more output at a lower price. (b) A single producer in the industry is a sure sign of monopoly.

Answers on pages 278–90

4-2 Imperfect competition and market structure

Learning outcomes

By the end of this section, you should understand:
- Imperfect competition and market power
- How differences in cost and demand affect market structure
- Monopolistic competition
- The tension between collusion and competition within a cartel
- Oligopoly and interdependence
- Games
- Commitment and credibility
- Why there is little market power in a contestable market
- Innocent entry barriers and strategic entry barriers

Perfect competition and pure monopoly are useful benchmarks of extreme kinds of market structure. Most markets lie between these two extremes. What determines the structure of a particular market? Why are there 10 000 florists but only a handful of chemical producers? How does the structure of an industry affect the behaviour of its constituent firms?

A perfectly competitive firm faces a horizontal demand curve at the going market price. It is a price-taker. Any other type of firm faces a downward-sloping demand curve for its product and is an *imperfectly competitive* firm.

> An **imperfectly competitive** firm recognises that its demand curve slopes down.

For a pure monopoly, the demand curve for the firm is the industry demand curve itself. We now distinguish two intermediate cases of an imperfectly competitive market structure.

> An **oligopoly** is an industry with only a few, interdependent producers. An industry with **monopolistic competition** has many sellers making products that are close but not perfect substitutes for one another. Each firm then has a limited ability to affect its output price.

Table 4-1 offers an overview of market structure. As with most definitions, the distinctions can get a little blurred. How do we define the relevant market? Was British Gas a monopoly in gas or an

Table 4-1

Market structure

Competition	Number of firms	Ability to affect price	Entry barriers	Example
Perfect	Many	Nil	None	Fruit stall
Imperfect:				
Monopolistic competition	Many	Small	None	Corner shop
Oligopoly	Few	Medium	Some	Cars
Monopoly	One	Large	Huge	Post Office

oligopolist in energy? Similarly, when a country trades in a competitive world market, even the sole domestic producer may have little influence on market price.

Why market structures differ

We now develop a general theory of how the economic factors of demand and cost interact to determine the likely structure of each industry. The car industry is not an oligopoly one day and perfectly competitive the next. It is long-run influences that induce different market structures. In the long run one firm can hire another's workers and learn its technical secrets. In the long run, all firms or potential entrants to an industry essentially have similar cost curves.

Chapter 2 discussed minimum efficient scale *MES*, the lowest output at which a firm's long-run average cost curve bottoms out. When *MES* is tiny relative to the size of the market, there is room for lots of little firms, each trivial relative to the whole, a good approximation to

perfect competition. Conversely, when *MES* occurs at an output nearly as large as the entire market, there is room for only one firm. A smaller firm trying to squeeze into the remaining space would be at too great a cost disadvantage because it gets inadequate scale economies.

A **natural monopoly** enjoys sufficient scale economies to have no fear of entry by others.

When *MES* occurs at say a quarter of the market size, the industry is an oligopoly, with each firm taking a keen interest in the behaviour of its small number of rivals. Monopolistic competition lies midway between oligopoly and perfect competition.

Monopolistic competition

The theory of monopolistic competition envisages a large number of quite small firms, each ignoring any impact of its own decisions on the behaviour of other firms. There is free entry and exit from the industry in the long run. In these respects, the industry resembles *perfect* competition. What distinguishes monopolistic competition is that each firm faces a *downward*-sloping demand curve in its own little niche of the industry.

Different firms' products are only limited substitutes. An example is the location of corner grocers. A lower price attracts some customers from other shops, but each shop has some local customers for whom local convenience matters more than a few pence on the price of a jar of coffee. Monopolistically competitive industries exhibit *product differentiation*. For corner grocers, differentiation is based on location. In other cases, it reflects brand loyalty or personal relationships. A particular restaurant or hairdresser can charge a slightly different price from other producers in the industry without losing all its customers.

Monopolistic competition requires not merely product differentiation, but also few economies of scale. Hence there are many small producers, ignoring their interdependence with their rivals. Many examples of monopolistic competition are service industries.

Each firm produces where its marginal cost equals marginal revenue. If firms make profits, new firms enter the industry. That is the competitive part of monopolistic competition. As a result of entry, the downward-sloping demand curve of each individual firm shifts to the left. For a given market demand curve, the market share of each firm falls. With lower demand but unchanged cost curves, each firm makes lower profits. Entry stops when enough firms have entered to bid profits down to zero for the marginal firm.

Figure 4-4 shows long-run equilibrium once there is no further incentive for entry or exit. Each individual firm's demand curve *DD* has shifted enough to the left to just be tangent to its *LAC* curve at the output *q** the firm is producing. Hence, it makes zero economic profits. Price *P** equals average cost. For a perfectly competitive firm, its horizontal demand curve would be tangent to *LAC* at the minimum point on the average cost curve. In contrast, the tangency for a monopolistic competitor lies to the left of this, with both demand and *LAC* sloping down. The firm chooses output such that marginal revenue equals long-run marginal cost. That is the monopolistic part of monopolistic competition.

Notice two things about the firm's long-run equilibrium. First, the firm is *not* producing at the lowest point on its average cost curve. It could reduce average costs by further expansion. However, its marginal revenue would be so low that this is unprofitable.

Figure 4-4

Tangency equilibrium in monopolistic competition

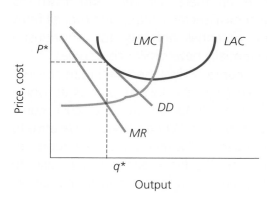

Second, the firm has some monopoly power because of the special feature of its particular brand or location. Price exceeds marginal cost. Hence, firms are usually eager for new customers prepared to buy more output at the *existing* price. It explains why we are a race of eager sellers and coy buyers. It is purchasing agents who get Christmas presents from sales reps, not the other way round.

Oligopoly and interdependence

Under perfect competition or monopolistic competition, there are so many firms in the industry that no single firm need worry about the effect of its own actions on rival firms. The essence of an oligopoly is the need for each firm to consider how its actions affect the decisions of its relatively few rivals. The output decision of each firm depends on its guess about how its rivals will react. We begin with basic tension between competition and collusion in such situations.

> **Collusion** is an explicit or implicit agreement between existing firms to avoid competition.

Initially, for simplicity, we ignore entry and exit, studying only the behaviour of existing firms.

The profits from collusion

The existing firms maximise their *joint* profits if they behave like a multi-plant monopolist. A sole decision-maker would organise industry output to maximise total profits. By colluding to behave like a monopolist, oligopolists maximise their *total* profit. There is then a backstage deal to divide up these profits between individual firms.

Having cut back industry output to the point at which $MC = MR < P$, each firm then faces a marginal profit $(P − MC)$ if it can expand a little more. Provided its partners continue to restrict output, each individual firm now wants to break the agreement and expand!

Oligopolists are torn between the desire to collude, thus maximising joint profits, and the desire to compete, in the hope of increasing market share and profits at the expense of rivals. Yet if all firms compete, joint profits are low and no firm does very well.

Cartels

Collusion between firms is easiest when formal agreements are legal. Such *cartels* were common in the late nineteenth century. They agreed market shares and prices in many industries. Such practices are now outlawed in Europe, the US and many other countries. However, secret deals in smoke-filled rooms are not unknown even today.

The kinked demand curve

In the absence of collusion, each firm's demand curve depends on how competitors react. Firms must guess these reactions. Suppose that each firm believes that its own price cut will be matched by all other firms in the industry but that an increase in its own price will induce no price response from competitors.

Box 4-3

Packaging holidays

In the UK the market for package summer holidays is now worth £7bn a year as people jet off in search of sand and sun. Whereas in 1986 the top five chains of travel agents had a combined market share of 25 per cent, it later soared to 87 per cent. Evidence of huge economies of scale? Not necessarily.

The industry integrated vertically, as travel agents (retail outlets) combined with tour operators (supplying airline and hotel services). Vertical integration can cut costs by allowing better co-ordination between different stages of the production chain, but it can also enhance market power. The two largest tour operators, Thomson and Airtours, bought the two largest travel agents (Lunn Poly and Going Places). Together, these two firms' market share rose to 49 per cent.

The market leaders were accused of unfair practices. For example, for a while Lunn Poly refused to display brochures of First Choice until a new agreement on commissions for travel agents was reached. Small operators had to pay up to 19 per cent commission to Lunn Poly, while Thomson paid only 10 per cent. Thomson and Airtours argued that their size let them keep prices lower, and that smaller competitors could not compete.

UK package tours (% market share)

Thomson	28
Airtours	21
Thomas Cook	19
First Choice	17
Other	15

Source: The Observer, 19 September 1999

Figure 4-5 shows the demand curve *DD* each firm then faces. At the price P_0 the firm makes Q_0. Since competitors do not follow suit, a price rise leads to a big loss of market share to other firms. The firm's demand curve is elastic above *A* at prices above P_0. However, a price cut is matched by its rivals, and market shares are unchanged. Sales rise only because the industry as a whole moves down the market demand curve as prices fall. The demand curve *DD* is much less elastic for price reductions from the initial price P_0.

Thus, marginal revenue *MR* is discontinuous at Q_0. Below Q_0 the elastic part of the demand curve applies, but at Q_0 the firm hits the inelastic portion of its kinked demand curve and marginal revenue suddenly falls. Q_0 is the profit-maximising output for the firm, given its belief about how competitors will respond.

The model has an important implication. Suppose the *MC* curve of a single firm shifts up or down by a small amount. Since the *MR* curve has a discontinuous vertical segment at the output Q_0, it remains optimal to make Q_0 and charge a price P_0. The kinked demand curve model may explain the empirical finding that firms do not always adjust prices when costs change.

It does not explain what determines the initial price P_0. It may be the collusive monopoly price. Each firm believes that an attempt to undercut its rivals induces them to cut prices to defend market share. However, its rivals are happy for it to charge a higher price and lose market share.

There is a difference between the effect of a cost change for a single firm and a cost change for all firms together. The latter shift the marginal cost curve up for the industry as a whole, raising the collusive monopoly price. Each firm's kinked demand curve shifts up since the monopoly price P_0 rises. Thus, we can reconcile the stickiness of a single firm's prices with respect to changes in its own costs alone, and the speed with which the entire industry marks up prices when all firms' costs are increased by higher taxes or wage rises in the whole industry.

Game theory and interdependent decisions

A good poker player sometimes bluffs. Sometimes you make money with a bad hand that your opponents misread as a good hand. Like poker players, oligopolists have to try to second-guess their rivals' moves to determine their own best action. To study how interdependent decisions are made, we use *game theory*.

> A **game** is a situation in which intelligent decisions are necessarily interdependent.

The *players* in the game try to maximise their own *payoffs*. In an oligopoly, the firms are the players and their payoffs are their profits in the long run. Each player must choose a strategy.

> A **strategy** is a game plan describing how the player will act or **move** in each situation.

Being a pickpocket is a strategy. Lifting a particular wallet is a move. As usual, we are interested in equilibrium. In most games, each player's best strategy depends on the strategies chosen by other players. It is silly to be a pickpocket in a police station.

> In **Nash equilibrium**, each player chooses his best strategy, *given* the strategies chosen by other players.

Figure 4-5

The kinked demand curve

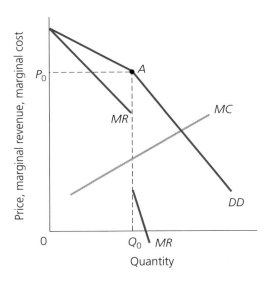

This description of equilibrium was invented by John Nash, who won the Nobel Prize for Economic Science for his work on game theory, and was the subject of the film *A Beautiful Mind*, starring Russell Crowe. Sometimes, but not usually, a player's best strategy is independent of those chosen by others. If so, it is a *dominant strategy*. We begin with an example in which each player has a dominant strategy.

Collude or cheat?

Figure 4-6 shows a game[1] that we can imagine is between the only two members of a cartel like OPEC. Each firm can select a high-output or low-output strategy. In each box the coloured number shows firm A's profits and the black number, firm B's profits for that output combination.

When both have high output, industry output is high, the price is low, and each firm makes a small profit of 1. When each has low output, the outcome is more like collusive monopoly. Prices are high and each firm does better, making a profit of 2. Each firm does best (a profit of 3) when it alone has high output; for then, the other firm's low output helps hold down industry output and keep up the price. In this situation we assume the low-output firm makes a profit of 0.

Now we can see how the game will

---

1 The game is called the Prisoners' Dilemma, because it was first used to analyse the choices facing two people arrested and in different cells, each of whom could plead guilty or not guilty to the only crime that had been committed. The penalties were such that each prisoner would plead innocent if only he or she knew the other would plead guilty.

Figure 4-6

The Prisoners' Dilemma game

Firm B output

		High		Low	
Firm A output	High	**1**	1	**3**	0
	Low	**0**	3	**2**	2

unfold. Consider firm A's decision. If firm B has a high-output strategy, firm A does better also to have high output. In the two left-hand boxes, firm A gets a profit of 1 by choosing high but a profit of 0 by choosing low. Now suppose firm B chooses a low-output strategy. From the two right-hand boxes, firm A still does better by choosing high, since this yields it a profit of 3 whereas low yields it a profit of only 2. Hence firm A has a dominant strategy. Whichever strategy B adopts, A does better to choose a high-output strategy. Firm B also has a dominant strategy to choose high output. Check for yourself that B does better to go high whichever strategy A selects. Since both firms choose high, the equilibrium is the top left-hand box. Each firm gets a profit of 1.

Yet both firms would do better, getting a profit of 2, if they colluded to form a cartel and both produced low – the bottom right-hand box. But neither can afford to take the risk of going low. Suppose firm A goes low. Firm B, comparing the two boxes in the bottom row,

Box 4-4

War games

Nintendo, Sony and Microsoft are pitting their video game consoles against each other, fighting for a global industry now worth £12 billion a year. Sony will spend £500 million in 2002 protecting its huge PlayStation franchise. Microsoft will spend even more launching its Xbox. Merrill Lynch estimates that Nintendo's 2001 profits will fall by a quarter because of money spent launching the GameCube. In the US alone, Sony hopes to have sold at least 7 million PlayStation 2 consoles before its rivals' consoles come out.

However, the key to success is not hardware but software. Microsoft's problem is that Sony and Nintendo have a history of popular games, such as the *Twisted Metal* and *Mario* series. As a late entrant, Microsoft needs to overcome these barriers. It is betting on the Xbox's online capability, allowing players to compete remotely over the internet. Whereas, with practice, people can learn to beat the artificial intelligence of a computer, Microsoft hopes that playing unpredictable humans online will be much more interesting.

There is also a bigger picture. The Xbox may be Microsoft's Trojan horse. The ultimate fight may not be about games consoles but set-top boxes. Sony and Microsoft are battling for control of the entire home entertainment industry.

Source: Financial Times, 19 May 2001

will then go high, preferring a profit of 3 to a profit of 2. And firm A will get screwed, earning a profit of 0 in that event. Firm A can figure all this out in advance, which is why its dominant strategy is to go high.

This is a clear illustration of the tension between collusion and competition. In this example, it appears that the output-restricting cartel will never get formed, since each player can already foresee the overwhelming incentive for the other to cheat on such an arrangement. How then can cartels ever be sustained? One possibility is that there exist binding commitments.

A **commitment** is an arrangement, entered into voluntarily, that restricts one's future actions.

If both players could simultaneously sign an enforceable contract to produce low output they could achieve the co-operative outcome in the bottom right-hand box, each earning profits of 2. Clearly, they then do better than in the top left-hand box, which describes the non-co-operative equilibrium of the game. Without any commitment, neither player can go low because then the other player will go high. Binding commitments, by removing this temptation, enable both players to go low, and both players gain. This idea of commitment is important, and we shall meet it many times. Just think of all the human activities that are the subject of legal contracts, a simple kind of commitment simultaneously undertaken by two parties or players.

This insight is powerful, but its application to oligopoly requires some care. Cartels within a country are illegal, and OPEC is not held together by a signed agreement that can be upheld in international law! Is there a less formal way in which oligopolists can commit themselves not to cheat on the collusive low-output solution to the game? If the game is played only once, this is hard. However, in the real world, the game is repeated many times: firms choose output levels day after day. Suppose two players try to collude on low output. Furthermore, each announces a *punishment strategy*. Should firm A ever cheat on the low-output agreement, firm B promises that it will subsequently react by raising its output. Firm A makes a similar promise.

Suppose the agreement has been in force for some time, and both firms have stuck to their low-output deal. Firm A assumes that firm B will go low as usual. Figure 4-6 shows that firm A will make a *temporary* gain today if it cheats and goes high. Instead of staying in the bottom right-hand box with a profit of 2, it can move to the top right-hand box and make 3. However, from tomorrow onwards, firm B will also go high, and firm A can then do no better than continue to go high too, making a profit of 1 for ever more.

But if A refuses to cheat today it can continue to stay in the bottom right-hand box and make 2 for ever. In cheating, A swaps a temporary gain for permanently lower profits. Thus, punishment strategies can sustain an explicit cartel or implicit collusion even if no formal commitment exists.

It is easy to say that you will adopt a punishment strategy in the event that the other player cheats. But this will affect the other player's behaviour only if your threat is credible.

> A **credible threat** is one that, after the fact, it is still optimal to carry out.

In the preceding example, once firm A cheats and goes high, it is then in firm B's interest to go high anyway. Hence B's threat to go high if A ever cheats is a credible threat.

Entry and potential competition

So far we have discussed imperfect competition between existing firms. What about potential competition from new entrants? Three cases must be distinguished: where entry is trivially easy, where it is difficult by accident, and where it is difficult by design.

Contestable markets

Suppose we see an industry with few incumbent firms. Before assuming it is an oligopoly, we must think about entry and exit.

> A **contestable market** has free entry and free exit.

Free exit means that there are no *sunk* or irrecoverable costs. On exit, a firm can fully recoup its previous investment expenditure, including money spent on building up knowledge and goodwill. A contestable market allows *hit-and-run* entry. If the incumbent firms, however few, are pricing above minimum average cost, an entrant can step in, undercut them, make a temporary profit, and exit. If so, even when incumbent firms are few in number, they have to behave as if they were perfectly competitive, setting $P = MC = AC$.

The theory of contestable markets is controversial. There are many industries in which sunk costs are hard to recover, or where expertise takes an entrant time to acquire. Nor is it safe to assume that incumbents will not change their behaviour when threatened by entry. But the theory does vividly illustrate that market structure and incumbent behaviour cannot be deduced by counting the number of firms in the industry. We were careful to stress that a monopolist is a sole producer *who can completely discount fear of entry*.

Innocent entry barriers

Entry barriers may be created by nature or by other rivals.

> An **innocent entry barrier** is one made by nature.

Absolute cost advantages, where incumbent firms have lower cost curves than entrants, may be innocent. If it takes time to learn the business, incumbents have lower costs in the short run

Scale economies are another innocent entry barrier. If minimum efficient scale is large relative to market size, an entrant cannot get into the industry without considerably depressing the price. It may be impossible to break in at a profit. The greater are innocent entry barriers, the more we can neglect potential competition from entrants. The oligopoly game then reduces to competition between incumbent firms as we discussed in the previous section.

Where innocent entry barriers are low, incumbent firms may accept this situation, in which case competition from potential entrants prevent incumbent firms from exercising much market power, or else incumbent firms will try to design some entry barrier of their own.

Strategic entry deterrence

The word 'strategic' has a precise meaning in economics.

> Your **strategic move** influences the other player's decision, in a manner helpful to you, by affecting the other person's expectations of how you will behave.

Suppose you are the only incumbent firm. Even if limited scale economies make it feasible for entrants to produce on a small scale, you threaten to flood the market if they come in, causing a price fall and big losses for everyone. Since you have a fat bank balance and they are just getting started, they will go bankrupt. Entry is pointless. You get the monopoly profits. But is your threat credible? Without spare capacity, how can you make extra output to bid down the price a lot?

Seeing this, the potential entrant may call your bluff. Suppose, instead, you build a costly new factory which is unused unless there is no entry. If, at some future date, an entrant appears, the cost of the new factory has largely been paid, and its marginal cost of production is low. The entrant succumbs to your credible threat to flood the market and decides to stay out. Provided the initial cost of the factory (spread suitably over a number of years) is less than the extra profits the incumbent keeps making *as a result of having deterred entry*, this entry deterrence is profitable. It is strategic because it works by influencing the decision of *another* player.

> **Strategic entry deterrence** is behaviour by incumbent firms to make entry less likely.

Is spare capacity the only commitment available to incumbents? Commitments must be irreversible, otherwise they are an empty threat; and they must increase the chances that the incumbent will fight. Anything with the character of fixed and sunk costs may work. Fixed costs artificially increase scale economies, and sunk costs have already been incurred.

Advertising to invest in goodwill and brand loyalty is a good example. So is product proliferation. If the incumbent has only one brand, an entrant may hope to break in with a different brand. But if the incumbent has a complete range of brands or models, an incumbent will have to compete across the whole product range. Sometimes deterring entry costs incumbents too much money. Entry will then take place, as in the example of monopolistic competition.

Summing up

Few industries in the real world closely resemble the textbook extremes of perfect competition or pure monopoly. Most are imperfectly competitive. Game theory in general, and notions such as commitment, credibility and deterrence, let economists analyse many of the practical concerns of big business.

What have we learned? First, market structure and the behaviour of incumbent firms are determined *simultaneously*. At the beginning of the section, we argued that the relation between minimum efficient scale and market size would determine market structure, whether the

Box 4-5

Freezing out new entrants?

Unilever is a major player in many consumer products from toothpaste to soap powder. One of its big winners is Wall's ice cream, which has two-thirds of the UK market and generates profits of £100 million a year; retailers' markups can also be as high as 55 per cent. In addition to established rivals such as Nestlé (www.nestle.com) and Haagen Dazs, Unilever has faced new challenges from frozen chocolate bars. Mars has 18 per cent of the market.

A critical aspect of these 'bar wars' is the freezer cabinets in which small shops store ice cream. As the leading incumbent, Unilever 'loaned' cabinets free of charge to small retailers. Unilever contended that its high market share reflected its marketing expertise (just one Cornetto); Mars argued that Unilever erected strategic barriers to entry, particularly effective in small shops with space for only one freezer cabinet, by requiring that only Unilever products were stocked in the cabinet it loaned to retailers. In January 2000 the UK government ordered Unilever to stop freezing out competitors.

industry was a monopoly, oligopoly, or displayed monopolistic or perfect competition. However, these are not merely questions of the extent of innocent entry barriers. Strategic behaviour can also affect the shape of cost curves and the market structure that emerges.

Second, and related, we have learned the importance of *potential* competition, which may come from domestic firms considering entry, or from imports from abroad. The number of firms observed in the industry today conveys little information about the extent of the market power they truly exercise.

Finally, we have seen how many business practices of the real world – price wars, advertising, brand proliferation, excess capacity, or excessive research and development – can be understood as strategic competition in which, to be effective, threats must be made credible by commitments.

Recap

- Imperfect competition exists when individual firms face down-sloping demand curves.
- When minimum efficient scale is very large relative to the industry demand curve, this innocent entry barrier may produce a natural monopoly in which entry can be ignored.
- At the opposite extreme, entry and exit may be costless. The market is contestable, and incumbent firms must mimic perfectly competitive behaviour, or be undercut by a flood of entrants.
- Monopolistic competitors face free entry and exit, but are individually small and make similar though not identical products. Each has limited monopoly power in its special brand. In long-run equilibrium, price equals average cost. Each firm's downward-sloping demand curve is tangent to the down-sloping part of its *LAC* curve.
- Oligopolists face a tension between collusion to maximise joint profits and competition for a larger share of smaller joint profits. Without credible threats of punishment by other collusive partners, each firm is tempted to cheat.
- Game theory describes interdependent decision-making. In the Prisoners' Dilemma game, each firm has a dominant strategy but the outcome is disadvantageous to both players. With binding commitments, both are better off by guaranteeing not to cheat on the collusive solution.
- In Nash equilibrium, each player selects her best strategy, given the strategies selected by rivals.
- Innocent entry barriers are made by nature, and arise from scale economies or absolute cost advantages of incumbent firms. Strategic entry barriers are made in boardrooms and arise from credible commitments to resist entry if challenged.

Review questions

1 An industry faces the demand curve:

Q	1	2	3	4	5	6	7	8	9	10
P	10	9	8	7	6	5	4	3	2	1

As a monopoly, with $MC = 3$, what price and output are chosen? (b) Now suppose there are two firms, each with $MC = AC = 3$. What price and output maximise joint profits if they collude? (c) Why do the two firms have to agree on the output each produces? Why might each firm be tempted to cheat?

2 With the above industry demand curve, two firms, A and Z, begin with half the market each when charging the monopoly price. Z decides to cheat and believes A will stick to its old output level. (a) Show the demand curve Z believes it faces. (b) What price and output would Z then choose?

3 Vehicle repairers sometimes suggested that mechanics should be licensed so that repairs are done only by qualified people. (a) Evaluate the arguments for and against licensing car mechanics. (b) Are the arguments the same for licensing doctors?

4 *Encyclopaedia Britannica* used to dominate the market, charging £1300 for its 32-volume set of books. Then Microsoft produced *Encarta*, an encyclopaedia on CD-ROM, for under £50. How do you think *Britannica* responded to this combination of entry and technical change?

5 A good-natured parent knows that children sometimes need to be punished, but also knows that, when it comes to the crunch, the child will be let off with a warning. Can the parent undertake any pre-commitment to make the threat of punishment credible?

6 *Common fallacies* Why are these statements wrong? (a) Competitive firms should collude to restrict output and drive up the price. (b) Firms wouldn't advertise unless it increased sales.

Answers on pages 278–90

5

Input markets and income distribution

5-1 The labour market

Learning outcomes

By the end of this section, you should understand:
- The demand for labour
- Labour supply and work incentives
- Why poverty traps arise
- What determines wages and employment
- Why David Beckham and Robbie Williams earn so much

In winning a tournament, Tiger Woods earns more in a weekend than a professor earns in a year. Students studying economics can expect to earn more than students studying philosophy. An unskilled worker in the EU earns more than an unskilled worker in India. Each of these outcomes reflects the supply and demand for that particular type of labour.

The demand for labour

By a single firm, in the long run

A firm's demand for inputs depends on the technology it faces, the price of each input and the demand for its output. Technology and input prices determine its costs. Demand determines the revenue from sales. The chosen output equates marginal cost and marginal revenue. In so doing, it determines the inputs that the firm demands.

In the long run, a firm can adjust its inputs and the technique it uses to produce output. If the wage rises, the firm substitutes away from labour towards capital that is now relatively cheaper than before. Mechanised farming economises on costly workers in the UK. However, with cheap abundant labour but scarce and expensive capital, Indian farmers use labour-intensive techniques.

At a given output, a higher wage makes a firm demand less labour and more of its other inputs. However, by raising the cost of making output, a higher wage also reduces the firm's chosen output level. This reduces the firm's demand for *all* inputs. In the long run, both effects reduce the quantity of labour demanded when the wage rises.

The effect of a higher wage on the demand for *other* inputs is ambiguous. The demand for capital rises as firms substitute away from labour, but lower output reduces the demand for capital input.

Similarly, a higher price of capital reduces the demand for capital. Firms substitute away from capital, and lower output also reduces the demand for capital. However, if the substitution effect is strong, the demand for labour may rise, despite lower output.

In the short run

In the short run, the firm has some fixed inputs. Suppose only labour input can be varied.

> The **marginal product of labour**
> **MPL** is the extra physical output when a worker is added, holding other inputs constant.

Beyond some point, the *diminishing marginal productivity* of labour sets in. With existing machines fully utilised, there is less and less for each new worker to do, and the marginal product of labour falls. However, profits depend on revenue, not just on physical output.

> The **marginal revenue product of labour MRPL** is the change in sales revenue when an extra worker's output is sold.

Thus, *MRPL* is the marginal benefit of hiring an extra worker. If the firm is perfectly competitive, it can sell more output without affecting its output price. *MRPL* is then simply *MPL* multiplied by the output price.

Figure 5-1 shows the marginal revenue product of labour for a competitive firm. It slopes down because of diminishing marginal productivity. The wage is the marginal cost of hiring another worker. The firm expands workers until the marginal cost of another worker equals the marginal benefit. At a wage W_0, the firm hires N_0 workers. At a wage W_1 the firm hires N_1 workers.

Thus, *MRPL* is the demand curve for labour for a competitive firm, showing how many workers it hires at each wage. Moving down this schedule shows how desired hiring rises as the wage falls.

This theory is easily amended when the firm has *monopoly power* in its output

Figure 5-1

A firm's demand for labour

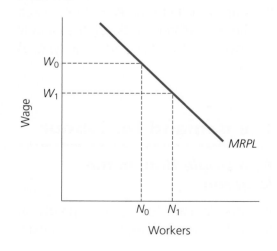

market (a down-sloping demand curve for its product) or *monopsony power* in its input markets (an upward-sloping supply curve for inputs because the firm's large scale affects the price of inputs).

> A **monopsonist** must raise the wage to attract extra labour.

The marginal cost of an extra worker exceeds the wage paid to that worker: if all workers must get the same wage, extra hiring also bids up the wage paid to the existing labour force.

Similarly, for a firm with monopoly power in its output market, the *MRPL* schedule is no longer the marginal product of labour multiplied by the output price. To sell extra output, facing a down-sloping demand curve the firm must cut its output price, even on existing output. To calculate the marginal revenue product of labour, it finds the marginal product of labour *MPL* then calculates the change in total revenue when it sells the extra output.

Figure 5-2 shows the schedules $MRPL_1$ and $MRPL_2$ for two firms with the same technology. Both schedules reflect diminishing marginal productivity – a property of technology – but $MRPL_2$ is steeper because an imperfectly competitive firm must also cut its price to sell more output. The marginal benefit of another worker is lower on $MRPL_2$ than on $MRPL_1$.

Similarly, although W_0 is the marginal cost of labour for a competitive firm taking the wage as given, a monopsonist faces a marginal cost of labour *MCL* in Figure 5-2.

Profit is maximised when the marginal revenue from an extra worker equals its marginal cost. Otherwise, the firm's hiring is inappropriate. A firm that is a price-taker in both its output and input markets hires L_1 workers in Figure 5-2. A firm with market power in its output market hires L_3 workers. A firm with market power in hiring labour input hires L_2 workers. And a firm with market power in both markets hires L_4 workers. For the rest of this chapter we assume both output and input markets are competitive. The analysis is easily amended for other cases.

Figure 5-2

Monopoly and monopsony power

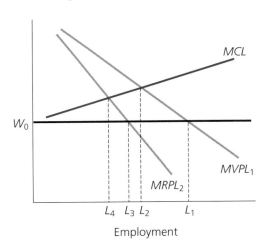

Employment

Changes in a firm's demand for labour

A higher wage moves a firm *along* its *MRPL* schedule, reducing the quantity of labour demanded. However, a rise in the output price raises the marginal benefit of labour and *shifts* the entire *MRPL* schedule upwards, raising its demand for labour.

Box 5-1

Good economists in short supply

In June 1999 the Bank of England warned that it was having difficulty recruiting staff with good postgraduate degrees in economics. British students account for only 10 per cent of PhD students in economics in leading UK universities. Why so low? Partly because a good undergraduate economics degree is now worth so much in the City. Professor Andrew Oswald of Warwick University has estimated that economics undergraduates earn about £35 000 a year in their mid-twenties, rising to over £100 000 a year by retirement. The Bank of England cannot match these salaries. Nor incidentally can universities. Some of us have to write textbooks to make a decent living!

For a given output price, two other things raise a firm's demand for labour. Technical progress makes labour more productive and raises its marginal benefit. So does a greater quantity of other inputs with which labour can work. When a firm gets more capital, this raises the demand for labour by shifting the $MRPL$ schedule up. At any wage, the firm hires more workers than before.

For the special case of a perfect competition, a firm hires labour until $W = MRPL = (P \times MPL)$. Hence, the marginal product of labour MPL equals the real wage W/P. If nominal wages and output prices both double, real wages and employment are unaffected. Nothing real has changed.

Demand for labour by an industry

Since all firms in the industry face the same wage as each other, you might think that we simply horizontally add each firm's labour demand schedule to get the industry demand schedule. This is

nearly correct but not quite. At a lower wage, each firm wants to hire more labour. This expands industry output, bidding down the output price. Even a competitive industry must cut its price to induce people to buy its higher total output.

This fall in the output price shifts to the left each individual firm's demand curve for labour. The marginal benefit of a worker is lower. We thus conclude that the industry demand curve for labour, relating the wage and the quantity of labour demand, is *steeper* than the horizontal sum of firms' individual labour demand curves.

Although each firm takes its output price as given, the entire industry bids down its output price when lower wages induce it to expand hiring and output. At industry level, this reduces the sensitivity of labour demand to the wage. Indeed, the more inelastic is the demand for the industry's output, the more inelastic will be the industry's demand for labour, because any given expansion will reduce prices by more, reducing the marginal benefit of hiring workers.

Labour supply

Labour supply depends both on how many people work and on their hours of work. To analyse labour supply, we ask how many hours do people in the labour force wish to work, and what makes people join the labour force at all?

The **labour force** is everyone in work or seeking a job.

Hours of work

How many hours a person in the labour force wants to work depends on the *real wage*, *W/P*, the nominal wage divided by the price of goods, which measures the amount of goods that can be bought as a result of working.

People not working can stay at home and have fun. Each of us has only 24 hours a day for work and leisure. More leisure is nice but, by working longer, we can get more income with which to buy consumer goods.

We can use the model of consumer choice in Chapter 2. The choice is now between goods as a whole and leisure. A higher real wage raises the quantity of goods an extra hour of work will buy. This makes working more attractive than before and tends to increase the supply of hours worked. But there is a second effect. Suppose you work to get a target real income to finance a summer holiday. With a higher real wage, you do not have to work so long to meet your target.

These two effects are the *substitution and income effects* of Chapter 2. A higher real wage raises the relative return on working, a substitution effect or pure relative price effect that makes people

want to work more. But a higher real wage also makes people better off, a pure income effect. Since leisure is a luxury good, the quantity of leisure demanded rises sharply when real incomes increase. This income effect tends to make people work less. Lottery winners quit their jobs.

The income and substitution effects pull in opposite directions. We need empirical evidence to see whether higher wages make people supply more hours of work. For most developed economies, this evidence says that, for men and women with full-time careers, the two effects largely cancel out. A change in the real wage has little effect on the quantity of hours supplied.

This conclusion applies to relatively small changes in real wage rates. In most Western countries, the large rise in real wages over the last 100 years has been matched by reductions of ten hours or more in the working week. The income effect has outweighed the substitution effect.

Workers care about take-home pay after deductions of income tax. A reduction in income tax rates thus raises after-tax real wages. Hence, the same empirical evidence implies that lower income tax rates will not lead to a big rise in the supply of hours worked! Tax cuts are not a magic solution to work incentives, and moderate tax rises should not be expected to have a major disincentive effect on hours of work.

Labour force participation

The effect of real wages on the supply of hours is smaller than often supposed. Real wages also affect labour supply by

Table 5-1

UK participation rates (%)

	1971	1985	2001
Men	92	89	84
Women: unmarried	72	74	
married	50	62	
all			72

Source: *General Household Survey, Labour Market Trends*

changing incentives to join the labour force.

> The **participation rate** is the fraction of people of working age who join the labour force.

Table 5-1 presents UK data on participation rates. Most men are in the labour force, though nowadays when older men lose their jobs they often give up completely and leave the labour force. A smaller but still quite stable percentage of unmarried women are in the labour force. There has been a big rise in the number of married women in the labour force, a trend continuing steadily since 1951 when only 25 per cent of married women were in the UK labour force. By 2001 over 70 per cent of all women were in the labour force.

Someone not in the labour force has lots of leisure, but how does she afford consumer goods? She may have inherited wealth, won the lottery, be supported by her working boyfriend, or get income support and housing benefit from the government.

If she joins the labour force and gets a job, she loses an hour of leisure for every hour she works. However, for every pound she initially earns she loses over 90 pence in withdrawal of government benefits. Since the Treasury coffers are not limitless, governments help the very poor but claw as much money back as they can once people's circumstances improve a little. Moreover, going out to work entails several costs – the right clothes, commuting to work, and paying for child care. It may simply not be worth it.

> The **poverty trap** means that getting a job makes a person worse off than staying at home.

Suppose the real wage rises. It may now be possible to pole vault over the poverty trap into work that pays. Conversely, lower real wages make the poverty trap worse. Hence, higher real wages increase the incentive to join the labour force.

What happened to income and substitution effects here? These tools compare two situations in which individuals can adjust their behaviour at the margin. The poverty trap is a high wall that entrants must clear to get into the labour force. Analysis of small changes is not the right procedure. Beginning from a low wage, a small rise in the wage makes no difference. As wages keep rising, eventually a person can soar over the wall and wants to join the labour force. Different people face walls of different heights. As wages in the economy rise, the aggregate labour supply response is continuous. A few more people join with each rise in real wages.

Why does Table 5-1 show so much more labour force participation by married women in recent decades? First, there was a social change in attitudes to married women working. Second, pressure for equal opportunities has raised women's wages. Third, the opportunity cost of working has fallen. Dishwashers and vacuum cleaners, and some limited assistance from men, has made it easier for women to go out to work.

To sum up, social influences matter and are one of the 'other things equal' that can change. For given attitudes, labour supply to the economy rises with the level of real wages, but not by a lot. It is rather inelastic. Many people are already in the labour force. Offsetting income and substitution effects mean that further changes in wages have a small effect on hours worked. The main reason aggregate supply of person-hours rises when real wages rise is that extra people can leap over the wall and join the labour force.

Labour supply to an industry

Suppose the industry is small relative to the economy, and wishes to hire workers with common skills. It must pay the going rate, adjusted only for the particular non-monetary characteristics of that industry. The *equilibrium wage differential* across two industries offsets differences in the desirability of jobs to workers, removing any incentive for workers to move between industries. Nasty and dangerous jobs have to pay more.

A small industry faces a horizontal labour supply curve at the appropriate wage. Paying this going rate, it can hire as many workers as it wants. In practice, few industries are this small. The construction industry is a significant user of roofers, and the haulage industry a significant user of lorry drivers. When an industry expands, it usually bids up

Box 5-2

Boosting UK labour supply

Under New Labour, current UK policies fall under two main headings, *Welfare to Work* and *Making Work Pay*. Both reflect a belief that work allows people to acquire skills and new opportunities: work is a ladder allowing people gradually to climb out of poverty. *Welfare to Work* has two elements, more help in finding a job and more pressure (threat of loss of social security benefits) on those thought to be making little effort to find work.

Both raise the incentive to participate in the labour force. *Making Work Pay* deals with incomes of people once they are in the labour force. The *Working Family Tax Credit* gives money to workers with children, provided the parent works a minimum number of hours a week (the limit being set roughly to make it possible for mothers to work while their children are at school).

Both measures attack the poverty trap. To pay for these schemes, the government could have taxed much richer people. Instead, part of the cost is being recouped by faster withdrawal of social security benefits just above the range of the poverty trap. Critics say this is still not a very good answer to the for-whom question.

wages for those skills by raising the whole economy's demand for a skill that, in the short run, is in limited supply. In the short run, an industry faces an upward-sloping labour supply curve.

In the long run, the industry's labour supply curve is flatter. When short-run expansion bids up the wages of computer programmers, more school-leavers train in this skill, enhancing the long-run supply of programmers. With more programmers available, an individual industry does not have to raise the wage so much to attract extra workers with this skill.

Labour market equilibrium in an industry

Figure 5-3 shows labour supply and demand for an industry. In equilibrium, the real wage is W/P_0 and employment is N_0. Shifts in these supply or demand curves change this equilibrium. In the market for Premier League footballers, the labour supply curve LS is steep since it is hard to find more good footballers, no matter how much the industry offers to pay.

Football clubs' revenue from TV depends in turn on the revenue that TV can earn from advertising. As the global economy slows down, even leading companies are reconsidering their spending on advertising. If they cut back, even David Beckham may feel the effects.

The arrival of Sky TV, paying vast sums to show games on TV, raised the demand for footballers from LD_0 to LD_1 and caused a large rise in their wages. Thus, Premier League footballers get high

wages for two reasons. First, the derived demand curve for their labour is high because football clubs can earn massive revenue from the success of their talented footballers.

Second, the labour supply curve for people with these skills is very steep. Even by paying a lot more, it is hard to attract many more Beckhams into the football industry. Beckham and Owen have few adequate substitutes. Thus, supply and demand explain the high wages of top stars.

Conversely, the collapse of ITV Digital can be expected to shift the demand curve for footballers down. Sooner or later their equilibrium wage will fall. One reason that many football clubs in the lower divisions of the English Football League feared bankruptcy was that they had awarded players multi-year contracts for high wages based on the expectation

Figure 5-3

Industry labour market equilibrium

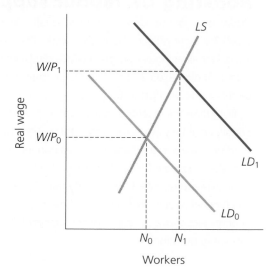

Box 5-3

Premiership wages

The golden egg that is the FA Carling Premiership may be about to cook its own goose. There are clear signs that exorbitant wage demands . . . are eating away at the financial wellbeing of the top-flight clubs.

The Times, 6 April 2001

The wage bill in UK Premier League football rose from £50 million in the 1992–93 season to £375 million in the 2000–01 season, while income of the clubs rose from £464 million to £689 million. Spiralling club incomes reflect not only increasing demand as satellite TV retails football to ever wider (and more profitable) audiences, but also greater proficiency in marketing ancillary products like replica shirts. Competition for top talent has seen players get their hands on all of the clubs' additional revenue, a dramatic example of how the demand for inputs is derived from the demand for output.

of fat fees from ITV Digital. They feared a sharp drop in revenue without being able to cut wages quickly enough.

Recap

- A higher wage has a substitution effect and an output effect. Both reduce the demand for labour.
- In the short run, the firm has some fixed inputs and varies output by varying its variable input, labour. Labour faces diminishing returns when other factors are fixed. Its marginal physical product falls as more labour is used.
- A profit-maximising firm produces the output at which marginal output cost equals marginal output revenue. Equivalently, it hires labour up to the point where the marginal cost of labour equals its marginal revenue product.
- A firm's *MRPL* schedule shifts up if its output price rises, if its capital stock rises, or if technical progress makes labour more productive.
- Higher industry output reduces the output price in equilibrium. The industry labour demand curve is steeper (less elastic) than that of each firm, and is more inelastic the more inelastic is the demand curve for the industry's output.
- For someone already in the labour force, a higher real wage has a substitution effect that raises the supply of hours worked, but an income effect that reduces the supply of hours worked. The two roughly cancel out.

- Participation rates rise with higher real wage rates, lower fixed costs of working and changes in tastes in favour of working rather than staying at home. All three have raised labour force participation, especially by married women.
- Equilibrium wage differentials are monetary compensation for different non-monetary characteristics of jobs across industries.
- When demand is high and supply is scarce, equilibrium wages will be high. Firms can still make profits provided demand continues to be high.

Review questions

1 Why is a firm's output supply decision the same as its labour demand decision?

2 (a) Why does the marginal product of labour eventually decline? (b) Show in a diagram how a rise in a firm's capital stock affects its short-run demand for labour.

3 Over the last 100 years, the real wage rose but the work week got shorter. (a) Explain this result using income and substitution effects. (b) Could labour input have risen despite shorter working hours?

4 A film producer says that the industry is doomed because Russell Crowe and Julia Roberts are paid too much. Evaluate the argument.

5 When might an industry face a horizontal supply curve for labour?

6 *Common fallacies* Why are the following statements wrong? (a) There is no economic reason why a sketch that took Picasso one minute to draw should fetch £100 000. (b) Higher wages must raise incentives to work.

Answers on pages 278–90

5-2 Different kinds of labour

Learning outcomes

By the end of this section, you should understand:
- The many different kinds of labour
- How human capital adds to skills
- When investment in education and training makes sense
- The role of trade unions
- How globalisation affects trade unions

In most European countries men earn more than women, and whites earn more than non-whites. Is this discrimination, or do different workers have different productivity? Workers differ not merely in sex and race but in age, experience, education, training, innate ability, and in whether or not they belong to a trade union.

Table 5-2 shows that UK women earn only two-thirds as much as men For men, the group on which most data are available, Table 5-3 highlights sources of pay differentials.

Table 5-2

Hourly earnings, UK, 2000

	Men	Women
Manual	£7.8	£5.7
Non-manual	£13.8	£9.7

Source: ONS, New Earnings Survey

Table 5-3

UK pay differentials

% extra pay for	Union	Non-union
Education and training		
GCSE	+5	+13
A-levels	+16	+21
University degree	+32	+47
Postgraduate degree	+50	+50
Other higher education	+18	+21
Apprenticeship	+11	+9
Personal		
Ethnic minority	−1	−5
Years experience		
5	+13	+10
10	+23	+20
15	+30	+28
30	+35	+32
Job character		
South East	+15	+16
London	+23	+15
Manual	+17	−21
Shift work	+12	+8

Source: A. Booth, 'Seniority, Earnings and Unions', Economica, 1996

People with more education and training earn more, whether or not they are in a trade union. Work experience adds to earnings, though at a diminishing rate, especially in manual work, where older workers cannot match their strong, young colleagues. But experience still matters, even in manual work. Job characteristics also affect pay. Manual workers, perhaps with fewer skills, earn less than non-manuals. And firms in the busy (and expensive) South East region, including London, have to pay workers more.

Human capital

> **Human capital** is the stock of accumulated expertise that raises a worker's productivity.

Human capital is the result of past investment in workers. It enhances their productivity and thus their current and future incomes. Education and training involve current sacrifices – both direct costs, and giving up opportunities to earn immediate income – but yield the benefit of higher future incomes because productivity is higher.

In long-run equilibrium, the extra benefit of acquiring skills must just cover the extra cost of acquiring them. Box 5-4 suggests that the payoff to education can be large. Don't quit now!

On-the-job training

Human capital can also be accumulated after people leave education and get a job. *Firm-specific skills* raise a worker's productivity only in that particular firm. A worker knows how that factory operates and what makes these particular teams of workers function effectively. These skills may be worthless on another firm. In contrast, *general skills*, such as knowing how to use *Windows 2000*, can be transferred to work in another firm.

A firm can afford to pay for training in firm-specific skills. Its workers' productivity rises, but they are unlikely to move to other firms since they will then get higher wages in the current firm where their productivity is higher. Conversely, the more general or transferable the skill, the more a firm will want the worker to pay the cost of training. No firm wants to invest heavily in training workers who then move to other firms.

An apprentice works for less than his immediate marginal product, thus paying for his own training. This investment raises his future productivity, raising his future income wherever he works. Firms do not mind if the worker quits since the worker bore the cost of the training.

Trade unions

Trade unions are worker organisations that affect pay and working conditions. Figure 5-4 shows UK union membership since 1910. After a steady rise until 1920, membership collapsed in the depression of the 1930s, but recovered strongly to peak in 1979 at about half the civilian labour force. Since then it has been in constant decline as the industrial economy gives way to the service economy and the public sector shrinks.

The traditional view of unions is that

Box 5-4

Higher education pays off

Nowadays most students must contribute to the cost of their higher education. What financial benefits are likely to accrue in the future? The table below shows the results of a major empirical study on determinants of people's wages by the time they are 33 years old.

Degrees add a lot to future earning power, but the subject also matters. Economics students can expect to earn much more than history or languages students.

% extra wage in Britain at age 33 for

	Men	Women
First Degree	+15	+32
Postgraduate degree	+15	+35
Extra effect by subject		
Arts	−0	+5
Economics	+10	+24
Chemistry/biology	−17	−11
Maths/physics	+9	+16

Source: R. Blundell *et al.*, 'Returns to higher education in Britain', *Economic Journal*, 2000

Figure 5-4

Union membership (% of civilian labour force)

Sources: Bain and Elsheik, *Union Growth and the Business Cycle*, Basil Blackwell, 1976 and ONS, *Labour Market Trends*

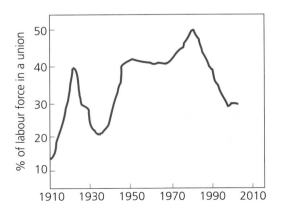

they offset the firm's power in negotiating wages and working conditions. A single firm has many workers. The firm is in a strong bargaining position if it can make separate agreements with each of its workers. By presenting a united front, the workers can impose large costs on the firm if they *all* quit. The firm can replace one worker but not its whole labour force. The existence of unions evens up the bargaining process.

A successful union must be able to restrict the firm's labour supply. If the firm can hire non-union labour, unions find it hard to maintain the wage above the level at which the firm can hire non-union workers. Hence, unions are keen on closed-shop agreements with individual firms.

Box 5-5

The unions flag

Figure 5-4 shows the steady fall in union membership. We can learn more about its possible causes by examining where this decline has occurred. The table examines various ways to disaggregate: male/female, part-time/full-time, manual/nonmanual, industry/services, and public/private.

Union membership (% of employees) 1990–2000

	1990	2000	Change
Male	43	30	−13
Female	32	29	−3
Full-time	43	33	−10
Part-time	22	22	0
Manual	42	27	−15
Nonmanual	35	30	−5
Industry	44	28	−16
Services	37	31	−6
Public	65	60	−5
Private	24	12	−12

Source: ONS, *Labour Market Trends*

A **closed shop** means that all a firm's workers must be members of a trade union.

By restricting supply and making workers scarce, a union can raise wages for the workers who still have jobs. How far will a union swap lower employment for higher wages in an industry? And what determines union power to control the supply of labour to particular industries?

The more the union cares about its *senior* members, the more it will raise wages by restricting employment. Senior workers are the least likely to be sacked. Conversely, the more a union is democratic, and the more it cares about potential members as well as actual members, the less it restricts employment to force up wages.

The more inelastic the demand for labour, the more a given restriction in jobs raises the wage. The incentive to unionise the labour force is strong when big wage rises are achieved with little loss of employment. Conversely, when labour demand is elastic, forcing up wages costs many jobs. Unions are then less attractive to their members.

Unions and globalisation

On 1 May each year, union members are well represented in the big marches against capitalism and globalisation. Now you understand why. In a small country, big firms may have significant monopoly power. This makes their demand for labour inelastic. Taking on extra workers and producing more output quickly bids down the output price, reducing the marginal benefit of another worker.

Conversely, at lower employment and output, the firm's output price rises since it no longer floods the small domestic market. With a higher output price, workers are more valuable and earn a higher wage. Thus the demand for labour: lower employment is accompanied by much higher wages, which is good news for the union. Restricting labour supply forces up the wage a lot.

Globalisation makes domestic firms swim in a much bigger pond with many foreign competitors. Facing this extra competition, the output price is much less sensitive to the output of domestic firms. Hence, when unions restrict labour supply, they scarcely manage to force up the wage. Globalisation thus weakens the power of domestic trade unions, which is why they mind about it.

Other effects of unions

Union wage differentials arise not only from the successful restriction of labour supply. Union work has certain characteristics – a structured work setting, inflexibility of hours, employer-set overtime, and a faster work pace – a whole set of conditions that might be regarded as unpleasant. Higher wages in such industries are partly *compensating wage differentials* for these non-monetary aspects of the job.

Thus, unions tend to emerge in industries where large productivity gains

would result from the introduction of unpleasant working conditions. The union exists not to restrict labour supply in total, but to negotiate productivity gains, ensuring that workers receive proper compensating differentials for the unpopular changes in working practices that firms find it profitable to introduce. On this view, the unions do not make separate deals for pay and working conditions; rather, their role is to secure pay increases *in exchange for* changes in working conditions.

From this perspective, unions play an important role in allowing firms to commit to what they promise. Without unions, there is the danger that workers would agree to new technologies and changes in work conditions but then find that the firm failed to honour its promise to offer higher wages in return. The existence of unions helps their members believe that firms will stick to their half of the bargain.

Recap

■ Different workers get different pay. This reflects personal characteristics such as education, job experience, gender, race, and union status.

■ Skills or human capital are the most important source of wage differentials. Human capital formation includes both formal education and on-the-job training. Workers with more education and training earn higher lifetime incomes.

■ Skilled labour is relatively scarce because it is costly to acquire human capital. Workers acquire human capital if the benefit exceeds the cost. Firms may pay for training if there is then little danger of the worker leaving the firm; otherwise, the worker may have to pay for it.

■ Under a third of the UK labour force now belongs to a trade union. Unions restrict the labour supply to firms or industries, thereby raising wages but lowering employment. Unions move firms up their demand curve for labour.

■ Unions achieve higher wages the more inelastic the demand for labour and the more they are willing or able to restrict the supply of labour. Globalisation makes labour demand elastic and reduces unions' incentive to raise wages.

■ Unions also raise wages by negotiating compensation for changes in work practices that raise productivity but reduce the pleasantness of the job. Without unions, workers might never agree to such changes, believing that firms would not honour their promise to raise wages after conditions were irreversibly altered.

Review questions

1 Suppose going to university adds nothing to productivity but reveals that you were simply born clever and determined. Would graduates earn more than non graduates? Would it matter if you studied philosophy or economics? What can be deduced from the fact that Arts graduates do earn less than economics graduates?

2 A worker can earn £20 000 a year for the next 40 years. Alternatively, the worker can take three years off to go on a training course whose fees are £7000 per year. If the government provides an interest-free loan for this training, what future income differential per year would make this a profitable investment in human capital?

3 Suppose economists form a union and establish a certificate that is essential for practising economics. Would this raise the relative wage of economists? How would the union restrict entry to the economics profession?

4 Young hospital doctors complain that the long hours they have to work are not adequately compensated by their initial salaries. Use the material of this section to discuss two theories of what is going on.

5 Why are trade unions highly visible in industries with monopoly power in their output market but not in competitive industries? What is the likely consequence of globalisation for the future of trade unions?

6 *Common fallacies* Why are these statements wrong? (a) Free schooling from 16 to 18 ensures that the poor can stay on in education. (b) Many low-paid workers belong to a trade union. Hence unions do not improve pay and conditions.

Answers on pages 278–90

5-3 Other input markets

Learning outcomes

By the end of this section, you should understand:
- The markets for capital and land
- Flows over time, and stocks at a point in time
- The markets for renting capital services and for buying new capital assets
- The required rental on capital
- How land is allocated between competing uses

We now examine other inputs used with labour in the production process. Having completed this analysis of factor markets, we discuss the *income distribution* in an economy. The price of an input, multiplied by the quantity used, is the income of that input. We need to know the prices and quantities of all inputs to understand how the economy's total income is distributed. First, we examine the market for capital.

> **Physical capital** is the stock of produced goods used to make other goods and services. **Land** is the input that nature supplies.

Physical capital includes machinery used to make cars, railway lines that produce transport services and school buildings that produce education services. Land is used in farming and in the supply of housing and office services. The distinction between land and capital is blurred. By applying fertiliser to improve the soil balance, farmers can 'produce' better land.

Capital and land are both assets. They do not completely depreciate during the time period in which we study output decisions by firms.

Physical capital

Fixed capital is plant, machinery and buildings. Inventories are stocks of working capital, goods awaiting further production or sale. Over time, the economy is becoming more *capital-intensive*. Each worker has more capital with which to work. Because capital depreciates, it takes some investment in new capital goods merely to stand still.

> **Gross investment** is the production of new capital goods and the improvement of existing capital goods. **Net**

investment is gross investment minus the depreciation of the existing capital stock.

If net investment is positive, gross investment more than compensates for depreciation and the capital stock is growing. However, very small levels of gross investment may fail to keep pace with depreciation; the capital stock then falls.

Rentals, interest rates and asset prices

Table 5-4 stresses two distinctions: between *stocks* and *flows*, and between *rental payments* and *asset prices*. The hourly wage is the *rental payment* to hire an hour of labour. There is no asset price for the asset called a 'worker' because we no longer allow slavery. However, for capital there are markets both to buy and sell capital goods and to lease capital services from other firms.

A **stock** is the quantity of an asset at a point in time (e.g. 100 machines on 1 January 2003). A **flow** is the stream of services that an asset provides in a given period. The cost of using capital services is the **rental rate** for capital. The **asset price** is the sum for which the stock can

be bought, entitling its owner to the future stream of capital services from that asset.

Buying a factory for £10 000 entitles the owner to a stream of future rental payments on the capital services that the factory provides. What will a purchaser pay for a capital asset?

If you borrow £10 000 to buy the machine, you face two costs. First, the opportunity cost of the funds tied up, which could instead have earned interest. If the interest rate is 10 per cent a year, this costs you £1000 a year in lost interest. Second, the value of the machine falls each year as its wears out with use and becomes obsolete. Suppose this depreciation is £500 a year. Although it cost £10 000 to buy the asset outright, it is effectively costing you £1500 a year then to use the flow of capital services that it generates during its lifetime.

If you enter the leasing business, you will buy the machine only if you can rent it for at least £1500 a year. The required rental is the price that connects the market for capital assets, in which capital goods are bought and sold, and the market for capital services, in which capital is hired out for use. Even where a business buys an asset for its

Table 5-4

Stock and flow concepts

	Capital	Labour
Flow input to hourly production	Capital services	Labour services
Payment for flow	Rental rate (£/machine hour)	Wage rate (£/labour hour)
Asset price	£/machine	£/slave, if purchase allowed

Box 5-6

The future's orange, but the present was in the red

How would you like to start a company, lose £229 million in your first year of trading, and watch your share price rise on the stock market? Not a bad beginning for Orange, the mobile phone operator. Because telecommunications was a growth area, stock market analysts forecast profits in the future even when the young company made massive losses in its early years. Orange's stock market value reflected guesses about the stream of future profits that shareholders expected to receive.

Even after the 1997 announcement of a £229 million loss that year Orange's total share value was £2.6 billion. Shareholders were banking on some pretty big profits in the future. Nor were they disappointed. By October 1999 Orange was worth £20 billion after a takeover by German competitor Mannesmann. After its subsequent sale to France Telecom, Orange's market value reached £21.6 billion, more than that of the whole of its new French parent company.

Because capital lasts a long time, the price of a capital asset has to value the stream of income that it will earn throughout its lifetime, not just the rentals that it is earning today. By 2002 people were much more pessimistic about future profits in telephony, and Orange's share price had fallen back a lot. Asset prices are volatile because they depend on beliefs about the asset's income over its entire future life.

own use, it should calculate whether the asset is covering its economic cost.

> The **required rental** is the income per period that allows the buyer of a capital asset to break even.

The required rental can change for three reasons. First, a higher price of new capital goods means that required rentals must rise: with more funds tied up, there is more interest and depreciation to offset. Second, a higher interest rate raises the required rental, since the interest foregone by owning the asset has risen. Third, a higher depreciation rate raises the cost per period of holding the asset, and hence the return it must earn to cover its costs.

The demand for capital services

The firm's demand for capital services is very like its demand for labour services. The rental rate for capital replaces the wage rate as the cost of hiring factor services. We emphasise the *use* of *services* of capital. The example to bear in mind is a firm renting a vehicle or leasing office space.

> The **marginal revenue product of capital *MRPK*** is the extra revenue from selling the extra output that an extra unit of capital allows, holding constant all other inputs.

The marginal revenue product of capital *MRPK* falls as more capital is used. First, physically there are diminishing marginal returns to adding more and more capital with other inputs held constant. Second, the firm may have to cut its output price to sell the extra output. The firm rents capital up to the point at which the rental rate equals its marginal revenue product. A lower rental rate makes the firm demand more capital services.

This entire demand curve for capital services shifts up if there is (a) a higher output price, making the extra physical output more valuable, (b) a rise in the quantity of other inputs that makes capital more productive, or (c) a technical advance that makes capital more productive.

The industry demand curve for capital services

As with labour, the industry demand for capital services adds together how much each individual firm demands at each rental rate. Again, the industry demand is less elastic than those of individual firms. Even if each firm thinks it has no effect on the output price, the industry as a whole must cut the price to sell more output. This reduces the marginal benefit of more capital, making demand less responsive to a fall in the rental rate on capital.

The supply of capital services

Capital services are produced by capital assets. In the short run, the total supply of capital assets (machines, buildings and vehicles), and thus the services they provide, is fixed for the economy as a whole. New factories cannot be built overnight. The economy's supply curve of capital services is vertical at a quantity determined by the existing stock of capital assets.

Some types of capital are fixed even for the individual industry. The steel industry cannot quickly change its number of furnaces. However, by offering a higher rental rate for delivery vans, the super-market industry can attract more vans from other industries, even in the short run, and thus faces an upward-sloping supply curve.

In the long run the total quantity of capital in the economy can be varied. New machines and factories can be built. Conversely, with no new investment in capital goods the existing capital stock will depreciate and its quantity will fall. Similarly, individual industries can adjust their stocks of capital.

Long-run equilibrium

The inherited stock of capital determines the vertical supply curve for capital services in the short run. Given the industry demand for capital services, this determines the equilibrium rental on capital services in the industry. If this matches the required rental on capital, this is a long-run equilibrium. Users of capital services are equating their marginal benefit and marginal cost. Owners of capital services are earning streams of income that just cover the cost of buying the capital asset. And producers of capital assets – the construction and machine tool industries – are selling new assets at a price that just covers the cost of making them.

Adjustment to changes

In Figure 5-5 greater import competition reduces the demand for domestic textiles. Beginning in long-run equilibrium at A, a lower output price shifts the derived demand curve for capital services to the left in the textile industry, from DD to $D'D'$. Overnight, the supply of capital services SS is vertical, determined by previous investment in capital assets.

The immediate effect is a big drop in rentals on textile machinery. The industry moves from A to B. Machine owners no longer get the required rental R^*, and stop building new machines. Depreciation gradually reduces the stock of existing machines. This makes capital services scarcer, and bids up the rental. When capital has fallen to K', the rental returns to the required rental R^* and long-run equilibrium is restored at C.

Producers of new machines make just enough new machines to cover depreciation of existing machines, and the capital stock remains constant.

Land

Since land is the input supplied by nature, we often treat its supply as constant, since it cannot be augmented by economic activity. This is not literally true. We can drain marshes, and improve land with fertiliser. However, it is much harder to add to the total supply of land than that of machines or buildings. We capture the key feature of land by treating its total supply as fixed.

Figure 5-6 shows the derived demand curve DD for land services. With a fixed supply, the equilibrium rental is R_0. A rise in the derived demand, for example

Figure 5-5

Adjustment of capital services

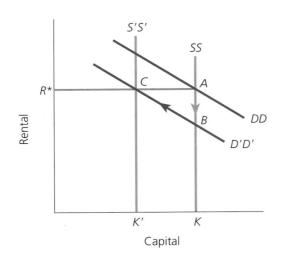

Figure 5-6

The market for land services

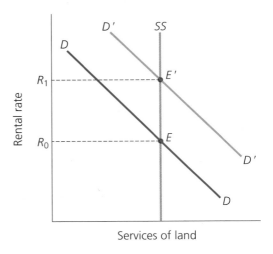

Box 5-7

The best address

Since land is in fixed supply, land prices are dearest where demand is greatest. Here are the ten dearest places to buy a two-bedroom apartment.

Rank and city		Area	Price (£)
1	London	Eaton Square	1 500 000
2	San Francisco	Pacific Heights	1 400 000
3	Hong Kong	Barker Road	1 300 000
4	New York	Fifth Avenue	1 200 000
5	Amsterdam	R. Wagnerstraat	1 200 000
6	Stockholm	Strandvagen	1 100 000
7	Sydney	Circular Quay	900 000
8	Chicago	Michigan Ave	800 000
9	Zurich	Zurichberg	700 000
10	Singapore	Scotts 28	700 000

Source: *BA Business Life*, August 2001

because wheat prices have risen, leads only to a rise in the rental to R_1. The quantity of land services is fixed by assumption.

Consider a tenant farmer who rents land. Wheat prices have risen but so have rents. The farmer may not be better off, and may complain that high rentals make it hard to earn a decent living. As in our discussion of footballers' wages, it is a combination of a strong derived demand and inelastic supply that leads to a high price for the input's services. Figure 5-6 implies that farm subsidies earned through the Common Agricultural Policy benefit the owners of land, for whom rentals are income, but may not benefit those who rent land in order to farm it.

Long-run trends explained

Modern economies are becoming more capital-intensive in production techniques. Why is capital intensity rising in the long run? First, in the long run we can raise the supply of capital more easily than that of labour or land. Hence, rising demand bids up wages more than rental rates for capital. Firms substitute away from labour as it gets relatively more expensive than capital. Second, firms then look for inventions that economise on expensive labour. Hence, new technologies often favour more capital-intensive methods.

Why does the price of a house in London keep rising, even after adjusting for inflation? The supply of land close to the city centre is fixed. As households and businesses get richer, their demand for land rises. With a fixed supply, the price has to rise to ration scarce land in London. And low-paid nurses complain that they cannot find affordable accommodation close to their job in hospitals located in central London.

Recap

- Stocks are measured at a point in time. Flows are measured during periods of time. Flows are the rate of change of the corresponding stock, and a stock is the cumulation of the relevant flows.

- A firm demands capital services up to the point at which the rental equals the marginal revenue product of capital. The latter rises if the output price rises, if capital has more of other inputs with which to work, or if technical progress makes capital more productive. The industry demand curve is less elastic than the horizontal sum of each firm's demand curve because an industry expansion also bids down the output price, reducing the marginal benefit of capital.

- In the short run the supply of capital services is fixed. In the long run, it can be adjusted by producing new capital goods or allowing the existing capital stock to depreciate.

- The required rental allows a supplier of capital services to break even on the decision to purchase the capital asset. The required rental is higher the higher is the interest rate, the depreciation rate, or the purchase price of the capital good.

- In long-run equilibrium, the asset price of a capital good is both the price at which suppliers of capital goods are willing to make new goods and the price at which buyers can earn the required rental.

- Land is the special capital good whose supply is fixed even in the long run.

Review questions

1 Classify each as a stock or a flow: (a) a four-bedroom house; (b) the annual output of the UK housebuilding industry; (c) a painting by Picasso; (d) a training video.

2 Discuss the main determinants of the firm's demand curve and the industry's demand curve for capital services. How do these determinants affect the way a tax on the industry's output will shift the industry demand for capital services?

3 The interest rate falls from 10 to 5 per cent. Discuss in detail how this affects the rental on capital services and the level of the capital stock in an industry in the short and long run.

4 Suppose a plot of land is suitable only for agriculture. Can it be true that the farming industry will experience financial distress if there is an increase in the price of land? How would your answer be affected if the land could also be used for housing?

5 How fixed is the supply of land?

6 *Common fallacies* Why are these statements wrong? (a) If the economy continues to become more capital-intensive, eventually there will be no jobs left for workers. (b) Land is freely supplied by nature, hence land rentals should be zero.

Answers on pages 278–90

5-4 Income distribution

Learning outcomes

By the end of this section, you should understand:
- The functional distribution of income
- The personal distribution of income
- Their relation to input markets

The income of an input is simply its rental rate multiplied by the quantity of the factor employed. We now use our discussion of input markets to analyse the distribution of income in the UK.

The functional distribution of income

The **functional income distribution** is the division of national income between the different production inputs.

Table 5-5 shows the income shares of the different inputs in the UK in 1999 and compares these shares of national income with their shares during 1981–89. The functional income distribution has been quite stable over time. As national income rose, the total income of each production input broadly kept pace.

Even higher wages hardly raised labour input during the period, whereas the UK capital stock grew much more. More capital, and technical progress, together raised labour productivity and the

Table 5-5

UK functional income distribution
(% of national income)

Input	1981–89 average	1999
Employment	64	63
Self-employment	6	6
Profits and property rentals	30	31

Source: ONS, *UK National Accounts*

demand for labour. With a near fixed supply, this bid up wages and labour income, roughly at the same rate as national income as a whole.

Profits and land rentals also grew in line with national income, but for different reasons. Physical investment added to the quantity of capital. For a given technology, this would have led to diminishing returns to capital and lower rentals. But technical progress boosted capital productivity, preventing rentals from falling. The higher quantity of capital then implied a higher income for capital. In contrast, the quantity of land was fixed, but stronger demand for land bid up land rentals enough to maintain the share of land rentals in national income.

The personal income distribution

> The **personal income distribution** shows how national income is divided between people, regardless of the inputs from which these people earn their income.

The personal income distribution is relevant to issues such as equality and poverty. Table 5-6 excludes the very poor, showing data only for those whose incomes are large enough to have to submit a tax return. Even within this group, pre-tax income is quite unequally distributed in the UK. Table 5-6 shows that the richest 20 per cent of taxpayers earn over half the total UK income, whereas the poorest 20 per cent earn only 3 per cent of total income. Why do some people earn so much while others earn so little?

Unskilled workers have little training and low productivity. Workers with high levels of training and education earn much more. Some jobs, such as coal mining, pay high compensating differentials to offset unpleasant working conditions. Pleasant, but unskilled, jobs pay much less since many people are prepared to do them. However, talented superstars in scarce supply but high demand earn big money.

Another reason for the disparities in Table 5-6 is that personal income is not just labour income but also income from owning capital and land. This wealth is even more unequally divided than labour income. In 1998 the most wealthy 1 per cent of the UK population owned 23 per cent of the nation's wealth. The stream of profit and rental income to which such wealth gives rise helps explain the disparities in personal income in Table 5-6.

Surely such an unequal distribution is unfair, and the government should intervene? This normative issue takes us beyond the positive economies studied in Chapters 2–4. Normative issues are the subject of Chapter 6.

Table 5-6

UK personal income distribution, 1999

Household group	Average income (£000)
Poorest 20%	3
Next 20%	7
Next 20%	17
Next 20%	27
Richest 20%	51

Source: ONS, *Social Trends*

Box 5-8

The invisible helping hand

After Labour lost the 1979 general election it moved to the left. This pleased party activists but took the party too far away from the preferences of most voters. The Conservatives were in power for the next 17 years. After heavy defeat in 1983, successive Labour leaders slowly moved the party back to the middle ground. New Labour focus groups interviewed people directly to clarify the majority view on different issues. The result? Landslide Labour victories in 1997 and 2001.

Did Labour abandon its principles to win and keep office? Initially, it gave up old traditions of high welfare spending and high, visible taxes. But Chancellor Gordon Brown helped the poor a lot without frightening the middle classes. As a result of his first four budgets, the post-tax income of the poorest 10 per cent of people rose by 9 per cent, the post-tax income of the next poorest 10 per cent rose by 8 per cent. He did this without raising income tax or VAT.

Some of it was financed by stealth taxes, such as the tax treatment of pension funds, which ordinary voters did not notice or understand. Some was financed by making transfer payments more selective. Instead of a universal benefit, scarce resources were concentrated only on those who really needed them. Some of it was financed by economic growth: as incomes grew, given tax rates yielded more tax revenue, which was mainly given to the poor.

Recap

- The functional distribution of income across different inputs reflects equilibrium prices and quantities in input markets. Each input's share of national income is quite stable over time.
- The personal distribution of income shows how income is distributed across individuals, through whichever input supply they earn this income.
- High incomes reflect ownership of attributes or assets in scarce supply and high demand. Markets do not produce equal equality across individuals.
- The bequest of wealth across generations perpetuates advantage and disadvantage. Across individuals, wealth is even more unequally distributed than income.

Review questions

1 Name three taxes that help equalise the after-tax personal income distribution. Do any taxes have the opposite effect? Did you remember inferior goods?

2 If land is fixed in quantity and quality, can land rentals keep pace with other factor incomes in a growing economy?

3 Brazil has an unequal personal income distribution. Suggest at least three reasons.

Answers on pages 278–90

6

Governing the market

6-1 Equity, efficiency and market failure

Learning outcomes

By the end of this section, you should understand:
- Horizontal equity and vertical equity
- Pareto efficiency
- When markets are efficient
- Sources of market failure
- Externalities and public goods
- Informational problems in markets
- Moral hazard and adverse selection

Are markets a good way to allocate scarce resources? What does 'good' mean? Is it fair that some people earn much more than others in a market economy? These are not positive issues about how the economy works, but normative issues based on value judgements by the assessor.

Left-wing and right-wing parties disagree about the market economy. The right believes the market fosters choice, incentives and efficiency. The left stresses the market's failings and how government intervention can improve market outcomes. Generally, outcomes are judged against the criteria of equity and efficiency.

Horizontal equity rules out discrimination between people with similar characteristics and performance. Vertical equity is the Robin Hood principle, taking from the rich to give to the poor.

Horizontal equity is the identical treatment of identical people. **Vertical equity** is the different treatment of different people in order to reduce the consequences of these innate differences.

An economy's *resource allocation* describes who does what, and who gets what. Equity always entails value judgements but Vilfredo Pareto suggested a definition of efficiency that might be free of value judgements.

For given tastes, inputs and technology, an allocation is **efficient** if no one can then be made better off without making at least one other person worse off.

Suppose we have ten apples to give Stan and Rudi. Failure to hand out all ten apples is inefficient. A free lunch is available. Stan can get more apples without Rudi having fewer. Giving Stan and Rudi five apples each is efficient. None are wasted. However, giving all ten to Rudi is also efficient, but many would think this unfair. Eight for Stan and two for Rudi is still efficient, but fairer.

Taxation and subsidies can redistribute apples, but may waste some in the process. If a free market yields seven for Rudi and three for Stan, suppose by redistribution we could then gain one more for Stan but only at the cost of losing two for Rudi. Reasonable people will disagree whether this is desirable. It is a pure value judgement.

The invisible hand

Adam Smith suggested that a market economy is efficient 'as if by an Invisible Hand'. Perfect competition may do the job. Each consumer buys goods until his marginal cost (the price of the good) equals the marginal benefit of the good to him. The demand curve shows how much consumers buy at each price. Thus at each quantity in Figure 6-1 the demand curve DD is also the marginal benefit to consumers of getting that quantity of films.

Perfectly competitive producers equate price to marginal cost. At each output in Figure 6-1 the supply curve SS thus shows

the marginal cost of making that amount of the good. At Q_1 films, the marginal benefit to consumers is P_1, above the marginal cost to producers. Society should make more films than Q_1. Where supply and demand intersect, the social marginal benefit P^* of using resources to make films equals the social marginal cost P^* of films. No free lunch is available by reallocating resources. The allocation is efficient.

No government decided this. Each consumer and each firm pursued their self-interest, buying and selling what made sense to them. Prices co-ordinated their decisions. Because every buyer and seller faced the *same* price, marginal benefits equalled marginal costs. Society got the efficient quantity produced and consumed.

Even so, the resulting allocation may well be very unequal, as the talented are rewarded more highly than the

Figure 6-1

Competitive equilibrium and Pareto-efficiency

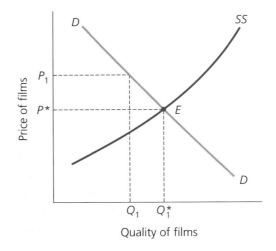

disadvantaged. The Invisible Hand applies to efficiency but not to equity. Quite often, it does not deliver efficiency either.

Market failures

> A **distortion** or **market failure** exists if society's marginal cost of making a good does not equal society's marginal benefit from consuming that good.

There are four principal sources of market failure.

Taxation

Governments levy taxes to finance public spending. A tax creates a gap between the price the buyer pays and the price the seller receives. If there is car tax of £2000, car buyers equate the marginal benefit of cars to the gross price, but car producers equate the marginal cost of cars to the lower net price received by producers. Hence the marginal cost of cars is £2000 less than the marginal benefit of cars. This is inefficient. Society should make more cars. Government spending is needed to offset other distortions in the market economy, and to redistribute income, but taxation itself usually creates a distortion.

Imperfect competition

Facing down-sloping demand curves, imperfect competitors set marginal cost equal to marginal revenue, which is less than the price they charge. Thus, price exceeds marginal cost, like a privately imposed tax. Again, such industries produce too little from the social view-point: in equilibrium, the marginal benefit of more output exceeds its marginal cost.

Externalities

Externalities are spillovers, such as pollution, noise and congestion. A person's decision ignores her effect on other people. There is no market for externalities like noise, secondary cigarette smoke or induced congestion on roads. Without a market in noise, prices cannot equate the marginal benefit of making a noise and the marginal cost of that noise to other people.

Other missing markets

People cannot always insure against the risks that they face, or find a loan on reasonable terms. Like externalities, these are examples of missing markets. The problem is often the fear market partici-pants have of being exploited by others with superior information. Again, with no market, price cannot equate society's marginal costs and benefits of these activities.

We now discuss market failures in more detail, and how policy might solve them. The rest of this section discusses externalities and other missing markets. The next two sections discuss taxation and imperfect competition.

Externalities

> An **externality** arises if a production or consumption decision affects the physical production or consumption possibilities of other people.

A chemical firm pollutes a lake, imposing an extra production cost on anglers (fewer fish) or a consumption cost on swimmers (dirty water). The firm pollutes until the marginal benefit of polluting (a lower cost of making chemicals) equals its marginal cost of polluting, which is zero. It ignores the marginal cost its pollution imposes on anglers and swimmers.

Conversely, you paint your house but ignore the consumption benefit to your neighbours, who now live in a nicer street. You paint up to the point where your own marginal benefit equals your marginal cost, but society's marginal benefit exceeds yours. There is too little house painting.

In both cases, the private costs or benefits differ from social costs or benefits. Figure 6-2 shows the marginal private cost *MPC* of making chemicals.

Figure 6-2

The social cost of a production externality

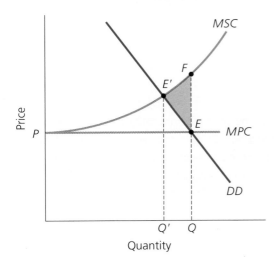

For simplicity, we assume it is constant. The marginal social cost *MSC* of chemical production is the marginal private cost plus the *marginal externality* from pollution at each output of chemicals. As chemical production rises, each extra unit of chemical output causes more pollution damage.

The curve *DD* shows the demand for chemicals. At the equilibrium output is *Q*, the marginal social cost *MSC* exceeds the marginal social benefit of chemicals (the private demand curve *DD*, since there are no consumption externalities). The output *Q* is inefficient. By reducing chemical production, society saves more in social cost than it loses in social benefit. Society could then make some people better off without making anyone worse off.

The efficient output is *Q'*, at which the marginal social benefit and cost of the last output unit are equal. By producing at the market equilibrium *E*, not the efficient point *E'*, society wastes the triangle *E'EF*, the excess of social cost over social benefit when output rises from *Q'* to *Q*.[1]

Production externalities make private and social cost diverge. Consumption externalities make private and social benefit diverge. Again, free market equilibrium is inefficient. Output is too low if externalities are beneficial, as with planting roses in your garden, but is too high if externalities are adverse, as with smoking in restaurants.

1 Beneficial production externalities help other producers. Pest control by one farm reduces pests on nearby farms. The marginal social cost of farm output is then *below* the marginal private cost. We could re-label the *MSC* curve as *MPC* in Figure 6-2 and re-label *MPC* as *MSC*. Free market equilibrium is at *E'* but *E* is now the efficient point.

Box 6-1

Atmosphere of pollution

Chlorofluorocarbons (CFCs), gases used in things like aerosols, are destroying the ozone layer. Without this sunscreen, more people get skin cancer. Organising international cutbacks in atmospheric pollution is difficult: each country wants to free ride, enjoying the benefits of other countries' cutbacks but making no contribution of its own. The Montreal Protocol was signed by nearly 50 countries in 1987. Before the Protocol, projected ozone depletion was 5 per cent by 2025 and 50 per cent by 2075. In the Protocol, countries agreed to take steps to reduce ozone depletion to 2 per cent by 2025 with no further deterioration thereafter. Dream on.

A second type of atmospheric pollution is the greenhouse effect from emissions of CFCs, methane, nitrous oxide and, especially, carbon dioxide. Greenhouse gases are the direct result of pollution and the indirect result of the atmosphere's reduced ability to absorb them. Plants convert carbon dioxide into oxygen. Chopping down forests to clear land for cattle, as global demand for hamburgers rises, has accelerated the greenhouse effect.

The consequence is global warming. People in London and Stockholm get better suntans; people in Africa face drought and famine. As icecaps melt, the sea rises, flooding low-lying areas. By 2070 the temperature will have risen by 4°C, and the sea by 45 centimetres. Again, organising collective international cutbacks has been difficult.

In 1997 the Kyoto Protocol agreed national targets for lower emissions of greenhouse gases. Becoming binding in 2008–12, the Kyoto deal would have cut emissions by 5 per cent relative to the 1990 level, but by much more relative to the growth that a do-nothing policy would have allowed. The table shows 1990 levels, actual behaviour in the 1990s, and the target for 2012.

	1990 emissions (million tonnes)	2012 target (% change from 1990 level)
Japan	1190	−6
US	5713	−7
Germany	1204	−21
UK	715	−12
Italy	532	−6
France	498	0
Spain	301	+15

In 2001 US President George W. Bush announced that the US would not ratify the Kyoto Protocol because it did not force poorer countries such as India and China to do their share of pollution reduction. In July 2001, after a meeting in Bonn, 178 countries decided to proceed with a weaker version of the Kyoto Protocol, despite the refusal of the US to participate.

Property rights and externalities

Can we set up a market in pollution? By pricing pollution itself, people could trade it until private marginal costs and benefits were equal. With nobody now ignored, private and social costs or benefits are the same again. Notice, in passing, that this implies that the efficient quantity of pollution is not zero. Eliminating the last little bit has a huge marginal cost and only a small marginal benefit. It is not worth cutting back to zero.

Why don't we have a market in pollution? Someone at your door says: 'I am collecting money from people who hate factory smoke in their gardens. We'll pay the factory to cut back. Will you contribute? I'm visiting 5000 houses nearby.' Even though you hate smoke, you pretend not to care and do not contribute. If everybody else pays, the factory cuts back and you get the benefit. If nobody pays, your small payment makes little difference. Whatever others do, you don't pay: you are a *free rider*. Everyone else reasons similarly. Nobody pays, even though you are all better off paying to get the smoke cut back.

> A **free rider**, knowing he cannot be excluded from consuming a good, has no incentive to buy it.

Taxing externalities

Cigarette smokers cause bad consumption externalities for those nearby. Figure 6-3 shows the supply curve *SS* of cigarette producers, which also shows marginal social cost. *DD* is the private demand curve, showing the marginal private benefit of cigarettes to smokers.

The marginal social benefit *DD'* of cigarette consumption is lower than *DD*.

Free market equilibrium is at *E*, but the efficient point is *E**. The government now levies a tax *E*F* per packet of cigarettes. With the tax-inclusive price on the vertical axis, the demand curve *DD* is unaffected, but the supply curve shifts up to *SS'*, which, subtracting the tax *E*F* from each price, returns producers to the original supply curve *SS*.

A tax rate *E*F* leads to market equilibrium at *F*. The efficient quantity *Q** is produced and consumed. Consumers pay *P'* and producers get *P''* after tax is deducted at *E*F* per unit. The tax rate *E*F* is exactly the marginal externality on the last unit when the efficient quantity *Q** is produced. Consumers behave as if they took account of the externality, though they look only at the tax-inclusive price.

Figure 6-3

Taxes to offset externalities

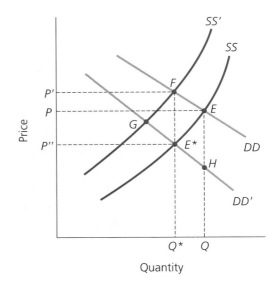

Box 6-2

Keeping pollution in check

Environmental protection has been a mixed success in the last 30 years. Smog has gone, and fish are back in many rivers. But coal-fired power stations still emit sulphur dioxide, and Greenpeace activities highlight many other examples that still cause concern. If we want to reduce pollution further, should we use quotas or taxes?

Facing the same pollution tax rate, each firm would adjust until the marginal cost of cutting pollution is the same across firms, a necessary feature of the efficient solution. However, in an uncertain world, the government might miscalculate, and set the wrong tax rate. If pollution beyond a certain critical level is disastrous, for example irreversibly damaging the ozone layer, direct regulation of the quantity of pollution is safer, even if it fails to cut pollution in the least-cost way. However, a clever compromise is possible.

The US Clean Air Acts include an *emissions trading programme* and *bubble policy*. The Acts specify a minimum standard for air quality, and impose pollution emission quotas on individual polluters. Any firm below its pollution quota gets an *emission reduction credit* (*ERC*) that can be sold to other polluters wanting to exceed their pollution quotas. Total pollution is regulated, but firms that can cheaply cut pollution do so, selling their *ERC* to firms for which pollution reduction is costlier. This reduces the total cost of pollution reduction.

When a firm has many factories, the *bubble policy* applies pollution controls to the firm as a whole, not to individual factories. A firm can cut back most in the plants where pollution reduction is cheapest. US policy combines 'control over quantities' for aggregate pollution where the risk and uncertainty are greatest, with 'control through the price system' for allocating efficiently the way these overall targets are achieved.

Taxes that offset externalities *improve* efficiency. The fact that alcohol and tobacco have harmful externalities is a reason to tax them heavily.

Public goods

Public goods are like a very strong externality. Most goods are private goods. The ice cream in your throat is now unavailable for eating by other people. Not so with public goods, such as clean air and national defence.

A **public good** is necessarily consumed in equal amounts by everyone.

Public goods have this special feature in consumption, in whichever sector they are produced. If the Navy patrols coastal waters, your consumption of national defence does not affect our quantity of national defence. We get different amounts of utility from it if our tastes differ, but must all consume the same quantity. Nobody can be excluded from consuming a public good once it exists, and the act of consumption does not deplete the quantity left for other people.

Public goods supplied in private markets are wide open to the free-rider problem. Since you get it, *whether or not you pay for it*, you never buy a public good that already exists. Private markets do not produce the efficient quantity. We need government intervention. The efficient quantity of a public good equates the marginal cost of making it to the marginal social benefit of having it, which is simply the *sum* of the marginal private benefit of each person consuming that quantity.

Democracies resolve this problem through elections. By asking 'How much would you like, given that everyone will be charged for the cost of providing public goods?' society tries to identify the efficient quantity of a public good. This may then be produced by the public sector, or contracted out to private suppliers.

Other missing markets

Information is not always free to acquire. People often know more about their own behaviour than others can easily find out. Fear that people will exploit this informational advantage may then prevent markets from developing. Here are two problems that crop up regularly.

Moral hazard

Insurance companies calculate the odds of various risks occurring. Is this how they calculate what premium to charge for house insurance? Sitting in a restaurant, you remember you left some chips frying in a pan. Why leave your nice meal to go home to switch the cooker off? You are fully insured against fire. Similarly, with full health insurance you may not bother with precautionary check-ups. The act of insuring raises the likelihood of the thing you are insuring against.

> **Moral hazard** exploits inside information to take advantage of the other party to the contract.

With complete information, the insurance company could refuse to pay out if you do not take proper care. With costly information, it is hard for the company to discover this key fact.

Actuarial calculations for the whole population, many of whom are uninsured, are now a poor guide to your behaviour once insured. Moral hazard makes it harder to get insurance and costlier if you get it. Insurance firms at best offer partial insurance, leaving you to bear part of the cost if the bad thing happens. This gives you an incentive to take care, reducing the odds of the bad outcome. Hence, insurance firms pay out less often and can charge you a lower premium.

Adverse selection

People who smoke are more likely to die young. Individuals know if they themselves smoke. If an insurance firm cannot tell who smokes, it must charge everyone the same price. Suppose this reflects mortality rates for the whole country. Non-smokers, with above-average life expectancy, find the price too dear. Smokers, knowing their looming health problems, realise that the price is a bargain.

> **Adverse selection** means individuals use their inside information to accept or reject a contract. Those accepting are no longer an average sample of the population.

Box 6-3

Economics: a Nobel science

The 2001 Nobel Prize for Economic Science was shared by three economists who pioneered the analysis of inside information.

George Akerlof first analysed *adverse selection* in the used car market, where sceptical buyers know sellers may try to offload useless cars about which the seller has much more information than the buyer. Akerlof showed that, in market equilibrium, buyers assume all cars are bad. Sellers of good cars cannot get a fair price. The same analysis helps us understand loan sharks, junk bonds and street traders offering supposedly genuine Armani perfume at silly prices.

Michael Spence showed that this problem is partly solved if those with good characteristics take costly actions to reveal credibly that they must be the good guys. Higher education can *signal* that you are smart and determined, valuable things in a worker. Investment banks hire history as well as economics graduates because they value these attributes, not because they want to know more about Queen Elizabeth I.

Joseph Stiglitz, until recently Chief Economist of the World Bank, developed another solution to adverse selection, relying on *screening* by the buyer rather than signalling by the seller. Offering lower initial wages but correspondingly higher salaries later in life is attractive only to those workers who plan to remain with the firm in the long run. It allows the firm then to invest in training, knowing that its workers will not then take years out to surf in Australia.

The insurance firm cannot distinguish the two groups, but knows that a price based on the national average will attract only smokers, a loss-making proposition. Instead, the firm assumes that all its customers smoke, and charges a suitably high price. It defends against the worst. Non-smokers cannot get insurance at a fair price.

To check the difference between moral hazard and adverse selection, which is which in the following examples? (1) A person with a fatal disease signs up for life insurance. (2) Already having insured his kids, a person then becomes unexpectedly depressed and commits suicide. (The first is adverse selection, the second moral hazard.)

Similarly, borrowers know if they are safe or risky, but this is hard for lenders to discover. Suppose a bank should charge safe borrowers an interest rate of 5 per cent, but risky borrowers an interest rate of 15 per cent. An accountant may tell the bank to charge something in between, like 10 per cent. An economist knows this will attract only risky borrowers. The only equilibrium is for the bank to charge 15 per cent, attracting only risky borrowers. Safe borrowers are fed up they cannot get a loan on decent terms. Adverse selection prevents a market for safe borrowers.

Moral hazard and adverse selection prevent some markets developing properly. Without markets, the Invisible Hand cannot equate marginal social benefit and marginal social cost.

Recap

- Horizontal equity is the equal treatment of equals, and vertical equity the unequal treatment of unequals.

- A resource allocation says who makes what and who gets what. It is efficient if no reallocation of resources could then make some people better off without making others worse off.

- For given inputs and technology, there are many efficient allocations, differing in fairness.

- With no market failures, free markets are efficient. Producers and consumers equate marginal costs and marginal benefits to the same price, and thus to each other.

- Governments face a conflict between equity and efficiency. Redistributive taxes drive a wedge between prices to buyers and sellers, undermining the invisible hand.

- Distortions occur if market equilibrium does not equate marginal social cost and benefit, an inefficiency or market failure. Distortions arise from taxation, imperfect competition, externalities, and other missing markets reflecting informational problems.

- Externalities imply one agent's decisions have direct but neglected effects on others. The free-rider problem usually inhibits markets in pollution or congestion. Imposing taxes (subsidies) to reflect the marginal adverse (beneficial) externality makes people act as if the market existed, restoring efficiency.

- Public goods are a strong externality in which everyone consumes the same amount and cannot be prevented from doing. Markets cannot handle this well. Having elections to decide the level of public goods is a possible solution.

- Inside information inhibits markets through moral hazard and adverse selection. Where markets are missing, prices cannot equate marginal social cost and benefit.

Review questions

1 An economy has ten goods to share between two people. The expression (x,y) denotes that the first person gets x and the second person y. For allocations (a) to (e) say if they are efficient, equitable, or neither: (a) (10,0) (b) (7,2) (c) (5,5) (d) (3,6) (e) (2,8). Would you prefer allocation (d) or (e)?

2 Driving your car in the rush hour, you slow down other drivers. Is this an externality? How might it be offset efficiently? Discuss the merits of fuel taxes that also penalise rural drivers on deserted roads.

3 Should it be compulsory to wear seat belts in cars?

4 Which of the following are public goods: a privatised coastguard system, a tolerant society, a state-owned post office. In each case explain your answer.

5 **Common fallacies** Why are these statements wrong? (a) Society should ban all toxic discharges. (b) Railways must be made completely safe. (c) Anything the government can do the market can do better.

Answers on pages 278–90

6-2 Taxation

Learning outcomes

By the end of this section, you should understand:
- Average and marginal tax rates; direct and indirect taxes
- Fair and unfair taxes
- Tax incidence
- Taxation, efficiency and waste

Table 6-1 shows UK government spending over nearly 50 years. Governments buy goods and services – schools, defence, the police, and so on – which directly use resources that could have been used in the private sector. Governments also spend on *transfer payments* – subsidies such as social security, state pensions and debt interest – that do not directly use scarce resources. Rather, they transfer purchasing power to people who then buy goods and services.

Table 6-1

UK government spending (% of GDP)

	1956	1976	2001
Total spending	33.9	46.9	40.4
Goods and services	20.7	25.9	22.2
Transfer payments	13.2	21.0	18.2

Sources: ONS, *UK National Accounts*; HM Treasury, *Budget 2001*

Between 1956 and 1976 the scale of government got bigger. Since then, the trend has been reversed. One reason has been the desire of governments to make tax cuts.

> If T is the amount paid in tax, and Y is income, then T/Y is the **average tax rate**. The **marginal tax rate** shows how total tax T increases as income Y increases.

Taxes are *progressive* if the average tax rate rises as income rises, taking proportionately more from the rich than from the poor. Taxes are *regressive* if the average tax rate falls as income level rises, taking proportionately less from the rich. Table 6-2 shows that the UK, like many other countries, has cut tax rates in the last two decades, especially for the very rich.

UK government spending, and the taxes that finance it, are now 40 per cent of national output. Nearly half of total government spending goes on transfer

Table 6-2

UK income tax rates, 1978–2000

Taxable income	Marginal tax rate	
(000s 2001 £)	1978–79	2001–02
1800	34	10
5000	34	22
20 000	45	22
30 000	50	40
40 000	70	40
70 000	83	40

Sources: ONS, *Financial Statement and Budget Report*; ONS, *Budget 2001*

Note: Taxable income after deducting allowances. In 2001–02 a single person's allowance was £4535

payments such as pensions and debt interest. Just over half goes to buy goods and services, especially health, defence and education. Most government spending is financed by taxation, mainly *direct taxes* related to income (income tax itself, national insurance contributions and corporation tax paid by firms) and *indirect taxes* on expenditure [value added tax (VAT) and excise duties on fuel, alcohol and tobacco].

> **Direct taxes** are taxes on income, **indirect taxes** are taxes on spending.

We now assess the UK tax system against our two criteria, equity and efficiency.

How to tax fairly

In taking proportionately more from the rich than from the poor, income tax reflects the principle of *ability to pay*, based on a concern about vertical equity. In contrast, the *benefits principle* argues that people who get more than their share of public spending should pay more than their share of tax revenues. Car users should pay more than pedestrians towards public roads.

The benefits principle often conflicts directly with the principle of ability to pay. If those most vulnerable to unemployment have to pay the highest contributions to a government unemployment insurance scheme, it is hard to redistribute income, wealth or welfare. If the main objective is vertical equity, the ability to pay principle must take precedence.

Two factors make the tax and benefit system more progressive than income tax alone. First, transfer payments actually give money to the poor. The old get pensions, the unemployed get jobseekers allowance and the poor get income support. Second, the state supplies some public goods available to the poor even if they do not pay taxes. The rich sunbathe in their own gardens, but the poor sunbathe in public parks.

There are some *regressive* elements that take proportionately more from the poor. Beer and tobacco taxes, and the National Lottery, are huge earners for the government. Yet the poor spend much more of their income on these goods than do the rich. These things effectively redistribute from the poor to the rich!

Tax incidence

The ultimate effect of a tax can be very different from its apparent effect.

Tax incidence is the final tax burden once we allow for all the induced effects of the tax.

Figure 6-4 shows labour demand *DD* and labour supply *SS*. With no tax, equilibrium is at *E*. Now an income tax is introduced. If we measure the gross wage on the vertical axis, the demand curve *DD* is unaltered since the gross wage is the marginal cost of labour to the firm.

However, it is the wage net-of-tax that induces workers to supply labour. *SS* still shows labour supply in terms of this net wage, so we must draw the higher schedule *SS'* to show the supply of labour in terms of the gross wage. The vertical distance between *SS'* and *SS* is the income tax on earnings from the last hour of work.

The new equilibrium is *E'*. The gross wage is *W'* at which firms demand *L'* hours. The vertical distance *A'E'* is the tax paid on the last hour of work. At the net wage *W''*, workers supply *L'* hours. Relative to the original equilibrium, a tax on wages raises the gross wage to *W'*, but cuts the net wage to *W''*. It raises the wage firms pay, but cuts the wage workers get.

> The **tax wedge** is the gap between the price paid by the buyer and the price received by the seller.

The incidence of the tax fell on *both* firms and workers even though, for administrative convenience, the tax was collected from firms. The incidence or burden of a tax does not depend on who hands over money to the government. Taxes alter equilibrium prices and quantities. These induced effects must also be taken into

Figure 6-4

A tax on wages

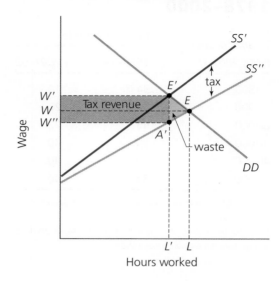

account. However, we can draw a general conclusion. The more inelastic the supply curve and the more elastic the demand curve, the more the final incidence will fall on the seller rather than the purchaser.

Figure 6-5 shows the extreme case of a vertical supply curve. Without a tax, equilibrium is at *E* and the wage is *W*. A vertical supply curve *SS* implies that a quantity of hours *L* are supplied whatever the net wage. A tax on wages leads to a new equilibrium at *A'*. Only if the gross wage is unchanged will firms demand the quantity *L* that is supplied. The entire incidence falls on the workers. To check you have got the idea of incidence, draw for yourself a market with a horizontal supply curve but down-sloping demand curve. Show that the incidence of a tax now falls only on consumers.

Taxation, efficiency and waste

Having examined taxation and equity, we now look at taxation and efficiency. We can use Figure 6-4 again. Before the tax, labour market equilibrium is at E. The wage W is both the marginal social benefit of the last hour of work and its marginal social cost. The demand curve DD shows the marginal benefit of labour, the value of extra output. The supply curve SS shows the marginal social cost of work, the value of leisure sacrificed to work another hour. At E marginal social cost and benefit are equal, which is socially efficient.

A tax shifts equilibrium to E'. The tax $A'E'$ raises the gross wage to firms to W' but cuts the net wage for workers to W''. The triangle $A'E'E$ is a deadweight loss or pure waste. By cutting hours from L to L', the tax stops society using hours on which the marginal social benefit, the height of the demand curve DD, exceeds the marginal social cost, the height of the supply curve SS. By driving a wedge between the wage firms pay and the wage workers get, the tax makes market equilibrium inefficient.

Figure 6-5

Taxing a factor in inelastic supply

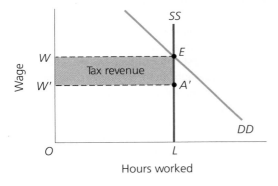

Box 6-4

Betting tax scrapped early

The tax on punters will be abolished three months ahead of schedule on the first weekend in October, the Financial Secretary Paul Boateng announced today (13 July 2001). Gordon Brown announced in his March Budget that by 1 January 2002, the current tax on betting stakes would be replaced with a tax on bookmakers' gross profits, a radical reform which means Britain's bookmakers will end the deductions they currently charge punters, and look to grow their domestic and international business from a UK base.

Source: www.hm-treasury.gov.uk

This example illustrates the limits to government sovereignty. Betting tax had been a big earner for the Treasury. Competition from offshore bookies offering online betting put an end to this. The government was forced to change betting tax to stop onshore bookies being wiped out. How the internet and globalisation are changing the nation state is a key issue of the new millennium. Economics helps you understand better what is going on.

Must taxes distort?

Most taxes do, but Figure 6-5 showed a tax when supply is completely inelastic. With equilibrium quantity unchanged, there is no distortion triangle. This is a general principle. If either the supply or the demand curve is inelastic, a tax induces a small change in quantity. Hence the deadweight loss triangle is small. Since the government needs some tax revenue, the smallest waste occurs if the goods most inelastic in supply or demand are taxed most heavily. Another reason for high taxes on alcohol and tobacco is that they have inelastic demand.

Finally, Section 6-1 showed that taxes actually improve efficiency if they offset externalities. By building marginal externalities into the prices to which private individuals react, such pollution taxes and congestion charges make people 'internalise' externalities.

Recap

■ Government revenues come mainly from direct taxes on personal incomes and company profits, and indirect taxes on purchases of goods and services. Government spending is partly purchases of goods and services and partly transfer payments.

■ A progressive tax and transfer system takes most from the rich and gives most to the poor. The UK tax and transfer system is mildly progressive.

■ By taxing or subsidising goods that involve externalities, the government can induce the private sector to behave as if it takes account of the externality, raising efficiency.

■ Except for taxes designed to offset externalities, taxes are generally distortionary. By driving a wedge between the selling price and the purchase price, they stop prices equating marginal cost and marginal benefit. The size of the deadweight burden is higher the higher is the marginal tax rate and the more elastic are supply and demand.

■ The incidence of tax is who ultimately pays the tax. The more inelastic is demand relative to supply, the more a tax falls on buyers not sellers, and vice versa.

Review questions

1 Which of the following are public goods? (a) The fire brigade; (b) clean streets; (c) refuse collection; (d) cable television; (e) social toleration; (f) the postal service. Explain and discuss alternative ways of providing these goods or services.

2 Classify the following taxes as progressive or regressive: (a) 10 per cent tax on all luxury goods; (b) taxes in proportion to the value of owner-occupied houses; (c) taxes on beer; (d) taxes on champagne.

3 There is a flat-rate 30 per cent income tax on all income over £2000. Calculate the average tax rate (tax paid divided by income) at income levels of £5000, £10 000 and £50 000. Is the tax progressive? Is it more or less progressive if the exemption is raised from £2000 to £5000?

4 (a) Suppose labour supply is completely inelastic. Show why there is no deadweight burden if wages are taxed. Who bears the incidence of the tax? (b) Now suppose labour supply is quite elastic. Show the area that is the deadweight burden of the tax. How much of the tax is ultimately borne by firms and how much by workers? (c) For any given supply elasticity show that firms bear more of the tax the more inelastic is the demand for labour.

5 *Common fallacies* Why are these statements wrong? (a) Taxes always distort. (b) If government spends all its revenue, taxes are not a burden on society as a whole.

Answers on pages 278–90

6-3 Dealing with monopoly power

Learning outcomes

By the end of this section, you should understand:
- The social cost of monopoly power
- UK competition policy in theory and practice
- Mergers
- Regulation of natural monopolies

Imperfectly competitive firms with some monopoly power must cut their price to sell more output. Since marginal revenue is less than the price for which the last good is sold, marginal cost is less than price and marginal consumer benefit. Such firms make less than the efficient quantity.

Moreover, when a competitive firm gets lazy it loses market share and may go out of business. When a monopoly gets lazy, it simply makes less profit. From the social viewpoint, its cost curves are then unnecessarily high.

> There are two **social costs of monopoly power**. The first is too little output, the second is wastefully high cost curves.

Society may not worry just about the inefficiency of imperfect competition. It may also care about the *political* power that large firms exert, and the *distri-*butional issue of the fairness of large monopoly profits.

Taxing monopoly profits

The way to maximise after-tax profits is to maximise pre-tax profits. Thus, for *given* cost curves, a monopolist's output is unaffected by a tax on monopoly profits. Since the demand curve for its output is unaffected, making the same output means charging the same price. Governments can tax away monopoly profits. High profits are not directly a social cost of monopoly power.

Must liberalisation help?

Is more competition always better? Suppose there are big economies of scale and a steadily down-sloping average cost curve. Suppose the government insists on more competition, say entry of a second producer. Greater competition reduces profit margins, but, with lower output, the firms cannot enjoy scale economies and have high average costs. Society may lose more from the cost increase than it gains from greater competition.

We thus discuss two approaches to policy. Where scale economies are not too big, promoting competition is indeed the answer. But where scale economies are vast, it is better to keep the monopoly but regulate its behaviour.

Competition policy

What do Durex, Valium and Cornflakes have in common with household gas supplies and mobile phones? All were investigated by the Competition Commission, which monitors the behaviour of big firms and checks for the possible abuse of monopoly power.

> **Competition policy** promotes efficiency through competition between firms. The **Competition Commission** examines whether a monopoly, or potential monopoly, is against the public interest.

UK policy was laid down in the 1973 Fair Trading Act, amended in the Competition Acts of 1980 and 1998. The Director-General of Fair Trading monitors company behaviour, and can refer cases to the Competition Commission for a thorough investigation. A company can be referred if it supplies over 25 per cent of the total market. The Commission can also be given cases where firms collude to restrict competition.

The UK is also subject to the monopoly legislation of the European Union. Article 85 of the Treaty of Rome is similar to UK legislation on restrictive practices, which must be declared and are usually then prohibited. Article 86 bans the abuse of a 'dominant position' as a monopolist.

UK competition policy in practice

The Competition Commission has wide powers, yet few firms were penalised after its investigation. The Commission has often relied on informal assurances that bad behaviour would stop.

Famous cases include the Unilever subsidiary Birds Eye Wall's (BEW), accused of freezing out the competition by distributing wrapped ice cream in corner-shop freezer cabinets from which products of competitors were excluded. The Commission found against BEW, and recommended that BEW practices should change.

Similarly, after examining charges from fixed phones to mobile phones, it concluded that emerging competition in telecommunications was not yet sufficient to discipline the top suppliers, whose charges were well above those justified by the public interest. The Commission recommended that the licences of Cellnet, Vodafone and BT be modified to impose price ceilings on these particular charges.

Should UK policy abandon this case-by-case approach, and ban monopolies altogether? Large scale is needed to achieve scale economies, and may also promote better management, co-ordination and research. Moreover, when import tariffs are low and transport costs moderate, domestic firms face severe international competition.

Box 6-5

Sky's the limit for Man United

In 1998, Sky launched a huge bid to take over Manchester United. The Competition Commission turned it down, arguing that if collective selling of Premier League rights continued, Sky would get an unfair advantage over other TV bidders through the influence and information it got from merging with Man United. Aware of this, potential bidders would then withdraw, further enhancing Sky's dominant position. The merger would also have given Sky too much influence over regulation of football by the Premier League.

The Commission asserted that 'the relevant football market in which Manchester United operates is no wider than the matches of Premier League clubs', but was this correct? In 1999 Man United were European champions, won on the cheap since so many of their young stars had grown up in the Man United youth programme. Sky's money would have let Man United match salaries in Italy. The Premier League still can't match salaries of Real Madrid, and thus has never attracted the top Brazilian stars.

Whereas European club teams simultaneously compete in national and European competitions, most American sports are hermetically sealed. World Series baseball is a US affair. The same goes for basketball or American football. This makes it easier to have salary caps and other rules that redistribute between clubs to prevent wide gaps persisting (the worst teams one year get the pick of the newcomers the next year). Within Europe, penalising the top team within a country helps the country's club competition, but may deprive it of honours on the European stage.

This example shows again the difficulty in defining the relevant market in which to assess competition policy. UK, Europe, or the global market? Once it extends beyond a single country, which competition authority should have jurisdiction? Easy questions with difficult answers.

Without knowing the size of the relevant market in which firms are competing, large size does not always imply uncompetitive behaviour.

Merger policy

Competition policy also scrutinises the formation of large new companies.

A **merger** is the union of two companies where they think they will do better by amalgamating.

A *horizontal merger* is the union of two firms at the same production stage in the same industry. A *vertical merger* is the union of two firms at different production stages in the same industry. In *conglomerate mergers*, the production activities of the two firms are essentially unrelated.

A horizontal merger may allow more scale economies. One large car factory may be better than two small ones. Vertical mergers may assist co-ordination and planning. It is easier to make long-term decisions about the best size and type of steel mill if a simultaneous decision is taken on car production for which steel is an important input. Conglomerate mergers involve companies with completely independent products,

Table 6-3

UK mergers 1972–2000 (annual averages)

	Number	Value (1998 £bn)
1972–78	640	1
1979–85	490	4
1986–89	1300	43
1990–94	590	10
1995–98	580	31
1999–2000	540	61

Sources: British Business 1989; Business Trends 1997; ONS, First Release

and have less scope for a direct reduction in production costs.

Merger policy must thus compare the social gains (potential cost reduction) with the social costs (larger monopoly power). Table 6-3 shows annual averages of mergers involving UK firms. It shows dramatic merger booms in the late 1980s and again after 1995.

Merger booms would have been impossible if policy had opposed them. Individual cases were again examined case by case. There are currently two grounds for referring a prospective merger to an investigation by the Competition Commission: (1) that the merger creates market share of at least 25 per cent, or (2) that the merger transfers at least £70 million worth of company assets.

Since 1965, only 4 per cent of merger proposals have been referred to the Competition Commission. UK policy has largely consented to mergers, reflecting two assumptions. First, cost savings from scale economies are big. Second, as part of an increasingly competitive world market, even large UK firms have little monopoly power.

Regulating natural monopolies

Sometimes, large domestic firms face little foreign competition, and the size of scale economies makes them natural monopolies.

> A **natural monopoly**, having vast scale economies, does not fear entry by smaller competitors.

The government can nationalise them, to control their behaviour in the public interest, or can leave them as private firms but appoint independent regulators to supervise their behaviour. After 1945, most European countries chose nationalisation. Since 1980 they have increasingly reverted to regulation of private monopolies.

To limit the exercise of monopoly power, regulators impose a price ceiling. After privatisation in 1984, BT had an '$RPI - X$' price ceiling. Its *nominal* prices could rise with the retail price index, minus X per cent. X is the annual fall in its *real* price. Since BT enjoyed rapid technical progress, it could cut costs year after year. During its first ten years as a private company, BT's real prices fell by 43 per cent.

Subsequent regulators used a similar approach. In regulating water companies, OFWAT adopted '$RPI + K$', letting the real price of water rise K per cent a year to finance much-needed investment in pipes and water purification. In 1999, after a Competition Commission report criticised charges for mobile phones,

Box 6-6

Off the rails

In 1997 rail privatisation broke up British Rail into many train operators but one company, Railtrack, to supply the track infrastructure. Railtrack's share price soared as investors expected it to prosper. By October 2001 Railtrack was bankrupt. What are the lessons of its failure?

After decades of underinvestment in rail infrastructure, massive investment was needed. Since both Railtrack and train operators were regulated, they were not allowed to raise fares enough to earn the revenue needed for this investment. Politicians were sensitive about the level of rail fares and unwilling to inject much public money.

Two things made a bad situation worse. First, everyone underestimated the cost of upgrading the track, notably the London to Glasgow line. Second, rail accidents, especially at Hatfield where the track was to blame, led to expensive but unanticipated programmes to improve safety rapidly.

The table shows the cumulative investment planned during 2001–10. With the Treasury refusing more help, the private sector was reluctant to invest £34 billion in an industry subject to outside regulation, with no guarantee of enough revenue to repay the investment with interest.

Planned rail investment, cumulative funding, 2001–10 (£ billion, 2000 prices)

	Public	Private
Rail infrastructure	3.5	25.5
New trains	11.5	8.5
Total	15.0	34.0

By withholding the next round of government money and forcing Railtrack into bankruptcy, the government took ultimate control when the going got tough. Some private investors claimed that this would make future partnerships between public and private sectors more difficult. Yet the private sector is happy to keep the profits when things go well. It is unclear that they have grounds for complaint when things happen to go the other way.

Source: The Economist, 20 October 2001

Vodafone and Cellnet were set a price ceiling of '*RPI* − 9' for two years.

Regulating behaviour is not the only option available to regulators. British Rail was broken up into many train operators and a track operator after privatisation. However, this has exposed problems of coordination that remind us that bigger is sometimes more beautiful.

Recap

- The social costs of monopoly power are too little output and high cost curves that waste resources.
- Competition policy tries to promote competition to discipline monopoly power. In the UK a firm with over 25 per cent of the market can be referred to the Competition Commission. The Commission weighs the costs of monopoly power against possible gains from larger scale.
- Anti-competition agreements between firms, such as collusive price-fixing, must be notified and are generally illegal.
- Mergers may be horizontal, vertical or conglomerate. Conglomerate mergers have the smallest scope for economies of scale. The recent merger boom was largely horizontal mergers to take advantage of larger markets caused by globalisation, European integration and deregulation.
- In principle, mergers can be referred to the Competition Commission if they will create a firm with a 25 per cent market share or they involve assets of over £70 million. In practice, few mergers satisfying these criteria are actually referred.
- Natural monopolies enjoy such scale economies that effective competition is impossible.
- Governments can nationalise such firms or regulate them as private monopolies. In the latter case, price ceilings help limit the abuse of monopoly power.

Review questions

1 With constant $AC = MC = £5$, a competitive industry makes 1 million cars. Taken over by a monopolist, output falls to 800 000 cars, and the price rises to £8. AC and MC are unchanged. By calculating an inefficiency triangle analogous to those in Section 6-1, quantify the social cost of monopoly in this case.

2 A regulator now imposes a price ceiling of £6. What happens to the social cost of monopoly? Could the regulator impose a ceiling of £5? Would this be efficient?

3 Now draw AC and MC for a natural monopoly that continues to enjoy scale economies as its output rises. What is the socially efficient output if cost curves do not shift? Could the regulator set a price ceiling that would achieve this?

4 Does globalisation always reduce the case for merger control?

5 *Common fallacies* Why are these statements wrong? (a) Monopolies make profits and must be well-run companies. (b) Mergers are beneficial; otherwise companies would not merge.

Answers on pages 278–90

7

The income and output of nations

7-1 Macroeconomic data

Learning outcomes

By the end of this section, you should understand:
- Measures of national income and output
- The circular flow of resources and payments
- Why leakages must equal injections
- What national income fails to measure

Microeconomics magnifies the detail in order to analyse particular markets. In contrast, macroeconomics simplifies the building blocks in order to focus on how they fit together as a whole. The media are always discussing problems of slow growth, inflation, unemployment, and the future of national currencies. These issues help determine the outcome of elections, and make some people interested in learning more about macroeconomics.

Macroeconomics studies the economy as a whole.

Table 7-1 shows both national income and income per person in the Group of Seven or G7, the largest of the rich industrial countries. In total, Americans earned $9.6 trillion in 2000, or about $34 000 a person. Japanese national income was $3.3 trillion, which implied about $26 000 a person. Although China, India and Russia are much less developed, and thus have lower incomes per person, they have such large populations that their total incomes are large. Table 7-1 shows that China now has the second largest national income in the world, despite the fact that its citizens each earn only a tenth as much as the average American.

We now explain what the concepts of national income and national output mean, and how they are measured.

Households and firms

Households own land, labour and capital, whose services they rent to firms as

Table 7-1

National income and income per citizen, 2000

		National income (US $ trillion)	Income per citizen (000s of US $)
G7:	US	9.6	34
	Japan	3.3	26
	Germany	2.1	25
	France	1.4	24
	UK	1.4	24
	Italy	1.3	23
	Canada	0.8	27
Other:	China	4.9	4
	India	2.4	2
	Russia	1.2	8

Source: World Bank, *World Development Report, 2002*

Figure 7-1

The circular flow between firms and households

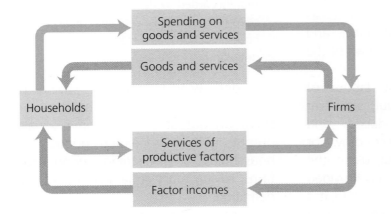

production inputs. Households spend this income buying the output of firms.

The **circular flow** is the flow of inputs, outputs and payments between firms and households.

In Figure 7-1, the inner loop shows the flows of real resources between the two sectors, and the outer loop shows the corresponding flows of payments.

This suggests three ways to measure the amount of economic activity in an economy: (a) the net value of goods and services produced; (b) the value of household earnings; and (c) the value of spending on the final output of firms. Whether we measure net output, incomes (including profit) or final spending, we get the same answer for GDP.

> **Gross domestic product (GDP)** measures an economy's output.

However, there are several complications. First, the output of firms is not all sold to households. The concept of value added avoids double counting the output that some firms buy from other firms.

> **Value added** is net output, after deducting goods used up during the production process.

From gross output we deduct the use of raw materials and partly finished goods, but not the cost of labour or capital. The steel in a car door was *already* counted as the output of the steel producer, and must not be counted again as part of the output of the car producer.

We do not deduct the labour of car workers from car output, since car workers were not produced and measured elsewhere in the economy. Nor do we deduct the cost of using the assembly line that made cars. Provided this capital input does not depreciate, it is available next period to make yet more cars, and hence was not used up.

Total value added is the net output of the economy. One way or another this is paid to households as income and profits, and this income is spent buying the final output that firms sell to end users. So far, households are the only end users.

Leakages and injections

> **Saving S** is the part of income not spent buying output. **Investment I** is firms' purchases of new capital goods made by other firms.

If households earn £7000 but spend only £5000 on consumption C, they must save the other £2000. To pay out incomes of £7000, firms must have value added of £7000 which is sold to end users. If £5000 is sold to households for consumption, the other £2000 must have been sold to firms buying new capital goods. These firms are end users because this capital is *not* then used up as a production input.

> Saving is a **leakage** from the circular flow, money paid to households but *not* returned to firms as spending. Investment is an **injection** to the circular flow, money earned by firms but *not* from sales to households. Leakages always equal injections, as a matter of definition.

The *only* way to measure saving is to measure the part of income not spent on output. Since income equals output, which is either goods for households or investment goods for firms, saving must equal investment. By definition.

Similarly, suppose firms do not sell all their output. We treat the flow of unsold goods as temporary *investment* by firms to add to their stock of working capital. Household consumption plus *total* investment still equal output and spending. When stocks are run down, this is negative investment, again keeping the accounting straight.

Adding the government and foreign countries

The government is also an end user, buying the output of firms (education, health, tanks). Governments also spend money on welfare benefits B for things like pensions, jobseekers allowance and income support. Not being physical output, these subsidies or *transfer payments* are not part of GDP. They get counted later when spent on household consumption. However, government purchases G of final output are part of GDP. Government spending, both on physical goods and services and on monetary transfer payments, are financed by taxes T.

Finally, we add trade with the rest of the world. Net exports add to GDP.

> **Exports X** are made at home but sold abroad. **Imports Z** are made abroad but bought at home.

Domestic output is bought for consumption C, investment I, government spending G, and exports X. Subtracting the import content Z in these goods, GDP is $(C + I + G + X - Z)$. This is paid out as

---

Box 7-1

How big is the hidden economy?

The gangster Al Capone, never charged with murder or gun running, was eventually convicted of income tax evasion. Taxes are evaded not only by smugglers and drug dealers but also by gardeners, plumbers, street vendors, and others working 'for cash'. Since estimates of GNP are derived from tax statistics, the 'hidden' economy is omitted from GNP.

To estimate the size of the hidden economy we can keep track of what people spend. Maria Lacko used the stable relationship between household consumption of electricity and its two main determinants – income and weather temperature – to estimate incomes by studying available data on electricity consumption and the weather. The hidden economy is large both in the former communist economies, where the new private sector is not yet part of official statistics, and in several Mediterranean countries with a long history of tax evasion.

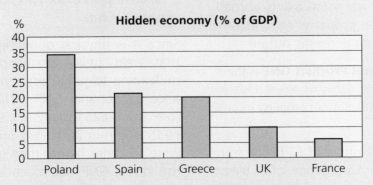

Source: M. Lacko, *The Hungarian Hidden Economy in International Comparisons*, Institute of Economics, Budapest, 1996

incomes and profits to households, who use it for consumption, saving or paying taxes net of benefits received. Thus GDP is also $(C + S + T - B)$. These two measures of GDP must be equal. Deducting consumption from both measures $(I + G + X - Z) = (S + T - B)$. Hence

$$\underset{\text{Total leakages}}{S + (T - B) + Z} = \underset{\text{Total injections}}{I + G + X}$$

Total leakages from the circular flow (saving, net tax payments and imports) are money from domestic firms that households do not recycle to domestic firms again. Total injections (firms' investment, government purchases and exports) are sources of firms' revenue not originating from households. Total leakages still equal total injections.

Saving need no longer equal investment. But we recover that special case if all transactions with government and foreigners are zero.

From GDP to GNP

To complete the national accounts, we deal with two final problems. First, foreigners own some of our capital and land, and we own some assets abroad. These assets or property earn income unconnected with domestic output.

> **Gross National Product GNP** is the total income of citizens wherever it is earned. It is GDP plus net property income from abroad.

If the UK has an inflow of £2 billion from foreign assets, but an outflow of £1 billion in property income to foreigners, UK GNP, the income of UK citizens, is £1 billion

more than UK GDP, the value of output in the UK.

The final complication is depreciation.

> **Depreciation** is the fall in value of the capital stock during the period through use and obsolescence.

Depreciation is an economic cost, reducing net output in any period. Deducting depreciation from GNP yields net national product NNP or national income.

> **National income** is GNP minus depreciation during the period.

Our national accounts are now complete, but can you remember them? Figure 7-2 will help to keep you straight.

What GNP measures

Depreciation, being hard to measure, is treated differently in different countries. Most international comparisons use GNP, which avoids the need to argue about depreciation.

> **Nominal GNP** is measured at the prices when income was earned. **Real GNP** adjusts for inflation by valuing GNP in different years at the prices prevailing at a particular date.

Since it is physical quantities of output that yield utility or happiness, it is misleading to judge economic performance by nominal GNP. GNP in the UK rose from £25 billion in 1960 to over £935 billion in 2001. Yet prices in 2001 were 15 times higher than in 1960. The rise in real GNP was much less dramatic than the rise in nominal GNP, much of which reflected inflation.

Figure 7-2

National income accounting: a summary

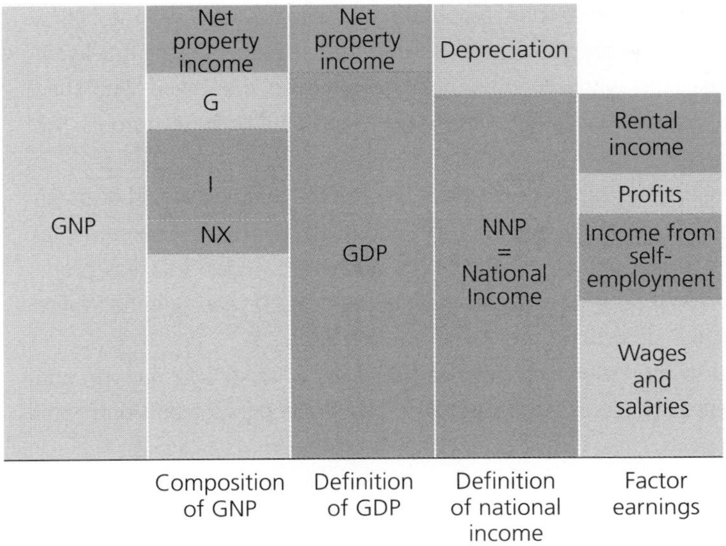

| Composition of GNP | Definition of GDP | Definition of national income | Factor earnings |

What GNP omits

In practice, GNP omits some things that ideally should be included. First, some outputs, such as noise, pollution and congestion, reduce true economic output and should be deducted from the usual GNP measure. This is logically correct but hard to implement. These 'bads' are not traded in markets, so it is hard to quantify them or value the costs they impose.

These activities include household chores, DIY activities and unreported jobs. Moreover, deducting environmental depreciation from measures of national output and income would radically alter our view of how well different countries are doing, and might affect the political incentives to pay more attention to such issues.

Leisure is also a valuable commodity. If two countries make the same output of consumer goods but one delivers more leisure for its residents, its net output of relevant economic goodies is higher. Yet conventional measures of GNP and GDP ignore leisure completely. Standard measures are confined to what is easily measured. Often national statistics are the byproduct of tax collection or other government activities. As macro-economists, we have to deal in the statistics that we have, which are not always the ones we would like to have.

Box 7-2

Asian snails

'Asia propelled to brink of environmental catastrophe' reported the *Financial Times* (19 June 2001). Well-run firms spend serious money on information systems to let their managers make intelligent decisions. Governments often make do with economic data gathered on the cheap. Published GDP data ignores valuable commodities like leisure, and omits important harmful outputs like environmental pollution.

Citing a study by the Asian Development Bank, the *Financial Times* noted that Asia would overtake the OECD as the world's biggest source of greenhouse-gas pollutants by 2015. Environmental degradation means that almost 40 per cent of the region's population now live in areas prone to drought and erosion. With the Asian population set to triple in the next 20 years, and half these people living in cities, air pollution will set new records. Clean water is also rare.

Asian countries, from Thailand to the Philippines, have had 40 years of rapid GDP growth, and so are often called the Asian tigers. If national accounts kept proper account of environmental depreciation, their growth would be much less impressive. We might call them Asian snails.

Recap

- Macroeconomics analyses the economy as a whole.
- Households supply inputs used by firms to make output. Households' income from firms is used to buy firms' output. There is a circular flow between households and firms.
- GDP, the value of output made in a country, is measured in three equivalent ways: value added in production, factor incomes including profits, or spending on final output.
- Leakages from the circular flow are household income from firms not then spent on the output of firms. Savings, net taxes and imports are leakages. Injections are revenue for firms not originating with household spending. Investment by firms, government purchases and exports are injections. Total leakages always equal total injections.
- GNP, a country's income, is its GDP plus its net property income from abroad.
- National income deducts depreciation from GNP.
- Nominal GNP is measured at current prices. Real GNP is measured at constant prices.

- In practice, GNP and GDP omit unmarketed activities – bads like pollution, valuable activities like leisure, and work in the home – and production unreported by tax evaders. Including these would give a better measure of income and output.

Review questions

1 The table shows final sales and purchases of intermediate goods in car production. What is the industry's contribution to GDP?

	Sales	Intermediate goods bought
Car producer	1000	330
Windscreen producer	200	10
Tyre producer	80	30
Steel producer	50	0

2 GNP is £300. Depreciation is £30 and net property income is −£3. Find the values of national income and GDP.

3 The output of the police is not marketed. GDP statistics use police wages to measure their output. If crime falls, we need fewer police. What happens to measured GDP? Is the country better off ?

4 Should the following ideally be in GNP? (a) Time spent by students in lectures; (b) the income of muggers; (c) time spent watching football; (d) the salary of traffic wardens; (e) dropping litter.

5 *Common fallacies* Why are these statements wrong? (a) Unemployment benefit raises national income in years when employment is low. (b) In 2002 Crummy Movie earned £1 billion more than *Gone With The Wind* earned 50 years ago. Crummy Movie is a bigger box office success.

Answers on pages 278–90

7-2 Output determination

Learning outcomes

By the end of this section, you should understand:
- Actual output and potential output
- Aggregate demand and equilibrium output
- The consumption function
- Shifts in aggregate demand
- The multiplier
- The paradox of thrift

Since 1960, annual real GDP growth in the UK has averaged 2.3 per cent. But there were cycles around this trend. In some years, output actually fell, but in other years it grew strongly. What determines national output, and why does it fluctuate? We distinguish *actual* output from *potential* output.

> **Potential output** is national output when all inputs are fully employed. The **output gap** is the difference between actual output and potential output.

Potential output tends to grow smoothly over time as inputs rise and technical progress occurs. Population growth adds to the labour force. Investment in education, training and new machinery raises the stock of human and physical capital. Technical advances make inputs more productive. Together, these explain why the UK has grown on average by 2.3 per cent a year since 1960.

Potential output is not the maximum we could be forced to produce. Rather, it is the output when all markets are in long-run equilibrium. Potential output includes an allowance for 'normal unemployment', probably around 5 per cent in the UK today. If actual output falls below potential output, workers become unemployed and firms have spare capacity.

Figure 7-3 shows the output gap in the UK during 1985–2002. In the Lawson boom of the late 1980s, UK GDP exceeded potential output so the output gap was positive. During the Major slump of the early 1990s, actual output fell well below potential output and the output gap was negative. However, since the late 1990s actual output has remained close to potential output. In part, this has reflected better macroeconomic policy.

To examine how policy affects output, we first need a model of what determines movements in output and causes deviations of output from potential output. To get started, we use the model invented by the great English economist John Maynard Keynes in the 1930s. There are two key assumptions, which we shall later relax. First, all prices and wages are fixed. Second, at these prices and wages, there are workers without a job wanting to work, and firms with spare capacity they want to use. With this excess capacity, any rise in demand is happily supplied. The actual quantity of total output is then *demand-determined*. It depends only on the level of *aggregate demand*.

Aggregate demand

Initially, we ignore the government and the foreign sector. The remaining sources of demand for goods are consumption demand by households, and investment demand by firms. Aggregate demand *AD* equals *C* + *I*, the sum of consumption demand and investment demand, but these are determined by different economic groups, and depend on different things.

Consumption demand

Households buy goods and services, from cars and food to holidays and heating. These consumption purchases take about 90 per cent of personal disposable income.

> **Personal disposable income** is household income from firms, plus government transfers, minus taxes. It is household income available to be spent or saved.

Given its disposable income, each household decides how to split this income between spending and saving. A decision about one is a decision about the other.

Figure 7-3

UK output gap (%), 1985–2002 (actual GDP − potential GDP)

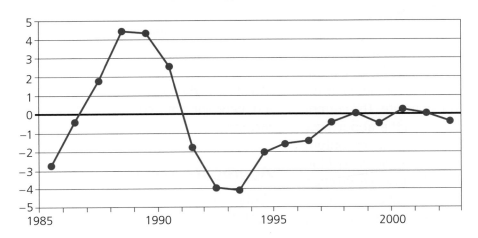

Initially, we assume that consumption demand rises with personal disposable income.

> The **consumption function** relates desired consumption to personal disposable income.

Our simple model has no transfer payments, or taxes. Personal disposable income is just national income. Figure 7-4 shows consumption demand C at each level of *national* income.

In this hypothetical example, $C = 10 + 0.9Y$. *Autonomous* consumption demand is unrelated to income. Needing to eat, households want to consume 10 even if income is zero. In Figure 7-5 the consumption function is a straight line with a constant slope. Each extra £1 of income leads to £0.9 of extra desired consumption spending. The slope of the consumption function is the marginal propensity to consume, which is 0.9 in Figure 7-4.

> The **marginal propensity to consume** *MPC* is the fraction of each extra pound of disposable income that households wish to consume.

Investment demand

Investment demand for fixed capital (plant and equipment) and working capital (inventories) reflects firms' current guesses about how fast the demand for their output will rise in future. The current *level* of output tells us little about how output will *change*. Sometimes output is high and rising, sometimes it is high and falling. With no close connection between the output level and investment demand, we initially assume that

Figure 7-4

Aggregate demand

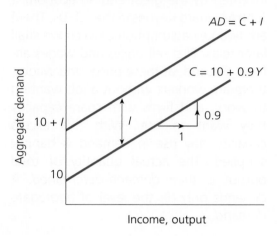

Income, output

Figure 7-5

Equilibrium output

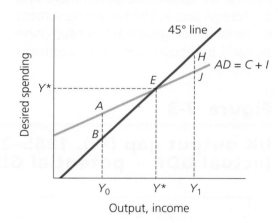

Output, income

investment demand is *autonomous*. It is independent of current output and income.

Aggregate demand

With only firms and households, aggregate demand is households' consumption demand C plus firms' investment demand I.

Aggregate demand is total desired spending at each level of income.

Figure 7-5 also shows the *aggregate demand schedule*. It adds the constant investment demand I to consumption demand C. The aggregate demand schedule is $AD = [(10 + I) + 0.9Y]$, parallel to the consumption function. The slope of both is the marginal propensity to consume, here 0.9. We now show how aggregate demand determines output and income.

Equilibrium output

When aggregate demand is below potential output, firms cannot sell all they would like. Suppliers are frustrated. But we can at least require that demanders are happy: actual output produced equals the output demanded by households for consumption and by firms for investment.

Short-run equilibrium output is where aggregate demand equals actual output.

Figure 7-5 shows income on the horizontal axis and planned spending on the vertical axis. The 45° line reflects any point on the horizontal axis into the *same* point on the vertical axis. The AD schedule crosses the 45° line only at point E. Equilibrium output and income are $Y*$. At this income, the AD schedule tells us that the demand for goods is also $Y*$.

At an output Y_0, less than $Y*$, the AD schedule is then above the 45° line. Aggregate demand at A exceeds actual output at B. There is excess demand, which firms initially meet by an *unplanned* reduction of inventories. Soon they raise output to meet the excess demand. When output rises to $Y*$, short-run equilibrium is restored. Aggregate demand again equals actual output.

Conversely, at any output Y_1 above $Y*$, the AD schedule is below the 45° line, desired spending at J is now below actual output at H, and firms cannot sell all their

Box 7-3

Movements along the *AD* schedule versus shifts in the *AD* schedule

The aggregate demand schedule is a straight line whose height reflects total autonomous spending: autonomous consumption demand plus investment demand. Its slope is the MPC. For a given autonomous demand, changes in income lead to movements along a given AD schedule.

The level of autonomous demand is not permanently fixed, but is independent of income. The AD schedule shows the change in demand directly induced by changes in income. All other sources of changes in aggregate demand are shown as shifts in the AD schedule. For example, if firms decide to invest more, the new AD schedule is parallel to, but higher than, the old AD schedule.

output. Initially, it piles up as *unplanned* additions to stocks. Then firms reduce their output. Once output is cut to Y^*, short-run equilibrium is restored. Aggregate demand again equals actual output.

At the short-run equilibrium output Y^*, firms sell all the goods they produce and purchasers buy all the goods they want. But Y^* may be *well below* potential output. Suppliers are still frustrated, and cannot sell what they would ideally like to make at the given wages and prices. A lack of aggregate demand prevents expansion of output to potential output. Since firms demand less labour input than at potential output, unemployment exceeds its long-run equilibrium level.

Another approach: equality of desired saving and investment

In short-run equilibrium, output Y^* equals desired investment plus desired consumption. However, income Y^* is devoted only to desired consumption and desired saving. Hence, in equilibrium, desired saving equals desired investment.

> The **saving function** shows desired saving at each income level. The **marginal propensity to save MPS** is the fraction of each extra pound of income that households wish to save.

If the consumption function is given by $C = 10 + 0.9Y$, the saving function must be $S = -10 + 0.1Y$. This ensures that desired $C + S = Y$. Households cannot plan what they cannot afford. For this saving function, the marginal propensity to save is 0.1.

Figure 7-6

Short-run equilibrium output Y^*

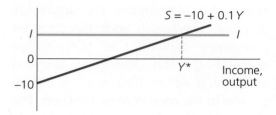

Figure 7-6 shows equilibrium output Y^*, using desired saving and desired investment. The latter is constant, a horizontal line at height I in Figure 7-6. When income is zero, the saving function implies that saving is -10, the counterpart to autonomous consumption of 10. Each extra unit of income adds 0.1 to desired saving, so the saving function is an upward sloping straight line with a constant slope of 0.1. The marginal propensity to save is 0.1. The remaining 0.9 of each extra unit of income is spent on consumption, as the marginal propensity consumed tells us.

Desired saving equals desired investment only at the income Y^*. If income exceeds Y^*, households want to save more than firms want to invest. But saving is the part of income not consumed. Saying that desired saving exceeds desired investment is the same as saying that aggregate demand is below actual output.

Unplanned stocks pile up and firms cut output. Conversely, if income is below Y^*, desired investment exceeds desired saving. Aggregate demand for output is now too high. Firms make unplanned cuts in stocks and raise output. Again, output adjusts towards its equilibrium level Y^*. This is the same level whether we use aggregate demand and actual output in Figure 7-5, or desired investment and desired saving in Figure 7-6.

Desired versus actual

Equilibrium output and income satisfy two equivalent conditions. Aggregate demand equals actual output; and desired investment equals desired saving. By definition *actual* investment is *always* equal to *actual* saving when only firms and households exist. But out of equilib-

rium, unplanned changes in inventories always make actual investment equal to actual saving, whatever their desired levels.

A fall in aggregate demand

What alters equilibrium output? After the terrorist attacks on New York in September 2001, firms became pessimistic about the future demand for their output. Their investment demand fell. How much should that have reduced equilibrium output?

Box 7-4

Spending like there's no tomorrow

Nowadays Nigel Lawson advertises diets. He used to be Chancellor of the Exchequer. At the height of the Lawson boom in the late 1980s, heady optimism and easy access to credit made UK consumers spend a lot. Personal saving collapsed as people bought champagne, sports cars and houses. The boom years did not last. As inflation got out of control, the government took action to slow the economy down. House prices fell below the value of people's mortgages. To pay off this 'negative equity', households had to raise saving sharply in the early 1990s. Since 1999 personal saving has been collapsing again. . . . Although in this chapter we assume a constant marginal propensity to save, Chapter 8 discusses more sophisticated theories of consumption and saving.

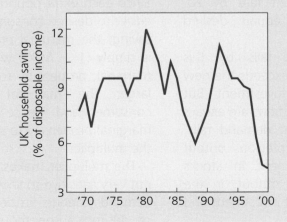

Figure 7-7

Lower investment reduces equilibrium output

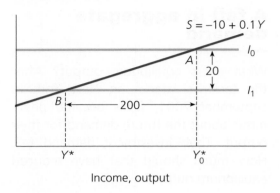

Income, output

To see the answer directly, we examine desired leakages and injections in Figure 7-7. Suppose the horizontal line showing desired investment shifts down by 20. Equilibrium moves from A to B, achieving a matching vertical fall of 20 in desired saving. Since the saving function has a slope of 0.1, it takes a horizontal leftward move of 200 in output to achieve a vertical fall of 20 in desired saving. Equilibrium output falls by 200 when desired investment falls by 20. Desired saving again equals desired investment.

Until actual output falls by this amount, desired saving exceeds the new lower level of desired investment. But *actual* leakages and injections are *always* equal. When investment demand falls, firms cannot sell their previous output and unplanned investment in stocks occurs. Firms then cut output. In the final equilibrium, desired investment and saving are equal again.

The multiplier

In this example, investment demand fell by 20 but equilibrium output fell by 200. The multiplier exceeds 1 because it takes a big change in income to alter desired saving by the amount that desired investment had changed.

> The **multiplier** is the ratio of the change in equilibrium output to the change in demand that caused output to change.

Equilibrium output fell by 10 times the original change in investment demand. The multiplier was 10 in this example. Notice that this is simply $[1/(0.1)]$ or $1/MPS$. This is indeed the formula for the multiplier for any saving function with a constant marginal propensity to consume. If investment demand falls by 1, eventually desired saving must fall by 1. Each fall in income by 1 reduces desired saving by the smaller amount MPS, so income must fall by $1/MPS$ in order to reduce desired saving by 1. In the new equilibrium, desired saving is again equal to desired investment. Hence:

$$\text{Multiplier} = 1/MPS = 1/(1 - MPC)$$

Since each extra pound of income adds either to desired consumption or desired saving, the marginal propensity to save is simply $(1 - MPC)$ where MPC is the marginal propensity to consume. The larger the marginal propensity to consume, and hence the lower the marginal propensity to save, the larger is the multiplier.

The multiplier makes equilibrium output very sensitive to shocks to aggregate demand (changes in desired investment or desired autonomous consumption).

However, if the multiplier were as large as 10 in the real world, the economy would be buffeted by every little shock that hit it. The next section explains why in practice the multiplier is lower than this section suggests.

The paradox of thrift

Suppose people want to save more at each income level, spending less at each income level. This reduces aggregate demand, shifting the AD schedule down because the consumption function shifts down. It also raises desired saving, shifting the saving function up.

Because aggregate demand falls, equilibrium income falls. This reduces equilibrium saving, since saving depends on income. We now have two effects: a desire to save more at each income, but lower equilibrium income, reducing desired saving. Which effect wins?

Think about desired investment and desired saving. Since nothing happened to desired investment, in the new equilibrium desired saving must be unaffected! A higher desire to save more, and spend less, reduces equilibrium income to the level that leaves desired saving at its original level. People save more out of any given income, but income is now lower. Desired saving stays the same.

> The **paradox of thrift** is that a change in the desire to save changes equilibrium output and income, but not equilibrium saving.

Recap

- Aggregate demand is planned spending on output. The AD schedule shows aggregate demand at each income level.
- Autonomous consumption is desired consumption at zero income. The marginal propensity to consume MPC, and the marginal propensity to save MPS, are the fractions by which desired consumption and saving rise when income rises by one unit. $MPC + MPS = 1$.
- For given prices and wages, short-run equilibrium output equates actual output and desired spending. Equivalently, it equates desired saving and desired investment.
- Equilibrium output is demand-determined in the short run if wages and prices are fixed at a level implying excess supply of goods and labour.
- A change in desired investment changes equilibrium output by a larger amount. The multiplier is the ratio of the change in output to the change in autonomous demand that caused it. With only households and firms, the multiplier is $1/(1 - MPC)$ or $1/MPS$. This is large since MPS is a small fraction.
- The paradox of thrift is that a change desired saving changes equilibrium output, but not equilibrium saving, which must still equal desired investment.

Review questions

1 $C = 0.7Y$ and $I = 45$. (a) Draw a diagram showing the AD schedule. (b) If actual output is 100, what unplanned actions occur? (c) What is equilibrium output?

2 $I = 150$. If people become thriftier, the consumption function shifts from $C = 0.7Y$ to $C = 0.5\,Y$. (a) What happens to equilibrium income? (b) What happens to the equilibrium proportion of income saved? (c) Show the change in equilibrium income in a saving–investment diagram. (d) Can you show the same change in a diagram using AD and the 45° line?

3 Which part of actual investment is not included in aggregate demand? Why not?

4 (a) Find equilibrium income when $I = 400$ and $C = 0.8Y$. (b) Would output be higher or lower if the consumption function were $C = 100 + 0.7Y$?

5 *Common fallacies* Why are these statements wrong? (a) If people would save more, investment would rise and we could get the economy moving again. (b) Lower output leads to lower spending and yet lower output. The economy could spiral downwards for ever.

Answers on pages 278–90

7-3 Fiscal policy and foreign trade

Learning outcomes

By the end of this section, you should understand:
- How government spending and taxes affect equilibrium output
- The balanced budget multiplier
- Automatic stabilisers
- Limits to active fiscal policy
- How foreign trade affects equilibrium output

In modern economies, governments are important and there is extensive trade with other countries. This section examines how the government and foreign countries affect aggregate demand and hence national output.

The government and aggregate demand

Figure 7-8 shows the evolution of government spending and tax revenue in the UK during 1987–2002. The gap

Figure 7-8

UK government spending and taxes, 1987–2002 (% of GDP)

Source: OECD, *Economic Outlook*, June 2002

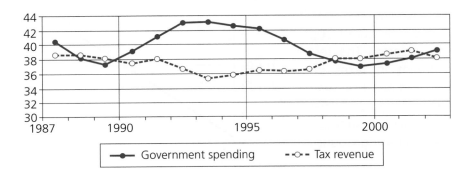

between spending and revenue measures the budget deficit. Figure 7-8 shows that the budget was nearly in balance in the late 1980s and again since the late 1990s. However, in the early 1990s there was a sharp increase in the budget deficit, both because government spending increased and because tax revenue fell.

> **Fiscal policy** is the government's decisions about spending and taxes.

We now examine the effects of fiscal policy in more detail. Government purchases G of final output add to aggregate demand. Hence, $AD = (C + I + G)$. The level of government demand reflects how many hospitals the government wants to build, how large it wants defence spending to be, and so on. In the short run, these decisions are not affected by changes in actual output. Now $(I + G)$ are desired injections, which in equilibrium must equal desired leakages. How are desired leakages affected by the government?

The government levies taxes and pays out transfer benefits. At given tax rates and benefit levels, tax revenue and benefit spending both vary with output. To capture this, assume net taxes $NT = tY$, where t is the net tax rate, which in practice is around 0.5. Households' disposable income YD is now $Y(1 - t)$. Households get to keep only about 50p of every £1 of gross income. The rest goes to the government in taxes on income and spending, and because, with higher gross income, people get fewer transfer payments for income support, housing benefit or help in paying Council Tax.

Suppose households still want to save 10 per cent of each extra pound of *disposable* income. However, with a 50 per cent net tax rate, £1 of gross income adds only 50p to disposable income and hence only 5p to saving. This is one leakage, but the 50p paid to the government is another leakage not reverting to firms as demand for their output.

In Section 7-2 each extra £1 of national income led only to an extra leakage of £0.10 in extra saving. Now it leads to an extra leakage of £0.55 in extra net tax payments and saving. Whereas each extra £1 of output was used to raise consumption demand by £0.90, now it raises it by only £0.45. That is extra desired spending by households on output after adjusting their desired saving and making their tax payments. Changes in income and output now induce much smaller changes in consumption demand. The multiplier is much smaller than in Section 7-1.

It used to be $(1/0.1) = 10$ but is now only $(1/0.55) = 1.82$. Figure 7-9 explains why. Desired injections are now $(I + G)$.

Figure 7-9

A fall in desired injections ($I + G$)

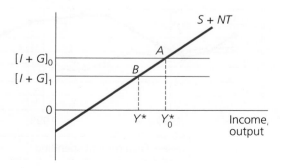

Desired leakages, reflecting the need to pay taxes and the desire then to save out of remaining disposable income, are shown by the desired leakage schedule $S + NT$ whose slope is now 0.55.

Equilibrium output is initially where the two lines cross at A. A fall in desired injections to $(I + G)_1$ has a smaller effect on equilibrium output the steeper is the desired leakages line. The multiplier is always 1/(marginal propensity to leak). With a marginal propensity to save of 0.1 and a net tax rate of 0.5, the value of the multiplier is now $1/(0.55) = 1.82$.

Because this is much smaller than the value of 10 in Section 7-1, equilibrium output is much less sensitive to shocks to aggregate demand. The net tax rate acts as an automatic stabiliser. When output rises, the government gets more tax revenue tY at a given net tax rate t. Similarly, when output falls, tax revenue also falls. By cushioning the disposable income of households, fiscal policy acts as a shock absorber, helping to stabilise aggregate demand and output.

> **Automatic stabilisers** reduce fluctuations in aggregate demand by reducing the multiplier. All leakages act as automatic stabilisers.

Changes in fiscal policy

Figure 7-9 showed how changes in desired injections change equilibrium output. For a given investment demand, lower government demand G cuts the planned injections from $(I + G)_0$ to $(I + G)_1$, reducing equilibrium output from Y_0^* to Y_1^*. Higher government demand has the opposite effect.

For given government purchases G, a higher net tax rate makes the desired leakages line steeper in Figure 7-9. It must cross a given desired injections line at a lower equilibrium output. With higher leakages at any output, output must fall to preserve desired leakages equal to the unchanged desired injections. A higher net tax rate reduces equilibrium output. Conversely, a tax cut raises equilibrium output.

Active or discretionary fiscal policy?

Although automatic stabilisers are always at work, governments may use *active* or *discretionary* fiscal policy to *alter* spending levels or tax rates to try to offset other shocks to aggregate demand. When aggregate demand is low, the government boosts demand by cutting taxes or raising spending. Conversely, when aggregate demand is high, the government raises taxes or reduces spending.

However, it is not always easy to change long-term fiscal plans quickly. Nowadays, much of the burden of stabilising output falls not on fiscal policy but on monetary policy, the subject of the next chapter.

The government budget

The budget is in surplus if revenue exceeds expenditure and is in deficit if spending exceeds revenue. Thus, the budget deficit is $G - tY$. For given levels of G, the budget varies with output Y because this automatically affects net tax revenue. Other things equal, high output means high tax revenue and a budget

Box 7-5

The limits to active fiscal policy
Why can't shocks to aggregate demand immediately be offset by fiscal policy?

Time lags It takes time to spot that aggregate demand has changed, then time to change tax rates and spending plans, then this policy change takes time to affect private behaviour.

Uncertainty The government does not know for sure the size of the multiplier. It only has estimates from past data. Moreover, since fiscal policy takes time to work, the government must forecast the level that aggregate demand will have reached by the time fiscal policy has had its full effects. Mistakes made in forecasting can frustrate good intentions of policy makers.

Induced effects on autonomous demand Treating investment, exports and autonomous consumption demand as fixed is only a simplification. Fiscal changes may affect private-sector confidence or force the Bank of England to alter interest rates. If the government estimates these induced effects incorrectly, fiscal changes have unforeseen effects.

The budget deficit Even if a fiscal expansion raises aggregate demand in a recession, it also adds to the budget deficit. The cure may be worse than the disease if people worry about the consequent rise in government debt or the temptation to print money to finance the budget deficit.

surplus; low output means low tax revenue and a budget deficit.

The balanced budget multiplier

Suppose government spending and tax revenue both rise by 1000. Since injections and leakages change by equal amounts, output is unaffected. Right?

Wrong! The higher tax rate also reduces disposable income, reducing desired saving. Desired injections rose by 1000, but desired leakages rose by *less* than 1000. Equilibrium output must rise, thereby raising both desired saving and tax revenue until desired leakages again equal desired injections.

The **balanced budget multiplier** means that a rise in government spending initially matched by higher taxes induces a rise in equilibrium output.

We can get the same answer by thinking about aggregate demand and actual output. A rise of 1000 in *G* adds a full 1000 to aggregate demand ($C + I + G$). Extra taxes of 1000 cut disposable income by 1000. Since the marginal propensity to consume out of disposable income is less than 1, desired consumption falls by *less* than 1000. Hence, aggregate demand ($C + I + G$) rises. The rise in *G* outweighs the fall in *C*. Equilibrium output rises because aggregate demand is higher.

This completes our introduction to fiscal policy, aggregate demand and equilibrium output. We conclude the chapter by bringing in foreign trade as well.

Box 7-6

'You've never had it so prudent' . . .

. . . as Prime Minister Tony Blair told the Labour Party Conference in 1999. Chancellor Brown not only gave the Bank of England independent control of interest rates (to stop politicians being tempted to boost the economy too much), but also introduced a Code for Fiscal Stability (for the same reason).

The **Code for Fiscal Stability** commits the government to a medium-run objective of financing all current government spending out of current revenues.

Borrowing-financed deficits are allowed only to pay for public-sector investment (which eventually pays for itself by raising future output, and thus future tax revenues). A medium-run perspective is needed because the actual deficit fluctuates over the business cycle even if tax rates are constant. Chancellor Brown's 'golden rule' means that government debt accumulation in the long run (borrowing to finance investment) should be accompanied by higher output and tax revenue without needing a change in tax rates.

Foreign trade and output determination

Figure 7-10 shows UK exports X, imports Z since 1950. Although exports and imports are each large relative to GDP, net exports $X - Z$ are usually small.

The **trade balance** is the value of net exports. When exports exceed imports, the economy has a trade surplus. When imports exceed exports, it has a trade deficit.

When a household spends more than its income, it runs down its assets (bank accounts, stocks and shares) or runs up its debts (overdrafts) to finance this deficit. Similarly, a country with a trade deficit must reduce its net foreign assets to finance this deficit.

Net exports $X - Z$ demand adds to aggregate demand, which becomes $AD = C + I + G + X - Z$. Desired

Figure 7-10

UK foreign trade (% of GDP)

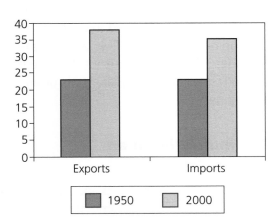

injections are now $(I + G + X)$ and desired leakages $(S + NT + Z)$

What determines desired exports and imports? Export demand reflects what is happening in foreign economies, which is largely unrelated to domestic output. Like other injections G and I, initially we treat export demand X as autonomous, or independent of domestic output.

Imports from abroad may be raw materials for domestic production or items consumed by UK households, such as a Japanese TV or French wine. Demand for imports rises when domestic income and output rise.

> The **marginal propensity to import (MPZ)** is the fraction of each extra pound of national income that domestic residents want to spend on extra imports.

Like the government budget, the trade balance varies with fluctuations in domestic income. Higher output and income raise imports, but leave exports unaffected. Hence, at low output, net exports are positive. There is a trade *surplus* with the rest of the world. At high output, there is a trade *deficit* and net exports are negative.

In Figure 7-11 the horizontal line $I + G + X$ shows desired injections. The up-sloping line $S + NT + Z$ is desired leakages. Equilibrium output Y^* makes desired leakages equal to desired injections.

The multiplier in an open economy

By adding a third leakage through imports Z, an open economy has planned leakages $(S + NT + Z)$ that are even more responsive to output than in our previous discussion. The line for planned leakages in Figure 7-11 is steeper than for planned leakages $(S + NT)$ in Figure 7-9, which in turn is steeper than for planned saving S in Figure 7-7.

The steeper the planned leakages line, the smaller is the effect on equilibrium output of any given upward shift in planned injections. The output multiplier is large in a closed economy with no government, much smaller in an open economy with a government sector.

Even so, a rise in planned injections, from $(I + G + X)_0$ to $(I + G + X)_1$ raises equilibrium output a bit, from Y_0^* to Y_1^*. Conversely, a higher savings rate, a higher tax rate or a higher marginal propensity to import make the planned leakages line steeper, reducing equilibrium output.

Import spending and jobs

Do imports steal domestic jobs? Cutting imports would raise aggregate demand $(C + I + G + X - Z)$ and create extra domestic output and jobs, a conclusion also seen using Figure 7-10, where a shift

Figure 7-11

Higher desired injections raise equilibrium output

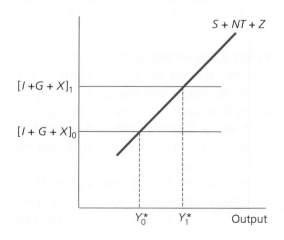

down in desired leakages $(S + NT + Z)$ would raise equilibrium output.

This view is correct, but dangerous. Other things equal, higher spending on domestic rather than foreign goods *will* raise demand for domestic goods. But import restrictions are dangerous because they may induce retaliation by other countries, which cuts demand for our exports. In the end, nobody gets more jobs but world trade shrinks, which hurts everyone.

Recap

- The government buys some output directly. It also levies taxes and makes transfers.
- Net tax revenue rises with income, reducing the marginal propensity to consume out of national income. This acts as an automatic stabiliser by reducing the value of the multiplier.
- A rise in government purchases raises desired injections, aggregate demand and equilibrium output. A higher tax rate raises desired leakages, reduces aggregate demand and reduces equilibrium output.
- An equal initial rise in government purchases and taxes raises output. This is the balanced budget multiplier.
- To stabilise aggregate demand and output, the government can set higher net tax rates, thus enhancing automatic stabilisers, or can make discretionary adjustments to government spending and tax rates to offset other shocks to aggregate demand. Discretionary changes are hard to implement quickly.
- Exports are an injection, adding to demand for domestic output. Imports are a leakage, domestic income spent on foreign output.
- Exports demand is autonomous spending unrelated to domestic income. The marginal propensity to import *MPZ* is the amount an extra unit of national income adds to import demand.
- Imports further reduce the value of the multiplier, and are another automatic stabiliser.
- Higher export demand raises equilibrium output. Higher import demand reduces it.
- The trade surplus (net exports) falls when domestic income rises. Higher export demand raises the trade surplus, but higher import demand reduces it.

Review questions

1 Equilibrium output in a closed economy is 1000. $C = 800$ and $I = 80$. (a) What level is G? (b) I now rises by 50, and the MPS out of national income is 0.2. What are the new equilibrium levels of C, I, G, and Y? (c) Suppose instead G had risen by 50. Would the effect on output have been the same? (d) What level of G makes equilibrium output 1200?

2 In equilibrium, desired savings equal desired investment. True or false? Explain.

3 Why does the government tax people when it could borrow to finance its spending?

4 Suppose $MPZ = 0.4$, $t = 0.2$ and $MPS = 0.2$. Investment demand rises by 136. (a) What happens to the equilibrium level of income and to net exports? (b) Suppose exports, not investment, rise by 100. How does the trade balance change?

5 *Common fallacies* Why are these statements wrong? (a) The budget raised taxes and spending by equal amounts. It was a neutral budget for output. (b) Countries with a trade deficit during an output boom are irresponsible, since things will get worse if output falls.

Answers on pages 278–90

8

Money, interest rates and output

8-1 Money and banking

Learning outcomes

By the end of this section, you should understand:
- The functions of money
- How banks create money
- The money multiplier
- Different measures of money

In songs and popular language, 'money' is a symbol of success, a source of crime and makes the world go around. Dogs' teeth in the Admiralty Islands, sea shells in parts of Africa, gold in the nineteenth century: all are examples of money. What matters is not the commodity used but the social convention that it is accepted, without question, as a means of payment.

Money is any generally accepted means of payment for delivery of goods or settlement of debt. It is the **medium of exchange**.

In exchanging goods or labour services for money, we accept money not to consume it directly but for its later use in buying what we really want. Imagine an economy without money.

A **barter economy** has no medium of exchange. Goods are simply swapped for other goods.

In a barter economy, if you want an economics textbook, not only must you find someone wanting rid of one, you must have what that person wants in exchange. People spend a lot of time and effort finding others with whom to swap. Time and effort are scarce resources. Using money makes trading cheaper and more efficient. Society can use the time and effort for better purposes.

Other functions of money

British prices are quoted in pounds, American prices are quoted in dollars. However, there are exceptions. During rapid inflation, people may quote prices in foreign currency even if they still take payment in local currency, the medium of exchange.

> The **unit of account** is the unit in which prices are quoted and accounts are kept.

Nobody would accept money as payment for goods today if the money was worthless when they tried to spend it later. But money is not the only store of value. Houses, paintings and interest-bearing bank accounts all store value. Storing value is necessary but not the key feature of money, which is its role as medium of exchange.

> Money is also a **store of value**, available for future purchases.

Different kinds of money

In prisoner-of-war camps, cigarettes served as money. In the nineteenth century, money was mainly gold and silver coins. These are examples of *commodity money*, ordinary goods with industrial uses (gold) and consumption uses (cigarettes) that also serve as a medium of exchange. But society need not waste valuable commodities by using them as money.

> A **token money** has a value as money that greatly exceeds its cost of production or value in consumption.

A £10 note is worth far more as money than as a 7.5 × 14 cm piece of high-quality paper. By collectively agreeing to use token money, society economises on the scarce resources required to produce money. A token money survives only if

private production is illegal. Society also enforces the use of token money by making it *legal tender*. In law, it must be accepted as a means of payment. Modern economies supplement token money by IOU money.

> An **IOU money** is a medium of exchange based on the debt of a private bank.

A bank deposit is IOU money. You pay for goods with a cheque, which the bank must honour when a shopkeeper presents it. Bank deposits are a medium of exchange, a generally accepted means of payment.

Modern banking

When you deposit your coat in the theatre cloakroom, you do not expect the theatre to rent your coat out during the performance. Banks lend out some of the coats in their cloakroom. A theatre would have to get your particular coat back on time, which might be tricky. A bank finds it easier because one piece of money looks just like another.

> **Bank reserves** are cash in the bank to meet possible withdrawals by depositors. The **reserve ratio** is the ratio of reserves to deposits.

Table 8-1 shows the balance sheet of UK commercial banks in 2001. Their assets were mainly loans to firms and households, and financial securities, such as bills and bonds, issued by governments and firms. Since many securities are very liquid – easily sellable at a predictable price – banks can lend short-term and still get their money back if depositors then

Table 8-1

Balance sheet of UK banks, March 2001

Assets	£bn	Liabilities	£bn
In foreign currency		*In foreign currency*	
Securities	747	Sight and time deposits	1202
Loans	938	Other liabilities	712
Other assets	240		
In sterling		*In sterling*	
Securities	240	Sight and time deposits	1086
Loans	1224	Other liabilities	478
Other assets	88		
Total	3477	Total	3477

withdraw their money. In contrast, many loans to firms and households are illiquid. The bank cannot easily get its money back in a hurry. Modern banks get by with tiny cash reserves in the vault. In Table 8-1 they are not even recorded separately.

Banks' liabilities are mainly sight and time deposits. Sight deposits mean a depositor can withdraw money 'on sight' without any notice; cheque accounts are sight deposits. Time deposits, which pay higher interest rates, need a period of notice before withdrawing money. Banks have more time to organise the sale of some of their high-interest assets in order to have the cash available to meet these withdrawals. The other liabilities of banks are various 'money market instruments', short-term and highly liquid borrowing by banks.

The business of banking

A bank is a business to make profits by lending and borrowing. To get money in, the bank offers favourable terms to potential depositors. UK banks increasingly offer interest on sight deposits, and often offer free cheque facilities to people whose sight deposits or current accounts are not overdrawn. And they offer better interest rates on time deposits.

Table 8-1 shows how the banks lend out this money. In sterling, most is lent as advances or overdrafts to households and firms, at high interest rates. Some is used to buy securities such as long-term government bonds. Some is more prudently invested in liquid assets, which pay less interest but can be easily sold if necessary. Some is held as cash, the most liquid asset of all.

The bank acquires a diversified portfolio of investments. Some of this income pays interest to depositors, the rest is for the bank's expenses and profits. Individual depositors have neither the time nor the expertise to decide which of these loans or investments to make.

UK banks' reserves are only 2 per cent

Box 8-1

Travellers' tales

This contrast between a monetary and barter economy is taken from the World Bank, *World Development Report*, 1989.

Life without money

'Some years since, Mademoiselle Zelie, a singer, gave a concert in the Society Islands in exchange for a third part of the receipts. When counted, her share was found to consist of 3 pigs, 23 turkeys, 44 chickens, 5000 cocoa nuts, besides considerable quantities of bananas, lemons and oranges. . . . as Mademoiselle could not consume any considerable portion of the receipts herself it became necessary in the meantime to feed the pigs and poultry with the fruit.' W. S. Jevons (1898).

Marco Polo discovers paper money

'In this city of Kanbula [Beijing] is the mint of the Great Khan, who may truly be said to possess the secret of the alchemists, as he has the art of producing money . . . He causes the bark to be stripped from mulberry trees . . . made into paper . . . cut into pieces of money of different sizes. The act of counterfeiting is punished as a capital offence. This paper currency is circulated in every part of the Great Khan's domain. All his subjects receive it without hesitation because, wherever their business may call them, they can dispose of it again in the purchase of merchandise they may require.' *The Travels of Marco Polo*, Book II.

---

of the sight deposits that could be withdrawn at any time. At short notice, banks can cash in *other* liquid assets easily and for a predictable amount. The skill in running a bank is judging how much to hold in liquid assets including cash, and how much to lend in less-liquid assets that earn higher interest rates.

Banks as creators of money

The **money supply** is money in circulation, namely cash outside the bank vaults, plus bank deposits on which cheques can be written.

For simplicity, suppose banks use a reserve ratio of 10 per cent. In Table 8-2,

initially citizens have £1000 in cash, which is also the money supply. This cash is then paid into the banks. Banks have assets of £1000 cash and liabilities of £1000 deposits, which is money they owe to depositors. If banks were like cloakrooms, that would be the end of the story. However, since all deposits are not withdrawn daily banks do not need then to be fully covered by cash in the bank.

In the third row, banks create £9000 of overdrafts. Think of this as loans to customers of £9000, an asset of the banks. But these are loans of deposits, against which cheques can be written, and hence also a liability of the banks. Now the banks have £10 000 of total deposits – the original £1000 of cash paid in, plus the £9000 deposits newly lent –

Box 8-2

A beginner's guide to financial markets

A *financial asset* is a piece of paper entitling the owner to a stream of income for a specified period. *Cash* is notes and coin, paying zero interest, but the most liquid asset of all. *Bills* are short-term financial assets paying no interest, but with a known repurchase date and a guaranteed repurchase price of £100. By buying it for less than £100, you earn a capital gain while holding the bill that gives a return similar to other market interest rates. Because bills have a short life, their price is never far below £100, and thus predictable. Bills are highly liquid.

Bonds are longer-term financial assets. A bond listed as Treasury 5% 2008 means that in 2008 the Treasury will buy it back for £100. Until then, the bondholder gets interest of £5 a year. Similarly, 2.5% Consolidated Stock (Consol) is a *perpetuity*, paying £2.5 a year for ever. Buying it for £100, you get a return of 2.5 per cent a year. You might happily buy it for £100 if other assets yield 2.5 per cent a year. Suppose other interest rates now rise to 10 per cent. To resell your Consol, you must cut the price to £25. The new buyer then earns £2.5 a year on a £25 investment, matching the 10 per cent yield available on other assets. Bonds are less liquid than bills not because they are difficult to buy and sell but because their future sale prices is less certain. Generally, the price of longer-term assets is more volatile.

Company shares (*equities*) earn dividends, the part of profits not retained by firms to buy new machinery and buildings. In bad years, dividends may be zero. Hence equities are risky and less liquid because share prices are volatile. Firms may even go bust, making the shares worthless. In contrast, government bonds are *gilt-edged* because the government can always pay.

Table 8-2

Money creation by the banking system

	Banks				Nonbank private sector			
Assets	Assets		Liabilities		Monetary assets		Liabilities	
Initial		0		0	Cash	1000		0
Intermediate	Cash	1000	Deposits	1000	Deposits	1000		0
Final	Cash	1000	Deposits	10 000	Cash	0	Loans from	
	Loans	9000			Deposits	10 000	banks	9000

and £10 000 of total assets, comprising £9000 to keep track of the loans plus £1000 cash in the vaults. The reserve ratio is now 10 per cent. It does not matter whether this ratio is imposed by law or is merely the profit-maximising behaviour of banks balancing risk and reward.

How did banks create money? Originally, the money supply was £1000 of cash in circulation. When paid into bank vaults, it went out of circulation as money. The public instead got £1000 of bank deposits against which to write cheques. The extra bank reserves were then used to create new loans and deposits, and the public had £10 000 of deposits in cheque accounts. The money supply rose from £1000 to £10 000. Banks created money.

The monetary base and the money multiplier

Cash is supplied by the *central bank*, which in the UK is the Bank of England. The government controls the issue of token money in a modern economy.

> The **monetary base** is the supply of cash, whether in private circulation or held in bank reserves. The **money multiplier** is the ratio of the money supply to the monetary base.

In our previous example, cash was £1000 and the money supply £10 000, so the money multiplier was 10. Suppose instead that banks operate on a 5 per cent reserve ratio. When £1000 cash is paid into the banks, they now create an extra £19 000 of new loans and deposits. Banks' assets are £1000 cash + £19 000 loans, and their liabilities are £1000 deposits when the cash was paid in, plus £19 000 deposits as counterparts to new loans. Now a monetary base of £1000 leads to a money supply of £20 000. The money multiplier has risen to 20.

Hence, a lower reserve ratio means that more loans and deposits are created for any given cash in the vaults. The money multiplier is larger. Conversely, the more cash the public keeps under the bed, the less of the monetary base goes into bank vaults, and the lower is the money multiplier for any given reserve ratio. Without cash reserves, banks cannot create additional money.

Measures of money

The money supply is cash in circulation (outside banks) plus bank deposits. It sounds simple, but it is not. Two issues arise: which bank deposits, and why only bank deposits?

There is a spectrum of liquidity. Cash is completely liquid. Sight deposits (cheque accounts) are almost as liquid, and time deposits (savings accounts) only a little less liquid than that. Where people can make automatic transfer between savings and cheque accounts when the latter run low, savings deposits are as liquid as cheque accounts.

Until the 1980s, everyone knew what a bank was, and whose deposits counted in the money supply. Financial deregulation has now blurred this distinction. 'Banks' lend for house purchase, 'Building societies' issue cheque books, and even supermarkets are joining the banking business.

Different measures of money draw different lines in the continuous spectrum of liquidity, and include the deposits of different institutions. The narrowest measure is M0, the *wide monetary base*. M0 measures all cash plus the banks' own deposits with the Bank of England.

Wider measures of money ignore bank

reserves but add various deposits to cash in circulation outside the banks. M1 adds sight deposits of banks. M3 also adds other banks deposits. Adding also the deposits in building societies we get the M4 measure of broad money.

Since we can no longer distinguish between banks and building societies, routine statistics are now published only for the narrow measure M0 and for the broad measure M4. Once we leave the monetary base, the first sensible place to stop is M4.

Table 8-3 gives data for 2001. Of the £33 billion monetary base, only £7 billion was in bank reserves. Since this was multiplied up into £904 billion of M4, the reserve ratio was below 1 per cent. Modern banks need little cash because financial markets and liquidity are so well developed. Hence, the money multiplier must be huge. In fact, Table 8-3 implies it was 904/33 = 27.

Table 8-3

Narrow and broad UK money, March 2001, sterling (£ billion)

	Wide monetary base (M0)	33
−	Banks' cash and balances at Bank	7
=	Cash in circulation	26
+	Banks' retail deposits	468
+	Building societies' deposits and shares	113
+	Wholesale deposits	297
=	Money supply (M4)	904

Source: Bank of England

Recap

- Money is the medium of exchange, for which it must be a store of value. It is usually also the unit of account.
- Bartering takes huge time and effort. Money reduces the resources used in trading. A token money's value as a money greatly exceeds it commodity value in other uses.
- Token money is used by social convention or because it is legal tender. The government has a monopoly on its supply.
- Modern banks attract deposits by offering interest and cheque facilities, but lend out funds at higher interest rates. If reserve ratios are below 100 per cent, banks create money by using their cash reserves to create extra loans and deposits.
- The money supply is currency in circulation plus relevant deposits. The monetary base M0 is currency in circulation and in banks. Broad money M4 is currency in circulation plus deposits at banks and building societies.
- The money multiplier is the ratio of the money supply to the monetary base. For M4 it is currently about 27. The money multiplier is larger (a) the smaller the reserve ratio and (b) the less of the monetary base is held outside banks and building societies.

Review questions

1 (a) Is a car taken in 'part exchange' for a new car a medium of exchange? (b) Could you tell by watching someone buying mints (white discs) with coins (silver discs) which is money?

2 How do commercial banks create money? What happens if their reserve ratio is 100 per cent?

3 (a) Are travellers' cheques money? (b) Season tickets? (c) Credit cards?

4 Sight deposits = 30, time deposits = 60, banks' cash reserves = 2, currency in circulation = 12, building society deposits = 20. Calculate M0 and M4.

5 *Common fallacies* Why are these statements wrong? (a) Since their liabilities equal their assets, banks do not create anything. (b) Tax evasion raises the money supply since people keep more cash under the bed.

Answers on pages 278–90

8-2 Interest rates and monetary policy

Learning outcomes

By the end of this section, you should understand:
- How a central bank affects the money supply
- What determines the demand for money
- How a central bank sets interest rates

Founded in 1694, the Bank of England was not nationalised until 1947. Usually called 'the Bank', it issues banknotes, sets interest rates and is banker to the commercial banks and the government, whose deposits are liabilities of the Bank. The Bank's assets are government securities and loans to commercial banks. Unlike commercial banks, the Bank cannot go bankrupt. It can always print more money to meet any claims upon it.

> A **central bank** is responsible for printing money, setting interest rates and acting as banker to commercial banks and the government.

The Bank and the money supply

The money supply is partly a liability of the Bank (currency in private circulation) and partly a liability of banks (bank deposits). The Bank could affect the money supply through reserve requirements, the discount rate or open market operations.

Reserve requirements

A *required* reserve ratio is a *minimum* ratio of cash reserves to deposits that the central bank requires commercial banks to hold. Banks can hold more than the required cash reserves but not less. If their cash falls below this limit, they must immediately borrow cash, usually from the central bank, to restore their required reserve ratio.

If set above the reserve ratio that prudent banks would anyway have chosen, a reserve requirement reduces the creation of bank deposits by reducing the value of the money multiplier, reducing the money supply for any given monetary base.

The discount rate

The discount rate is the interest rate at which the Bank lends cash to commercial banks. By setting the discount rate at a penalty level above market interest rates, the Bank makes commercial banks hold larger cash reserves to reduce the risk of having to borrow from the Bank. Bank deposits are now a lower multiple of banks' cash reserves. The money multiplier is lower, reducing the money supply for any level of the monetary base.

Open market operations

The previous two policies alter the value of the money multiplier. Open market operations alter the monetary base. For a given money multiplier, this alters the money supply.

> An **open market operation** is a central bank purchase or sale of securities in the open market in exchange for cash.

The Bank buys £1 billion of bonds by printing new cash, which adds £1 billion to the monetary base. Some of this ends up in circulation and some in bank reserves. The latter lets banks create new deposits. The broad money supply rises by more than the £1 billion of extra cash.

Conversely, if the Bank sells £1 billion of bonds in exchange for cash that disappears back into the Bank, the monetary base falls by £1 billion. Bank reserves fall, and commercial banks cut back on lending and deposits. The broad money supply falls by more than £1 billion.

There are three ways for a central bank to change the money supply – by changing reserve requirements, by changing the discount rate or by open market operations. In practice, modern central banks rely almost exclusively on open market operations.

Lender of last resort

Modern money is mainly bank deposits. Since banks have insufficient reserves to meet a simultaneous withdrawal of all their deposits, any hint of large withdrawals may be a self-fulfilling prophecy as people scramble to get their money out before the banks go bust. The threat of financial panics is reduced if the Bank will act as a lender of last resort.

> The **lender of last resort** lends to banks when financial panic threatens the financial system.

This is useful in helping banks that face a temporary liquidity crisis but whose underlying balance sheet is perfectly sound. When the balance sheet is unsound, that particular bank is usually allowed to go bankrupt. However, the Bank will lend to other banks until confidence recovers.

Of these functions, the main role of the central bank is to affect the money supply, and hence set interest rates. To explain the connection, we need to introduce the demand for money.

The demand for money

The UK stock of money M4 was 52 times higher in 2001 than in 1965. Why did UK residents hold so much more money in 2001 than in 1965? Money is a stock, the

Box 8-3

The repo market

In American movies, people in arrears on their loans have their cars repossessed by the repo man. In the mid 1990s, London finally established a repo market, catching up with other European financial centres, such as Frankfurt and Milan. Surely central banks are not major players in dubious car loans?

A repo is a sale and repurchase agreement. A bank sells you a long-lived bond with a simultaneous agreement to buy it back soon at a specified price on a particular day. You pay cash to the bank today and get back a predictable amount of cash (plus interest) at a known future date. You effectively made a deposit in the bank, a short-term loan to the bank secured or guaranteed by the bond that you temporarily own. Repos use the stock of long-term assets as backing for secured short-term loans.

Reverse repos work the other way. Now you get a short-term loan from the bank by initially selling bonds to the bank, agreeing to buy them back at a specified date in the near future at a price agreed now. Reverse repos are secured short-term loans from the bank.

Repos and reverse repos augment short-term assets and liquidity. As the cost of lending and borrowing fell, more people made deposits to banks and borrowed from banks. The Bank of England estimated that this raised the money supply M4 by as much as £6 billion at the start of 1996 when the gilt repo market began in the UK. The Bank of England now uses the repo market for most of its open market operations.

quantity of money *held* at any given time. Holding money is not the same as *spending* it. We hold money now to spend it later. We focus on three determinants of desired money holdings: interest rates, the price level and real income.

For simplicity, suppose money pays no interest and 'bonds' are all other assets that pay interest. How do people split their assets between money and bonds? Holding money means not earning more interest from holding bonds instead.

The **cost of holding money** is the interest given up by holding money rather than bonds.

People hold money only if there is a benefit to offset this cost. What is the benefit?

Transactions and precautionary benefits

Holding money economises on the costs of barter. The size of money holdings to meet this *transactions motive* depends mainly on the scale of our anticipated future spending, which we can proxy by real income Y.

The **demand for money** is a demand for *real* money balances M/P.

To lubricate a given flow of real transactions, we need a given amount of real money, which is nominal money M, divided by the price level P. If the price level doubles, other things equal the demand for *nominal* money balances doubles, leaving the demand for *real* money balances unaltered since the anticipated flow of real transactions has not changed.

People want money because of its purchasing power over goods and services. A higher real income raises the benefit of real money *M/P*, because more transactions occur. Having too little money raises the cost of transacting.

A second reason to hold money is the *precautionary motive*. If you see a bargain in a shop window, you need real money to grab the opportunity. Waiting while you cash in some bonds means that someone else gets the bargain. You hold money to cater for unforeseeable contingencies that require a rapid response. If these situations increase with the scale of economic activity, higher real income also strengthens the precautionary motive for holding money.

The transactions and precautionary motives are the main reasons to hold narrow money. The wider the definition of money, the less important is the role of money as a medium of exchange. We also have to take account of money as a store of value.

The asset motive to hold broad money

Forget the need to transact. Imagine someone deciding in which assets to hold wealth, to be spent at some distant date. A wise portfolio of assets will include some high-earning, but potentially risky, assets, such as company shares, but also some safer assets with a return that is lower on average but also less volatile. Holding some wealth in interest-bearing bank accounts is part of a well-diversified portfolio. Higher income and wealth give people more to invest, raising

the demand for broad money, such as M4.

Equating the marginal cost and benefit of holding money

The transactions, precautionary and asset motives affect the benefits of holding money. The cost is the interest forgone by not holding higher-interest-earning bonds instead. People hold money up to the point at which the marginal benefit of holding more money just equals its marginal cost in interest forgone. Figure 8-1 shows how much money people want to hold.

The horizontal axis plots real money *M/P*. The horizontal line *MC* is the marginal cost of holding money, the interest forgone by not holding bonds. *MC* shifts up if interest rates rise.

The *MB* schedule is the marginal benefit of holding money, for a given real

Figure 8-1

Desired money holdings

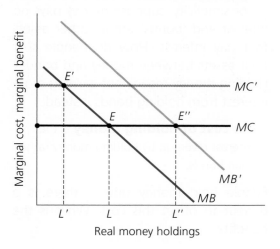

income and transactions flow. With low real money holdings, we put lots of time and effort into trading, being quick to invest money coming in, and alert to sell bonds just before every purchase. Also, with little precautionary money, we may miss out on unexpected chances to grab a good deal.

With low real money holdings, the marginal benefit of money is high. More money lets us put less effort into managing our transactions, and we have more money for unforeseen contingencies. However, for a given real income, the marginal benefit of money falls as we hold more real money. Life gets easier. The marginal benefit of yet more money is lower.

Given our real income and transactions, desired money holdings are L in Figure 8-1. Only at E are the marginal cost and benefit of money equal. How do changes in prices, real income and interest rates affect the quantity of money demanded?

Higher prices

Suppose all prices and wages double. Since interest rates are unaltered, MC stays the same. With real income unaltered, the MB schedule is unaffected. Hence, the desired holding of *real* money remains L. People hold twice as much nominal money M when prices P double. Real income and real money M/P are unaffected.

Higher interest rates

If interest rates on bonds rise, the cost of holding money rises. Figure 8-1 shows an

upward shift from MC to MC'. The desired point is now E', and desired real money holdings fall from L to L'. Higher interest rates reduce the quantity of real money demanded.

Higher real income

At each level of real money, higher real income raises the marginal benefit of money. With more transactions and more need of precautionary balances, a given stock of real money no longer simplifies transacting as much as before. The MB schedule shifts up to MB' when real income rises. At the original interest rate and MC schedule, desired real money holdings are now L''. Higher real income raises the quantity of real money demanded.

Broad money

So far we have implicitly been discussing the demand for narrow money M0. To explain the demand for M4, which is mainly bank (and building society) deposits, we re-interpret MC as the average *extra* return from risky assets rather than safer deposits that pay a lower interest rate. MB is the marginal benefit of bank deposits in reducing the risk of the portfolio.

A rise in the average *interest differential* between risky assets and deposits shifts the cost of holding broad money from MC to MC', reducing the quantity of broad money demanded. Higher income and wealth shift the marginal benefit from MB to MB'. More time deposits are demanded.

Table 8-4 summarises our discussion of the determinants of money demand.

Table 8-4

The demand for money

Quantity demanded	Effect of rise in		
	P	Y	r
Nominal money M	Rises in proportion	Rises	Falls
Real money M/P	Unaffected	Rises	Falls

Money market equilibrium

The money market is in equilibrium when the quantity of real money demanded equals the quantity supplied. For a given real income, Figure 8-2 shows real money demand MD. A higher interest rate raises the cost of holding money and reduces the quantity demanded.

Through open market operations, the central bank can determine the nominal money supply. If the price level is given, this also determines the real money supply. Hence the central bank can set an interest rate r_0 by supplying a quantity of real money L_0. To set an interest rate r_1 the central bank simply raises the money supply to L_1.

Changes in money demand

What would raise the demand for money at each interest rate? Either higher real income, which would raise the marginal benefit of money, or more banking competition, which would raise interest rates paid on deposits, reducing the cost of holding money at any level of interest rates on bonds and other assets.

Figure 8-2

Money market equilibrium

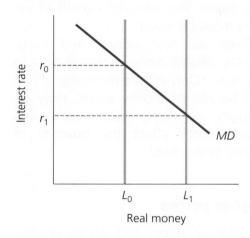

In Figure 8-3 a rise in money demand shifts MD up to MD'. With an unchanged real money supply, interest rates rise from r to r' in order to reduce the quantity of real money demand back to the level of the unchanged real money supply.

However, if the central bank wishes to maintain the interest rate at its original level r, it simply undertakes an open market operation to raise the real money supply from L to L'. When the central bank wants to 'set' interest rates, it

Box 8-4

Explaining the rise in money holdings from 1965 to 2001

To explain why nominal M4 holdings were 52 times higher in 2001 than in 1965, we need to examine changes in prices, real income and nominal interest rates. Because of inflation, the price level was more than 11 times higher in 2001 than in 1965. Hence, real money was only 4.5 times its initial level. Yet it still grew much more than real GDP, which rose only to 2.5 times its initial level, despite the fact that interest rates hardly changed. Why the discrepancy?

A big rise in competition forced banks to pay higher interest rates on *deposits*. For a given interest rate on bonds, a higher interest rate on bank deposits, the bulk of M4, *reduced* the cost of holding broad money, which is now *much* smaller than the 5 per cent shown in the table. People now get interest on bank deposits, especially on savings accounts. A lower cost of holding money made people hold more real money.

Holdings of M4, 1965–2001

	1965	2001
Index of:		
Nominal M4	1	52
Real M4	1	4.5
Real GDP	1	2.5
Interest rate	6%	5%

Source: ONS, *Economic Trends*

Figure 8-3

A rise in money demand

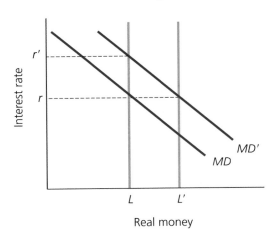

therefore passively supplies whatever money is demanded at that interest rate.

Monetary policy

Interest rates are the instrument of monetary policy.

The **monetary instrument** is the variable over which a central bank exercises day-to-day control.

The *ultimate objective* of monetary policy could in principle be a combination of low inflation, output stabilisation, manipulation of the exchange rate, or more stable house prices. The Bank of

England now has operational independence from government to set interest rates. But the Chancellor has decided the Bank's ultimate objective. It must set interest rates to try to keep inflation close to 2.5 per cent a year.

In making decisions, a central bank tries to get up-to-date forecasts of as many variables as possible. Sometimes, however, it concentrates on one or two key indicators, such as the recent behaviour of prices, the exchange rate or the money supply.

New data on the money supply (largely bank deposits) come out faster than new data on the price level or real output. If the true, but not yet observable, behaviour of output and prices feeds reliably into money demand, then recent data on what happened to the stock of money may be a useful leading indicator of what is happening to the economy.

In the heyday of *Monetarism*, central banks responded rapidly to new data on the nominal money stock. When it rose too quickly, the central bank inferred that rises in income or prices had boosted money demand, requiring the passive supply of extra money to maintain the previous interest rate. Given this signal, the central bank then raised interest rates to prevent the economy growing too quickly and bidding up inflation.

Throughout the world, over the last decade there have been two key changes in the design of monetary policy. First, central banks have been told that their ultimate objectives should concentrate more on low inflation control and less on other things.

Second, money has become much less reliable as a leading indicator. Rapid changes in the financial services sector keep changing the demand for money. When we see the money stock rising, we no longer know whether this signals imminent growth of prices and output, or whether it reflects a structural change that is making people hold more money even at constant levels of prices and output. Measures of money growth no longer have pride of place in central banks' assessments of whether to change interest rates.

Recap

- The Bank of England is the UK central bank acting as banker to the banks and to the government. Since it can print money it can never go bust. It acts as lender of last resort to the banks.

- The Bank mainly controls the monetary base through open market operations, by buying and selling government securities. It could also change the money multiplier by imposing reserve requirements on the banks, or setting the discount rate at a penalty level.

- The demand for money is a demand for real balances. It rises if real income rises, but falls if the interest rate rises.

- To set the interest rate, the central bank passively adjusts the money supply to the level of money demand at that interest rate.

- Interest rates are the instrument of monetary policy. Ultimate objectives usually include low inflation. Nominal money is now less reliable as a leading indicator of future price and output data.

Review questions

1 If commercial banks hold 100 per cent cash reserves against deposits, and the public holds no cash, what is the value of the money multiplier?

2 How do credit cards affect the precautionary demand for money?

3 Suppose banks raise interest rates on time deposits whenever interest rates on other assets rise. How much does a general rise in interest rates affect the demand for M4?

4 What are the desirable properties of a good leading indicator?

5 *Common fallacies* Why are these statements wrong? (a) Since higher interest rates on bank deposits make people hold less cash, they reduce the money supply. (b) Cash can never pay a decent rate of return.

Answers on pages 278–90

8-3 Interest rates, aggregate demand and output

Learning outcomes

By the end of this section, you should understand:
- How interest rates affect aggregate demand
- How monetary and fiscal policy interact to determine aggregate demand

Chapter 7 explained why equilibrium output can fluctuate, and how fiscal policy can affect the level of output. What about monetary policy? Section 8.2 discussed how the central bank can affect interest rates, but how do interest rates affect aggregate demand?

> The **transmission mechanism** of monetary policy is the process by which interest rates affect aggregate demand and output.

Figure 8-4 shows the behaviour of actual or nominal interest rates in the UK during 1985–2002. However, part of the interest rate is simply to allow lenders to keep pace with inflation.

> The **real interest rate**, the difference between the nominal interest rate and inflation, is what measures the real cost of borrowing and the real return on lending.

For example, the nominal interest rate is 10 per cent and inflation is 6 per cent,

the real interest rate is only 4 per cent. Figure 8-4 shows both inflation and nominal interest rates, and hence also shows the real interest rate as the difference between nominal interest rates and inflation.

Real interest rates were very high in the early 1990s when the UK was temporarily pegging the exchange rate against European currencies. European interest rates were high because of huge government spending by Germany on German unification. The German central bank deliberately raised interest rates in order to prevent aggregate demand getting too far above potential output in Germany.

Central banks, of course, only set the nominal or actual interest rate. They do not set the real interest rate directly. But they can make good forecasts of inflation. For any given inflation rate, a higher nominal interest rate implies a higher real interest rate. For simplicity, we can think of the central bank as setting the real interest rate too.

We now explain why higher real interest rates are likely to reduce aggregate demand.

Interest rates and consumption demand

In Chapter 2 we argued that changes in interest rates have two effects. The *substitution effect* makes everybody want to consume less today because the relative reward for saving has risen. The *income effect* also makes people consume less if initially they were borrowers. Higher interest rates make borrowers poorer, so they have to consume less. Both effects reduce consumption demand by borrowers.

However, higher interest rates make lenders *richer*. For them, the income effect makes them consume *more* today, whereas the substitution effect – a more attractive return on saving than before – makes them want to spend *less* today. For lenders, the effect of higher interest rates on consumption demand is ambiguous.

Aggregating borrowers and lenders, higher interest rates may reduce consumption demand, but perhaps by less than you expected.

However, a change in interest rates has another effect. Income and substitution effects do not apply if you are initially rationed and cannot borrow at the going interest rate. Lenders fear moral hazard (you borrow, then vanish with the money) and adverse selection (having inside information that you are a bad risk, you borrow an above-average amount). To combat both problems, lenders often require collateral.

> Borrowers offer **collateral** to lenders by handing over legal title to assets that the creditor can seize if the borrower fails to repay the loan.

For example, building societies usually keep the deeds to a property until a mortgage is paid off.

Lower interest rates boost the demand for assets, and thus their price, by reducing the opportunity cost of funds

Figure 8-4

Nominal and real UK interest rates (%)

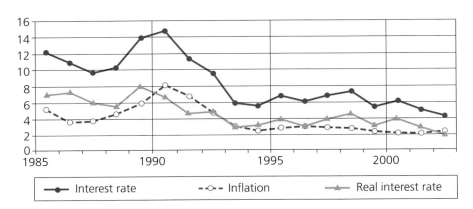

tied up in owning assets. Higher asset prices raise their value as collateral, allowing people to borrow more than before. A boom in house prices lets people remortgage their house, and spend the money on fancy cars and foreign holidays. This is a second channel through which interest rates affect consumption demand by households and investment demand by firms.

> The **credit channel** of monetary policy is the effect of lower interest rates in boosting aggregate demand by raising the value of collateral and thus the ability to borrow and spend.

Interest rates and investment demand

Chapter 7 treated investment demand as given, but this was only a simplification. We still treat as given investment by the government, which is part of G, but now focus on the effect of interest rates on investment demand by private firms.

Firms add to their plant and equipment because they expect profitable opportunities to raise future output or reduce future costs. Higher real interest rates raise the cost of investment by increasing the opportunity cost of the funds tied up in a new capital good. Other things equal, investment demand falls.

At any instant there are many investment projects that a firm *could* undertake. Suppose it ranks these projects, from the most profitable to the least profitable. At a high interest rate, only a few projects earn enough to cover depreciation and the opportunity cost of funds employed. As the interest rate falls, more and more projects are profitable to undertake.

Figure 8-5

The investment demand schedule

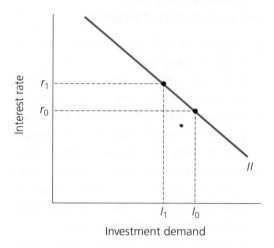

Figure 8-5 plots the investment demand schedule II showing how a lower interest rate raises investment demand. If the interest rate rises from r_0 to r_1, desired investment falls from I_0 to I_1.

> The **investment demand schedule** shows desired investment at each interest rate.

The height of the schedule II depends on the cost of new capital goods and the stream of profits to which they give rise. A higher price of new capital goods ties up more money, raising the opportunity cost of the funds employed. Investment demand is lower at any interest rate, shifting the investment demand schedule II downwards. Similarly, more pessimism about future demand reduces the flow of likely profits from new investment, again shifting the entire investment demand schedule downwards.

The slope of the investment demand schedule *II* depends mainly on the life of the asset. For short-lived capital goods, high rates of depreciation dominate the cost of investment. Changes in interest rates may have only a small effect on investment demand. However, for long-lived capital goods, with low depreciation rates, the interest cost of funds used is the main cost of investment, and investment demand is more sensitive to interest rates.

Hence, the *II* schedule is flatter for long-lived assets, but could be quite steep for short-lived capital assets. When the dot.com bubble burst, central banks worried that interest rates cuts might not help the sector recover quickly from excess capacity in the computer servers that handle e-mail traffic and data transmission. With high rates of depreciation due to rapid technical obsolescence, changes in interest rates and the cost of funds tied up had only a small effect on demand for new computer servers.

Inventory investment

There are two reasons why firms *plan* to hold inventories of raw materials, partly finished goods and finished goods awaiting sale. First, the firm may be speculating, or betting on future price rises.

Second, firms may plan to hold stocks to avoid costly changes in production levels. Suppose demand for the firm's output suddenly rises. A firm would have to pay big overtime payments to meet an upsurge in its order book. It is cheaper to carry some stocks in reserve with which to meet an upswing in demand. Similarly, in a temporary downturn, it is cheaper to maintain production and stockpile unsold goods than to incur redundancy payments, only to rehire workers in the next upswing.

As with physical capital, the cost of holding inventories is depreciation (and storage costs) plus the opportunity cost of the funds tied up. The investment demand schedule *II* in Figure 8-5 is thus also relevant to planned investment in stockbuilding. Other things equal, a higher interest rate raises the cost of holding inventories and reduces desired investment in inventories.

Thus, higher interest rates reduce all types of investment demand, a move left along the investment demand schedule. A rise (fall) in the cost of capital goods or fall (rise) in expected future profit opportunities shifts this schedule down (up). Since ideas about future profits can change a lot, the investment demand schedule shifts around quite a lot.

Money, interest rates and equilibrium output

By cutting interest rates, monetary policy can boost output and income. Suppose the central bank reduces interest rates. With given wages and prices, this is both a reduction in nominal interest rates and in real interest rates. Lower real interest rates raise investment demand and autonomous consumption demand (the part of consumption demand not explained by output and income). Hence, in Figure 8-6(a) aggregate demand rises, raising equilibrium output.

Equivalently, lower interest rates increase desired investment at any output, but also, by reducing desired

Figure 8-6

Lower interest rates raise equilibrium output

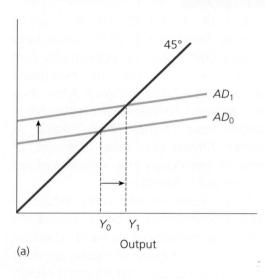

(a)

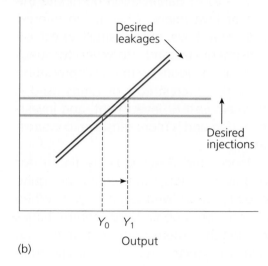

(b)

Box 8-5

The big issue

Japan had a huge property price boom in the late 1980s and then an even more severe collapse in the early 1990s. Japanese banks took a big hit. The value of their loans and other assets fell drastically. Consumers lost confidence in banks and private spending collapsed.

The chart shows that the Bank of Japan slashed interest rates to try to get people spending again. On one day in March 1999 it issued 1800 billion yen (about £9 billion), driving short-term interest rates to 0.02 per cent! With interest rates down to zero, further open-market operations between money and short-term securities were pretty pointless. The Bank of Japan then started discussing whether it should buy government bonds as a device for pumping yet more money into the economy.

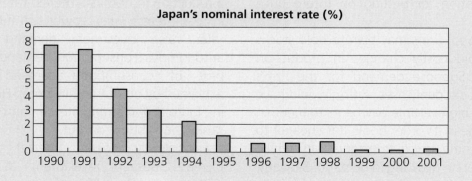

consumption, they raise (by a little) the desire to save at any output. For both reasons, desired injections exceed desired leakages at the original output level. In Figure 8-6(b) equilibrium output rises to raise desired leakages by enough to equal the new higher level of desired injections.

Fiscal policy and crowding out

Section 7-3 showed how fiscal policy affects aggregate demand and output. Now we have seen how monetary policy can also affect aggregate demand and output. What about the interaction of the two policies?

If a fiscal expansion has no effect on interest rates, the analysis of Section 7-3 remains relevant. The interest rate is simply only one of the other things equal. However, by raising aggregate demand and output, a fiscal expansion may affect the interest rate that the central bank then wishes to set. We discuss the central bank's reaction in detail in the next chapter.

For the moment, it seems plausible that, if fiscal policy boosts aggregate demand, it is no longer necessary for the central bank to set such a low interest rate to ensure that aggregate demand is at an appropriate level. If a fiscal expansion *induces* a rise in interest rates, demand for private spending on investment and consumption will fall. Higher government spending has partly crowded out private spending.

Crowding out is a fall in private demand caused by higher government spending that induces the central bank to raise interest rates.

The rise in government spending induces a *smaller* fall in private spending. If interest rates had risen enough to reduce private demand by as much as the rise in government demand, total demand would be unaltered. But then there would have been no reason for the central bank to raise interest rates! Without higher interest rates, there is no reason for private demand to fall. In the Keynesian model, crowding out is only partial.

Demand management and the policy mix

Demand management is the use of monetary and fiscal policy to stabilise output near the level of potential output.

Nevertheless, monetary and fiscal policy are not interchangeable. First, interest rates can be changed frequently, whereas changing tax rates and spending levels is more complicated and undertaken less frequently. Second, even in the longer run, monetary and fiscal policy affect aggregate demand through different routes and have different implications for the *composition* of aggregate demand.

A given level of aggregate demand can be achieved either by loose or expansionary fiscal policy (high government spending, low tax rates) combined with tight monetary policy (high interest rates); or by tight or contractionary fiscal policy (low government spending, high tax rates) combined with loose monetary policy (low interest rates).

Loose fiscal policy with easy monetary policy will mean that the public sector is large (high government spending) but the private sector is smaller (high interest rates reduce investment and consumption). Tight fiscal policy plus easy monetary policy will mean that the public sector is smaller but the private sector larger. Thus, different combinations of monetary and fiscal policy affect not only the level of output and spending, but also its composition across sectors.

Taking stock

We have now completed the first stage of macroeconomics. You have learned how to analyse the demand side of the economy. For simplicity, we assumed that there is spare capacity, and that prices and wages are fixed. To relax these assumptions we now need to introduce supply. Even once the analysis is more complete, the demand analysis of the previous two chapters remains an important part of the story, especially in the short run.

Recap

- A higher interest rate reduces consumption demand by borrowers but its effect on lenders is ambiguous. In the aggregate, consumption demand falls a bit. This is reinforced by the fact that higher interest rates reduce the value of collateral, making borrowing harder.
- The investment demand schedule shows how a higher interest rate reduces investment demand by raising the opportunity cost of funds tied up in new capital goods. Higher expected future profits, or a lower price of new capital goods, shift the investment demand schedule upwards.
- A lower interest rate raises aggregate demand and equilibrium output.
- A fiscal expansion raises demand and output, partly damped by an induced rise in interest rates that crowds out a smaller amount of consumption and investment demand.
- A given output can be attained by easy monetary policy and tight fiscal policy or by the converse. In the former case, interest rates are lower and private spending higher.

Review questions

1 People not previously allowed to borrow get credit cards with a £500 borrowing limit. What happens to the consumption function? Why?
2 After consumers go on a spending spree, they have large debts. How does this affect the effectiveness of monetary policy in future years?
3 Suppose the UK joins the euro, and that the single European interest rate then rises. What happens to UK aggregate demand? (b) Ideally, what should UK fiscal policy then do?
4 Suppose firms expect a huge boom in a couple of years. What happens today to investment and output today? How is the Bank of England likely to respond? Which types of investment will then be most affected?
5 *Common fallacies* (a) Consumers are crazy: their spending is up despite lower disposable income. (b) Borrowing should depend on the price of credit but not on the quantity of credit available.

Answers on pages 278–90

9
Aggregate supply, inflation and unemployment

9-1 Aggregate supply and equilibrium inflation

Learning outcomes

By the end of this section, you should understand:
- The classical model of output and inflation
- How inflation affects aggregate demand
- The equilibrium inflation rate
- Why wage adjustment is sluggish in the short run
- How temporary output gaps emerge
- How the economy eventually returns to potential output

For simplicity, our model of output determination treated prices and wages as given. Yet in practice there is inflation, a rise in the general level of prices. We need to think harder about what determines inflation. Figure 9-1 shows annual inflation rates in several countries since 1990. In these countries, like many others, inflation is lower than it used to be. This chapter explains why.

Once we stop treating prices as given, it no longer makes sense to treat output as demand-determined, which was anyway misleading since it appeared to suggest that higher aggregate demand can always raise output. However, with finite resources, the economy cannot expand output indefinitely. We now introduce aggregate supply – firms' willingness and ability to produce – and show how demand and supply *together* determine output. Introducing supply means that we finally abandon the simplifying assumption that output is determined by demand alone. And the balance of supply and demand tells us what is happening to inflation too.

Initially, we swap the Keynesian extreme, with fixed wages and prices, for

Figure 9-1

Annual inflation, 1990–2002 (%)

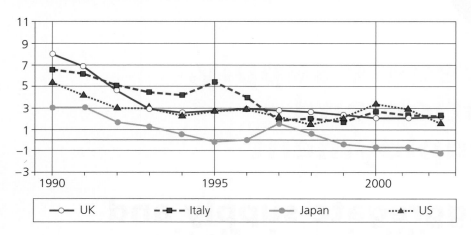

the opposite extreme, full wage and price flexibility.

> The **classical model** of macro-economics assumes wages and prices are completely flexible.

In the classical model, the economy is *always* at potential output. Any deviation of output causes instant changes in inflation to restore output to potential output. In the short run, before prices and inflation adjust, the Keynesian model is relevant. In the long run, after all adjustment is complete, the classical model is relevant. We examine how the economy evolves from the Keynesian short run to the classical long run.

Aggregate supply

> The **aggregate supply schedule** shows the output firms wish to supply at each inflation rate.

With complete flexibility, output has always adjusted back to potential output. All inputs are fully employed. This is the long-run equilibrium output of the economy. Potential output reflects technology, the quantities of available inputs in long-run equilibrium and the efficiency with which resources and technology are exploited. Chapter 11 studies how potential output grows in the long run. In the short run, we treat potential output as given.

How does more rapid growth of prices and nominal wages affect the incentive of firms to supply goods and services? We assume that people do not suffer from inflation illusion.

> **Inflation illusion** exists if people confuse nominal and real variables.

If wages and prices both double, real wages are unaffected. Neither firms nor workers change their behaviour.

Figure 9-2

The vertical *AS* schedule

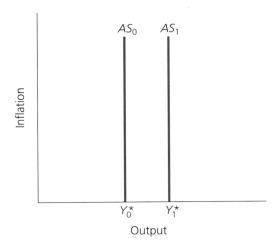

Output

Aggregate supply is unaffected by *pure* inflation, as shown in Figure 9-2.

In the classical model, the **aggregate supply schedule** is vertical at potential output.

Equilibrium output is *independent* of inflation. Since nobody has inflation illusion, people adjust nominal variables to keep pace with inflation. Nothing real changes, and output is constant. If potential output increases, the aggregate supply schedule shifts from AS_0 to AS_1 in Figure 9-2.

Inflation and aggregate demand

In the classical model, inflation does not affect aggregate supply but it does affect aggregate demand. To explain why, we need to discuss what is meant by a given monetary policy. Chapter 8 argued that monetary policy sets the nominal interest rate, thereby implicitly setting the real interest rate.

However, a *given* monetary policy is not the pursuit of a *given* real interest rate. The Bank of England, like many central banks, has been asked by the government to pursue an inflation target.

Following an **inflation target**, a central bank raises real interest rates if it expects inflation to be too high, and cuts real interest rates if it expects inflation to be too low.

By a *given* monetary policy, we mean the way the Bank systematically adjusts real interest rates to offset movements in inflation that would otherwise occur. Monthly variations in interest rates may simply be the implementation of this given strategy. A *change* in monetary policy is a decision to react differently to movements in inflation or other economic variables.

Figure 9-3 illustrates the aggregate demand schedule *AD*. When inflation is high, the Bank implements a given monetary policy by raising real interest rates, reducing aggregate demand and equilibrium output.

Movements *along* the schedule reflect interest rate changes in pursuit of a given inflation target. Interest rate changes take time to affect output and inflation, so the central bank cannot keep inflation perfectly on track, though it hopes to be moving in the right direction. In contrast, *shifts* in AD reflect a switch to a *different* monetary policy with a *different* inflation target.

Figure 9-3

Inflation and aggregate demand, for a given monetary policy

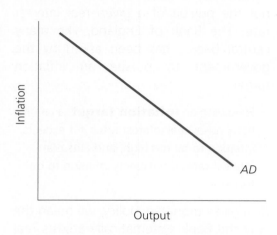

Figure 9-4

Equilibrium inflation

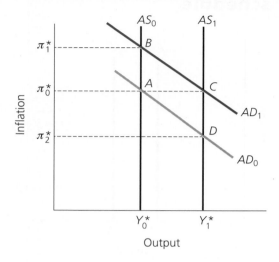

The equilibrium inflation rate

The equilibrium inflation rate π^* reflects the positions of the AD and AS schedules.

With aggregate supply AS_0 and aggregate demand AD_0, inflation is π_0^* and output is Y_0^*. Long-run equilibrium is at A. Although movements along the macroeconomic demand schedule show how interest rates are varied to start to offset inflation, the *average* level of interest rates and height of the macroeconomic demand schedule is chosen to hit the inflation target π_0^*, at least in the long run.

A permanent supply shock

Supply shocks may be beneficial, such as technical progress, or may be adverse, such as higher real oil prices or loss of capacity after an earthquake. Suppose

potential output rises. In Figure 9-4 the AS schedule shifts to the right, from AS_0 to AS_1. For a *given* AD schedule, it appears that equilibrium inflation falls to π_2^* and that the new equilibrium is at D.

To maintain the target inflation rate π_0^*, the central bank *loosens* monetary policy, setting a lower interest rate than before at any level of actual inflation. This raises demand, shifting AD_0 to AD_1 meeting the original inflation target π_0^* in long-run equilibrium at C not D.

> Monetary policy **accommodates** a permanent supply change by reducing the average level of real interest rates, thereby raising aggregate demand in line with higher aggregate supply.

A demand shock

For a given aggregate supply AS_0, a rise in demand from AD_0 to AD_1 takes the economy from A to B. The rise in inflation to π_1^* violates the long-run inflation target at π_0^*. The central bank has to *tighten* monetary policy, setting a higher real interest rate at each possible output level. This shifts AD_1 back to AD_0 and restores equilibrium at A, letting the central bank continue to meet its inflation target.

If the initial cause of the upward shift in demand was a fiscal expansion, the eventual result in the classical model is complete crowding out of the same amount of private expenditure.

> In the classical model, there is **complete crowding out**. Higher government spending causes an equivalent reduction in private spending, since total output cannot change.

To keep hitting its inflation target, the central bank must raise real interest rates enough to depress consumption and investment demand so that aggregate demand remains at potential output despite higher government spending.

If government spending falls, we can use Figure 9-4 in reverse. Beginning at A, tighter fiscal policy shifts AD_1 down to AD_0. To prevent inflation falling below the target π_0^*, the central bank must loosen monetary policy, which shifts demand back up to AD_1. Lower government spending then *crowds in* an equal amount of private spending because of lower real interest rates.

A rise in the inflation target

Suppose the inflation target is raised from π_0^* to π_1^*. The central bank no longer needs such high interest rates at any particular level of inflation. Real interest rates fall and the macroeconomic demand schedule shifts up from AD_0 to AD_1. With an unchanged AS schedule, equilibrium moves from A to B in Figure 9-4.

Inflation is higher but real output is unaltered. Since this is a full equilibrium, all real variables, including real money M/P, are then constant. In the classical model, higher inflation is accompanied by a similar rise in nominal money growth. The idea that nominal money growth is associated with inflation, but not higher output, is the central tenet of *Monetarists*. Figure 9-4 shows this is correct in the classical model with full wage and price flexibility.

Sluggish adjustment in the short run

In practice, prices and wages are not instantly flexible, so output can deviate from potential output in the short run. Some firms, in long-run relationships with their customers, prefer not to vary prices with short-run market conditions. It takes times and effort to decide how to react, to inform people of changes and to alter catalogues.

Wages are even slower to adjust than prices. Since wages are the main part of costs, which in turn affect prices, sluggish wage adjustment also helps explain sluggish prices adjustment. Long-run relationships matter a lot in the labour market. Teambuilding, trust and the acquisition of firm-specific skills take time to develop. It makes more sense for workers' pay to reflect longer-term considerations. Nor can a firm and its workforce continuously negotiate how wages should next be changed. Too much time negotiating means too little time producing. Costly negotiations are only undertaken at intervals, often once a year.

Short-run aggregate supply

In Figure 9-5 the economy is at potential output at A. In the short run, the firm inherits a given rate of nominal wage growth (not shown) that had anticipated staying at A with inflation π_0. By keeping up with inflation, nominal wage growth expected to maintain the correct real wage for labour market equilibrium.

If inflation exceeds the expected inflation rate π_0, firms have higher prices and nominal wages have risen less than they should. Firms take advantage of their good luck by supplying a lot more output. They pay overtime to buy workforce co-operation, and may also hire temporary extra staff.

Figure 9-5

Short-run aggregate supply

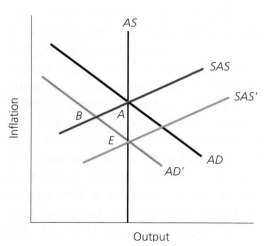

Conversely, if inflation is below π_0, the real wage is now higher than anticipated when the nominal wage was agreed. Since labour is now costly, firms cut back output a lot. In Figure 9-5 they move along the short-run supply schedule SAS in the short run.

> The **short-run supply curve SAS** shows how desired output varies with inflation, for a given inherited growth of nominal wages.

Suppose the economy begins at A, but then the central bank adopts a lower inflation target, shifting macroeconomic demand down from AD to AD'. After full wage and price adjustment, the final equilibrium is at E.

In the short-run, firms inherit given nominal wage settlements, now higher than ideal, and move down their short-run supply curve to B. Output is now below potential output, just as in the simple Keynesian model. Instead of assuming output is entirely demand-determined, it is now determined by demand and short-run supply.

> The **output gap** is actual output minus potential output.

Lower output and employment gradually bid down wages and prices. After a while, the short-run supply schedule shifts down to SAS'. Eventual equilibrium at E is a point on the new demand schedule AD', but also on both the supply schedules SAS' and AS. Shifts in short-run supply reconcile it eventually with long-run supply at potential output. The output gap disappears.

How long it takes to make the transition from short run to long run is a key issue in macroeconomics. Some

Box 9-1

OECD estimates of output gaps 1980–2000

The figure shows the UK slump of the early 1980s, as the Thatcher government reduced demand to defeat inflation, and the Lawson boom of the late 1980s, forcing the brakes on again in the early 1990s. Since then there has been steady recovery.

Germany also experienced a slump in the early 1980s as demand was reduced to fight inflation after the second oil shock. At the end of the 1980s, German Unification boosted demand since a large budget deficit was needed to finance restructuring in East Germany. The Bundesbank responded to overheating by raising interest rates, causing a big fall in demand. We also show data for Finland, which boomed with the opening of trade to the east, but then collapsed after its export markets disappeared in the early 1990s as the former Soviet Union imploded.

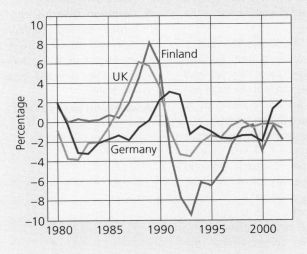

economists think it is rapid, so that the insights of the classical model quickly become relevant. Others think the Keynesian model of the previous chapter remains relevant for a long time. The mainstream view is somewhere in the middle. Within a year, price adjustment has begun. But it takes between two and four years to get to the new long-run equilibrium.

Recap

- Higher inflation reduces aggregate demand because the central bank raises real interest rates to get inflation back on target. The height of the aggregate demand schedule reflects the inflation target.

- In the classical model with complete wage and price flexibility, output is always potential output and the vertical long-run supply curve is valid immediately.

- The equilibrium inflation rate thus occurs at the inflation target. For a given monetary policy, a rise in demand caused by fiscal expansion or private optimism induces a rise in real interest rates to reduce aggregate demand back to the level of potential output.

- The short-run supply curve shows how higher inflation temporarily raises output because inherited nominal wages have not yet had time to adjust. Over time, shifts in the short-run supply curve restore long-run equilibrium at potential output and the inflation target.

- How quickly wage adjustment returns output returns to potential output is a key issue in macroeconomics. If this is rapid, demand management is unnecessary. If it is slow, demand management is essential.

- Permanent supply shocks change potential output. To preserve the target inflation rate, monetary policy must accommodate the shock, thus providing the required change in aggregate demand.

Review questions

1 The New Deal leads large numbers of extra people to join the labour force. Discuss the effects on output and inflation, in the short run and in the long run.

2 Suppose the Bank wants to keep inflation constant during this transition. How should interest rates be adjusted?

3 Is a rise in nominal money always accompanied by an equivalent rise in prices?

4 Discuss the effect of a rise in export demand when the Bank maintains a given monetary policy. What happens to (a) investment, (b) tax revenue?

5 *Common fallacies* Why are these statements wrong? (a) Higher inflation reduces output by making it more expensive for firms to produce. (b) Higher inflation reduces output because consumers demand fewer goods when prices are higher.

Answers on pages 278–90

9-2 Inflation

Learning outcomes

By the end of this section, you should understand:

- The quantity theory of money
- How inflation affects nominal interest rates
- Long-run and short-run Phillips curves
- The costs of inflation
- Why central banks were made independent

Persistent inflation is quite a recent phenomenon. The UK price level was the same in 1950 as in 1920. Figure 9-6 confirms that UK inflation was negative in some of the interwar years. Yet since 1945 annual UK inflation has never been negative. Since 1945 the price level has risen 25-fold, more than its rise in the previous 300 years. A similar story applies in most advanced economies.

Inflation and money growth

The real money supply M/P shows the quantity of goods that money will buy. Demand for real money rises with real income Y, but falls with the nominal interest rate r.[1] If real money demand is

1 Inflation at the rate π reduces the purchasing power of money. The cost of holding money, the real interest rate $(r - \pi)$ on bonds minus the real interest rate $(-\pi)$ on money, is thus the nominal interest rate r.

Figure 9-6

UK annual inflation, 1920–2002

Sources: B. R. Mitchell, *European Historical Statistics 1750–1970*, Macmillan, 1975, and OECD, *Economic Outlook*

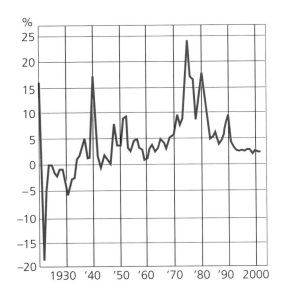

constant, any change in nominal money must be matched by a change in prices to keep the real money supply constant. This quantity theory of money is believed to date back at least to Confucius.

> The **quantity theory of money** says that changes in the quantity of nominal money *M* lead to equivalent changes in prices *P*, but have no effect on real output.

Section 9-1 showed that all nominal variables move together provided the classical model holds. However, the quantity theory needs interpreting with care. Nowadays, central banks set interest rates in pursuit of inflation targets and then passively supply whatever money is demanded at that interest rate. Causation thus runs from prices to money, not the other way round.

Moreover, real money demand can change, either because of short-run changes in real income, or because monetary policy has changed nominal interest rates. When real money demand changes, nominal money and prices must behave *differently* in order to *alter* the real money supply.

In the long run, the correlation of money and prices is stronger. Eventually, output is fixed at potential output, which changes only slowly. If inflation is permanently high, nominal money must grow at a similar rate. Otherwise, the real money stock is permanently changing, which is incompatible with long-run equilibrium.

In this sense, long-run inflation is always a monetary phenomenon. Take away the monetary oxygen and the inflationary fire goes out. Central banks with high inflation targets have to print lots of money to maintain the real money stock in line with real money demand. Those with low inflation targets need to print less money.

Hyperinflation

Ukraine's annual inflation reached 10 000 per cent in 1993. The most famous hyperinflation was in Germany during 1922–23.

> **Hyperinflation** is high inflation, above 50 per cent *per month*.

After the First World War, the German government had a big deficit, financed largely by printing money. Eventually, the government had to buy faster printing presses. In the later stages of the hyperinflation they took in old notes, stamped on another zero, and reissued them as larger-denomination notes in the morning. By October 1923 it took 192 million marks to buy a drink that had cost 1 mark in January 1922. People shopped by carrying money around in wheelbarrows. Muggers took the barrows but left the near-worthless money behind!

During hyperinflation, since inflation is so high, nominal interest rates are huge. People try to get by with low real cash balances. In 1923 Germans were paid twice a day so they could shop at lunchtime before the real value of their cash depreciated. Any unspent cash was quickly deposited in a bank where it could earn interest. People spent a lot of time at the bank.

Hyperinflations arise because governments can no longer raise enough taxes to finance their spending commitments, including interest on accumulated government debts. They try to print more and more money to cover the growing budget deficit. The additional money causes more and more inflation. The 'solution' often involves defaulting on the old debt, which dramatically reduces government spending and the need to print money.

Inflation and unemployment

In 1958, using UK data on inflation and unemployment, a professor at the London School of Economics discovered an empirical relationship that became famous, since it seemed also to work for other countries. It still bears his name today.

> The **Phillips curve** shows that higher inflation is accompanied by lower unemployment.

The Phillips curve in Figure 9-7 shows the trade-off that people thought they faced in the 1960s. It suggested that UK

Figure 9-7

The Phillips curve

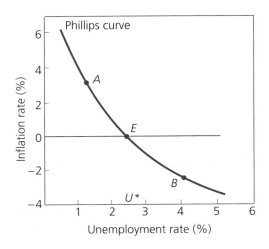

inflation would fall to zero if only people would tolerate unemployment as high as 2.5 per cent. If only! Since then, we have had years when *both* inflation and unemployment exceeded 10 per cent. The simple Phillips curve ceased to fit the facts.

We now realise that this Phillips curve is simply the mirror image of the aggregate supply curve. The latter relates inflation to output, the former relates inflation to unemployment. The two are connected because high output goes with low unemployment.

> **Equilibrium unemployment $U*$** is the level of unemployment in long-run equilibrium.

Section 9-3 explains why equilibrium unemployment is above zero. Once all variables can adjust, the market returns to equilibrium unemployment. There is no *long-run* trade-off between inflation and unemployment. Just as the long-run aggregate supply curve for goods is vertical at potential output, the long-run Phillips curve is vertical at equilibrium unemployment $U*$ in Figure 9-8. An increase in equilibrium unemployment shifts the long-run Phillips curve to the right.

> The **long-run Phillips curve** is vertical at equilibrium unemployment.

The height of a *short-run* aggregate supply curve reflects the inflation expectations already built into nominal wages. The same holds in the labour market.

> Each **short-run Phillips curve** is a negative relation between inflation and unemployment, given the inflation expectations already built into nominal wages.

Figure 9-8

The short-run Phillips curve

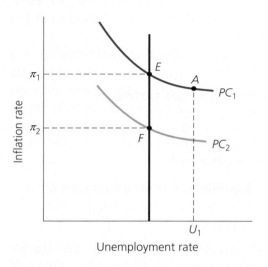

In Figure 9-8, inflation expectations π_1 are already embodied in nominal wages and the short-run Phillips curve is PC_1. Suppose the central bank adopts a lower inflation target. Initially, this is below the previous level of expected inflation. Hence, nominal wages have been set too high. The economy moves from E to A along the short-run Phillips curve. High real wages reduce output and raise unemployment.

If people expect lower inflation to be sustained, new wage settlements eventually embody lower inflation expectations, the Phillips curve shifts down to PC_2 and the eventual equilibrium is at F. Unemployment and output are back in long-run equilibrium, and inflation expectations have adjusted to the new policy. Since F is vertically below E, in the long run there is no trade-off between inflation and unemployment.

The original Phillips curve of Figure 9-7 was not a *permanent* trade-off between inflation and unemployment. It showed a temporary trade-off, for a given level of inherited inflation expectations and nominal wages. During the long historical period examined by Phillips, expected inflation happened to be low. In the second half of the twentieth century, inflation was higher on average and more variable. Hence, the short-run Phillips curve shifted up and down as inflation expectations changed.

Inflation got out of control because monetary growth was no longer tied to growth in the stock of gold, as it had been in the nineteenth century. Governments could print money. Workers, perceiving that governments were fearful of unemployment, kept raising nominal wages. Frightened to put on the monetary brakes and raise real interest rates, governments instructed their central banks to print money and accommodate nominal wage increases. The expectation of this behaviour became a self-fulfilling prophecy.

This example shows the crucial role of expectations, and explains why governments now go to such lengths to try to convince the public of their good intentions. Before discussing smart ways to do this, we examine why people hate inflation so much in the first place.

The costs of inflation

Inflation illusion?

Voters may suffer from inflation illusion, confusing nominal and real changes. It is wrong to say that inflation is bad because it makes goods more expensive. If *all* nominal variables rise together, people have larger nominal incomes and can buy the same physical quantity of goods as before.

In other cases, inflation does indeed have costs. Their size depends on whether inflation is anticipated, and whether economic and political institutions let people adapt to foreseen inflation.

Adaptation and anticipation

If everyone sees inflation coming, and can adapt fully, all nominal variables adjust to restore real variables to their former levels. Nominal wages and nominal interest rates are set at appropriate levels; with unchanged real wages and real interest rates, workers and savers are protected. Nominal taxes and nominal government spending are adjusted regularly to maintain the real level of taxes and welfare benefits. Does inflation hurt anyone?

Cash cannot be protected from inflation since its zero interest rate cannot be adjusted. Higher inflation makes people hold less real cash, thus raising the time and effort needed for transacting.

> **Shoe-leather costs of inflation** is shorthand for the extra time and effort in transacting when inflation reduces desired real cash holdings.

In addition, when prices are rising, price labels have to be changed and catalogues reprinted. Higher inflation means these costs are incurred more frequently.

> **Menu costs of inflation** are the physical resources used in changing price

tags, reprinting catalogues and changing vending machines.

Even with complete adaptation and full anticipation, we cannot avoid shoe-leather and menu costs of inflation. These are big if inflation is high, but are probably small when inflation is low.

Anticipation without adaptation

Sometimes, our institutions are not inflation-neutral. This stops full adjustment to foreseen inflation, raising the distortions that inflation creates. For example, if nominal tax allowances do not rise with prices, people are driven into higher real tax payments. If the government taxes all interest income (only the real interest rate is a genuine profit on lending, the rest is just for keeping up with inflation), or taxes all capital gains (only the gain in excess of inflation is real profit), then higher inflation raises effective tax rates. The government gains from the failure to use proper inflation accounting, but the private sector changes its behaviour as a result. These institutional imperfections imply that even anticipated inflation has costs for society.

Unexpected inflation

Surprise inflation alters the real value of nominal contracts. Lenders lose out, having failed to charge an adequate nominal interest rate. Workers lose out, having failed to settle for an adequate nominal wage. Conversely, borrowers and firms benefit. One person's gain is another person's loss. In the aggregate these cancel out. But unexpected inflation redistributes income and wealth, for example from lenders to borrowers.

Uncertain inflation

Uncertainty about future inflation makes long-term planning harder. People also dislike risk itself. The extra benefits of the champagne years are poor compensation for the years of starvation. People would rather average out these extremes and live comfortably all the time. Uncertain inflation makes the real value of the contract less certain. This is another cost of inflation. There is some empirical evidence that inflation that is high on average also tends to be more volatile and harder to predict. One benefit of low inflation is that the institutional changes necessary to deliver it also tend to make it more predictable.

Committing to low inflation

Box 9-2 provides evidence that central bank independence is a useful commitment to tight monetary policy and low inflation. Institutional commitment has succeeded in keeping inflation in many countries in recent years.

The euro zone

Euro zone countries have to obey the Stability Pact, which commits them to avoid large budget deficits, so that they have no need of large money creation to finance their fiscal policies. The European Central Bank is constitutionally indepen-

dent of political control, and has a mandate to pursue low inflation.

UK policy 1992–97

In 1992 UK monetary policy first moved towards inflation targeting, but the Chancellor of the Exchequer still had the final say in setting interest rates. Even so, these arrangements partially committed the government to low inflation. Minutes of the monthly meeting between the Chancellor and the Governor of the Bank of England were published a few weeks later, so any objections by the Bank were highly publicised. Moreover, the Bank was told to publish a quarterly *Inflation Report*, completely free from Treasury control. This Report soon became very influential, because it was transparent and used good economic analysis.

UK policy since 1997

In May 1997, the new Chancellor, Gordon Brown, gave the Bank of England 'operational independence' to set interest rates in pursuit of the inflation target that he laid down. Any change in the target will be politically difficult, except in truly exceptional circumstances. Operational central bank independence is a commitment to low inflation.

UK monetary policy is now set by the Bank of England's Monetary Policy Committee, meeting monthly to set interest rates to try to hit the inflation target (currently 2.5 per cent, plus or minus 1 per cent). If it misses the target range, the Governor must write to the Chancellor to explain why.

Most people give the Monetary Policy Committee high marks for its perform-

Box 9-2

Central bank independence

Central bankers are cautious people unlikely to favour rapid money growth and inflation. So why do these occur? Either because the government cares so much about unemployment that it never tackles inflation, or because it is politically weak and has a budget deficit which has to be partly financed by printing money. Essentially, inflation arises when governments overrule cautious bankers. Proposals for central bank independence mean independence *from the government*.

Since the aggregate supply curve and the Phillips curve are vertical in the long run, permanently lower inflation should not permanently reduce output or add to unemployment. Eventually, better institutional design yields a benefit without a cost. The two figures below confirm this reality – countries with more independent central banks have lower average inflation, but long-run output growth does not systematically suffer.

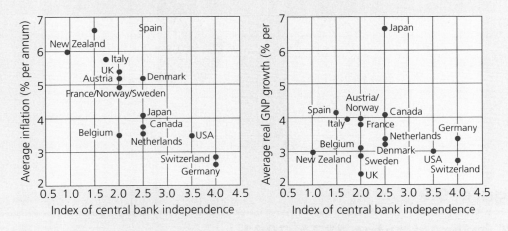

Source: A. Alesina and L. Summers, 'Central bank independence and macroeconomic performance: some comparative evidence', *Journal of Money, Credit, and Banking*, May 1993

ance so far. It was prepared to change interest rates even when this was unpopular, and inflation has stayed close to 2.5 per cent as a result. With low expected inflation, nominal interest rates are lower than for decades. Figure 9-9 shows the history of UK interest rates since 1974. Although the Bank's operational independence since 1997 has helped, the decisive break seems to have been 1992, when sterling left the Exchange Rate Mechanism and first moved towards inflation targeting.

Box 9-3

The Bank of England's fan chart

The *Inflation Report* includes the famous fan chart for inflation. A fan chart shows not just the most likely future outcome, but indicates the probability of different outcomes. The darker is the projected line, the more likely the outcome. Thus the Bank was expecting UK inflation to average around 2 per cent in 2002, but by the end of 2003 the range of possible outcomes had widened to between 1 per cent and 3.5 per cent. The chart shows how quickly uncertainty increases as we look into the future.

Percentage increase in prices on a year earlier

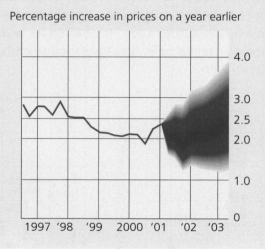

Figure 9-9

UK interest rates 1974–2001

Source: *Financial Times*, 11 June 1999

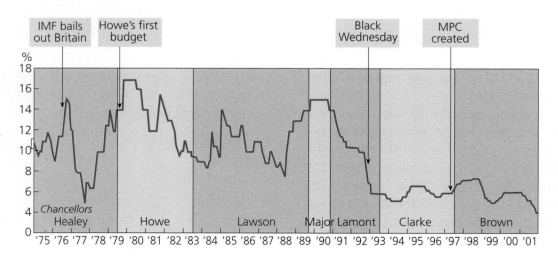

Recap

- In the short run, there may be little correlation of nominal money and prices, since real money demand can change. In the long run, the correlation is stronger. There is no close correlation of budget deficits and money growth if the government can finance deficits by borrowing.
- The long-run Phillips curve is vertical at equilibrium unemployment. The height of the short-run Phillips curve, a temporary trade-off between unemployment and inflation, depends on expected inflations built into nominal wage growth. This curve shifts down if inflation expectations fall.
- Some 'costs' of inflation are illusory. The true costs of inflation depend on whether it was anticipated and on whether an economy's institutions are inflation-neutral. Uncertain inflation is also costly. Uncertainty may be greater if inflation is already high.
- Operational independence of central banks removes the temptation faced by politicians to boost the economy too much.

Review questions

1 (a) Your real annual income is constant. You borrow £200 000 for 20 years to buy a house, paying interest annually, repaying the £200 000 in a final payment at the end. In one scenario, inflation is 0% and the nominal interest rate is 2 per cent a year. In a second scenario, annual inflation is 100 per cent and the nominal interest rate 102 per cent. Are the two scenarios the same in real terms?

2 (a) Explain the following data. (b) Is inflation always a monetary phenomenon?

2001	Money growth %	Inflation %
Euro area	3	2
Japan	12	−3
UK	6	2
US	8	2

Source: The Economist

3 Looking at data on inflation and unemployment over ten years, could you tell the difference between supply shocks and demand shocks?

4 Name three groups that lose out during inflation. Does it matter whether this inflation was anticipated?

5 *Common fallacies* Why are these statements wrong? (a) Inflation stops people saving. (b) Inflation stops people investing. (c) Foreseen inflation is costless.

Answers on pages 278–90

9-3 Unemployment

Learning outcomes

By the end of this section, you should understand:
- Classical, frictional and structural unemployment
- Voluntary and involuntary unemployment
- Determinants of UK unemployment
- Private and social costs of unemployment

In the early 1930s, over a quarter of the UK labour force was unemployed, which was both a waste of output and the cause of misery, social unrest and hopelessness. Postwar policy was geared to avoiding a rerun of the 1930s. Figure 9-10 shows that it succeeded.

In the 1970s, unemployment began to rise, but boosting demand failed to help. Instead, it caused high and rising inflation. Hence, by the 1980s many governments had embarked on tighter policies to get inflation under control. The combination of tight demand policies and adverse supply shocks initially caused a dramatic rise in unemployment, shown in Figure 9-11. However, since 1990 unemployment has fallen, and in the UK is now back to low levels.

> The **labour force** is everyone who has a job or wants one. The **unemployment rate** is the fraction of the labour force without a job.

Labour force growth since 1950 conceals two opposite trends: a steady rise in women wanting to work and a somewhat smaller fall in the number of men in the labour force.

Stocks and flows

Unemployment is a stock, measured at a point in time. Like a pool of water, it rises when inflows (the newly unemployed) exceed outflows (people getting new jobs or quitting the labour force entirely). Table 9-1 shows that the pool of unemployment is not stagnant.

Even with 1.7 million unemployed, many more people than this enter and leave the pool *every* year. Most people escape quickly, though those with few skills may visit the pool many times in their working lifetimes. However, some people get stuck in the pool, lose confidence and get stigmatised as a poor bet for an employer. Sometimes this is because the labour market has identified a worker who is genuinely less willing or able, but sometimes it just reflects bad luck that then becomes self-reinforcing.

Figure 9-10

UK unemployment (%)

Source: B. R. Mitchell, *Abstract of British Historical Statistics* and B. R. Mitchell and H. G. Jones, *Second Abstract of British Historical Statistics*, Cambridge University Press; ONS, *Economic Trends*

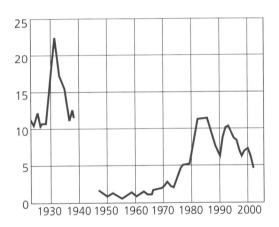

Types of unemployment

Unemployment can be frictional, structural, demand-deficient, or classical.

> **Frictional unemployment** is the irreducible minimum unemployment in a dynamic society.

It includes some people with handicaps that make them hard to employ, but also includes people spending short spells in unemployment as they hop between jobs in an economy where both the labour force and the jobs on offer are continually changing.

Table 9-1

UK unemployment (millions), 2000

Inflow to employment	2.2
Outflow from unemployment	3.3
Stock of unemployed	1.7

Source: ONS, *Labour Market Trends*

Figure 9-11

Unemployment (%)

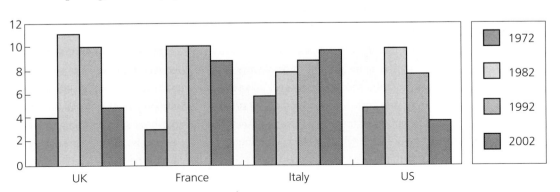

Structural unemployment reflects a mismatch of skills and job opportunities when the pattern of employment is changing.

Frictional unemployment arises from temporary impediments; structural unemployment reflects medium-run forces. A skilled welder made redundant at 50 in the north of England may have to retrain or move south to find work. Firms are reluctant to take on and train older workers, and housing in richer areas may be too dear. Such workers are victims of structural unemployment.

Demand-deficient unemployment occurs when output is below full capacity.

Until wages and prices adjust to their new long-run equilibrium level, a fall in aggregate demand reduces output and employment. Some workers want to work at the going real wage rate but cannot find jobs.

Classical unemployment arises when the wage is kept above its long-run equilibrium level.

This may reflect trade union power or minimum wage legislation. If wages cannot adjust, the labour market can restore low unemployment in long-run equilibrium.

The modern analysis of unemployment takes the same types of unemployment but classifies them differently, distinguishing between *voluntary* and *involuntary* unemployment.

Equilibrium unemployment

Figure 9-12 shows the market for labour. The labour demand schedule *LD* slopes downwards, since firms hire more workers at a lower real wage. The schedule *LF* shows how many people join the labour force at each real wage. A higher real wage makes (a few) more people want to work. The schedule *AJ* shows how many people accept a job at each real wage. It must lie left of the *LF* schedule, since the labour force is the employed plus the unemployed. The horizontal gap between *AJ* and *LF* shows

Box 9-4

A weak idea

Those with no economics training often think there is an easy way to cut unemployment. Shorten the working week, so that the same amount of total work is shared between more workers, leaving fewer people unemployed. But a shorter work-week is a very weak idea. The demand for labour (in person-hours) depends on the cost of hiring workers. Shortening the working week without cutting wages raises the cost of labour, so firms hire fewer workers. A daily eight-hour shift probably has an hour of dead time (coffee breaks, tidying the desk, chatting up colleagues, sneaking out to the shops). With a six-hour shift, dead time rises from 1/8 to 1/6, making labour more expensive.

Figure 9-12

Equilibrium unemployment

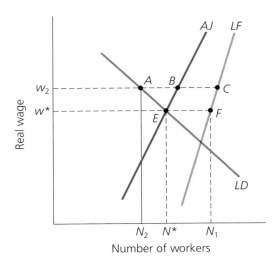

voluntary unemployment at each real wage.

> **Voluntary unemployment** is people looking for work who will not yet take a job at that real wage.

People house hunting do not take the first house they see. Similarly, some people invest in searching a bit longer for a more suitable job. At high real wages, people grab job offers quickly and the *AJ* and *LF* schedules are close together. At low real wages, people are more selective about accepting offers, especially if the offer is little above the benefits available to those out of work. Hence, the *AJ* and *LF* schedules are further apart at low real wages.

Labour market equilibrium is at *E*. Employment is *N** and unemployment is the distance *EF*.

> **Equilibrium unemployment** is unemployment when the labour market is in equilibrium.

Since it is the gap between the desire to accept jobs and the desire to be in the labour force, this unemployment is entirely voluntary. At the equilibrium real wage *w**, N_1 people want to be in the labour force but only *N** want to accept job offers; the remainder do not want to work at the equilibrium real wage.

Equilibrium unemployment includes frictional and structural unemployment. What about classical unemployment, for example if unions keep wages at w_2, above *w**? Total unemployment is now *AC*, which exceeds *EF*. At the wage w_2, *BC* workers are voluntarily unemployed, but *AB* workers are now involuntarily unemployed. Firms hire at point *A*, but individual workers want to be at point *B*.

> **Involuntary unemployment** means the unemployed would take a job offer at the existing wage.

However, through their unions, workers collectively have chosen wage w_2 in excess *w**, thus reducing employment. For workers as a whole, this extra unemployment is voluntary. It has raised equilibrium unemployment from *EF* to *AC*.

Keynesian or demand-deficient unemployment is entirely involuntary, and arises when wages have not yet adjusted to restore labour market equilibrium. Suppose in Figure 9-12 that the original labour demand schedule goes through points *E* and *F*. Equilibrium employment is at *B*, and equilibrium unemployment is *BC*. Now labour demand falls to *LD*. Until wages adjust, *BC* remains voluntary unemployment but *AB* is involuntary unemployment, pure spare capacity. Boosting labour demand again could move the economy from *A* back to *B*. Without such a boost to demand, involuntary unemployment will slowly bid wages down, moving the economy from *A* down to *E*. If this takes a long time, policies to boost demand may be preferable.

Thus, total unemployment is equilibrium unemployment plus demand-deficient unemployment. Only the latter is spare capacity that could be mopped up by shifting demand upwards. When the labour market is already in equilibrium, shifting demand up makes hardly any difference to the gap between the nearly parallel *AJ* and *LF* schedules. We then need *supply-side policies* that can close the gap between these two schedules that together reflect labour supply to the economy.

Why was unemployment so high?

Did high unemployment reflect inadequate demand or a rise in equilibrium unemployment? Figure 9-13 shows the average unemployment rate during eight periods, from 1956–59 through to 1996–2002. It shows how actual unemployment rose dramatically before eventually falling back. Clearly, most of this was explained by the rise and fall of equilibrium unemployment, which had many causes

Unions got more powerful after the 1960s, but were then undermined by globalisation, privatisation and legal changes to diminish their power. Mismatch and structural unemployment arose in regions and skills in which manufacturing decline had severe effects. More generous welfare benefits undermined work incentives at the lower end of the wage scale, and disconnected people from the labour market.

Recent policy has laid heavy emphasis on encouraging people back into work. *Welfare to Work* seeks to help people get off benefit, and *Making Work Pay* has tried to reduce disincentives for poorer workers. People out of work but on income support, housing benefit and Council Tax assistance lose benefits rapidly as they begin to earn income. The interaction of different policies used to impose effective tax rates of over 90 per cent on initial income work. Recent reforms have reduced this to below 70 per cent.

Governments need revenue to provide benefits for the very poor, including those out of work. But why do we tax the nearly poor so very heavily? We long ago abandoned 70 per cent tax rates on the rich, who now pay 41 per cent. In practice, middle class voters are more likely to be the swing voters who decide the outcomes of elections. Hence, they have significant political power. In contrast, the poor-in-work are unlikely to vote for parties associated with support for the well-off, and hence have less political influence.

Figure 9-13 also shows a few periods when demand-deficient unemployment was important, particularly in the early 1980s, when the Thatcher government first adopted tough policies to defeat inflation, and in the early 1990s when monetary and fiscal policy were

Figure 9-13

UK unemployment (%)

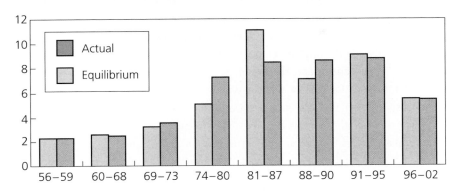

again tightened sharply. During these recessions, Keynesian unemployment existed.

Conversely, in the 1970s, despite the rise in unemployment, the economy was actually overheating and unemployment was less than its equilibrium level. Policy-makers, assuming that rising unemployment had been caused by deficient demand, boosted demand to mop up the slack. Since there was no slack, this merely added to inflation. Similarly, Figure 9-13 shows the Lawson boom at the end of the 1980s was another period of overheating, which is why the brakes had to go on in the early 1990s.

Figure 9-13 suggests that policy has subsequently done better. One reason was the switch to central bank independence and inflation targeting, which took the politics out of monetary policy and provided macroeconomic stability. The other reason is that governments gradually learned about the importance of supply-side policies to reduce equilibrium unemployment again.

Supply-side economics

Keynesians believe that the economy can deviate from full employment for quite a long time, certainly for a period of several years. Monetarists believe that the classical full-employment model is relevant much more quickly. Both agree that the long-run performance of the economy depends on aggregate supply and thus on what happens to potential output and equilibrium unemployment.

Tax cuts

Would lower tax rates improve work incentives and labour supply? Figure 9-14 again shows labour demand *LD*, the labour force schedule *LF*, and the job acceptances schedule *AJ*. As in Figure 9-13, the horizontal distance between *AJ* and *LF* shows voluntary unemployment, which decreases as the real wage rises relative to the given level of welfare benefits.

Box 9-5

'The graphs the EU Commission dare not publish'

'Brussels riven by job market row – A controversial report linking unemployment to rigidities in the labour market has split the Commission' reported the *Financial Times*. The first graph shows, for 14 EU members, the correlation between the degree of labour market regulation and the percentage of the labour force with jobs. The second graph shows, for some OECD countries, the correlation between the employment rate and the cost of firing a worker. The figures show a high degree of regulation and high costs of dismissal are each associated with a lower employment rate. If correlation proved causality, this would clinch the case for deregulation.

Suppose you had to make the case for labour market regulation. If the labour market worked perfectly there would be no need for intervention. Regulations may have been designed to offset existing market failures thereby enhancing efficiency. The countries with the largest distortions have the lowest employment rates, but also the largest government intervention to ameliorate the consequences of these distortions. Of course, to be persuasive, you'd have to identify exactly what these distortions were (market power of large employers, externalities in training, etc.) and explain why the particular forms of regulation made things better not worse. You might or might not be able to show this.

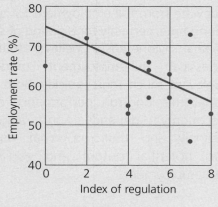

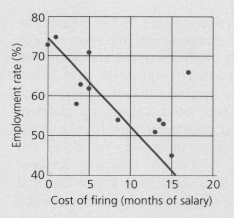

Source: Financial Times, 8 November 1996

Now imagine an income tax equal to the vertical distance *AB*. Equilibrium employment is now N_1, which is both the number of workers that firms want to hire at the gross wage N_1 and the number of workers wanting to take jobs at the corresponding after-tax wage w_3. The horizontal distance *BC* is now equilibrium unemployment, people in the labour force but not taking a job at the going rate of take-home pay.

If income tax is abolished, the gross wage to the firm now coincides with the take-home pay of a worker, and labour

Figure 9-14

A cut in marginal income tax rates

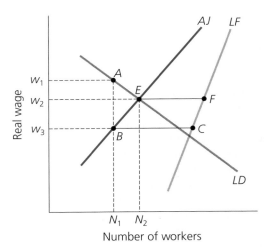

market equilibrium is at *E*. Equilibrium employment rises, and equilibrium unemployment falls from *BC* to *EF*. Higher take-home pay, relative to unemployment benefit, reduces voluntary unemployment.

Trade unions

By restricting job acceptances and making labour more scarce, trade unions shift the *AJ* schedule to the left, widening the gap between *AJ* and *LF*. Imagine a new *AJ'* schedule through point *B* in Figure 9-14. Point *B* is now labour market equilibrium. Since labour is scarcer, the real wage has risen, but equilibrium has increased from *EF* to *BC*. Conversely, equilibrium unemployment falls if union power is weakened. Unions are less successful in restricting labour supply and forcing up wages.

Welfare to work

Recent UK policies have tried to reconnect unemployment to the labour market, both by offering assistance and by removing the option to be in permanent receipt of unemployment benefit without making an effort to look for work. In effect, this shifts the *AJ* schedule to the right, by inducing or forcing more of the labour force to take jobs.

Costs of unemployment

The private cost of unemployment

Voluntary unemployment has a private cost to those unemployed, the sacrifice of the wage they would get by taking a job. The private benefit is that they may find a better job offer by looking longer; they also get some state benefits in the meantime. Whereas the voluntarily unemployed prefer not to take a job just yet, those involuntarily off work would prefer immediate employment and may be much worse off in unemployment. When unemployment is involuntary, people are suffering more.

The social cost of unemployment

This also varies with the nature of unemployment. Voluntary unemployment, by definition, is preferred by the individual, but should society value it too? Whereas these individuals count their benefit cheque as part of the gain from unemployment, socially this transfer payment does not contribute to national output or income.

Even so, society should not eliminate voluntary unemployment completely. First, transfer benefits may compensate for *other* market failures, such as difficulties in borrowing to acquire proper training. Second, society benefits directly from some voluntary unemployment. A changing economy needs to match up the right people to the right jobs, thus raising productivity and total output. The flow through the pool of unemployment is one way in which this is done.

Involuntary or Keynesian unemployment has a higher social cost. An economy producing below full capacity is wasting resources, which adds to the social cost of unemployment.

Recap

- People are either employed, unemployed, or out of the labour force. Unemployment rises when inflows to the pool of the unemployed exceed outflows. Inflows and outflows are large relative to the pool of unemployment.
- Unemployment may be frictional, structural, classical, or demand-deficient. The first three types are voluntary unemployment, the last is involuntary, or Keynesian, unemployment. Equilibrium unemployment is voluntary unemployment in long-run equilibrium.
- In the long run, a sustained rise in unemployment must reflect higher equilibrium unemployment. In temporary recessions, Keynesian unemployment also matters.
- Supply-side economics aims to raise potential output, and reduce equilibrium unemployment, by improving microeconomic incentives.
- Some unemployment allows a better match of people and jobs, especially if inflows and outflows to the unemployment pool are large.
- Keynesian unemployment is involuntary and represents wasted output. Society may also care about the human misery inflicted by involuntary unemployment.

Review questions

1 'The microchip has caused a permanent rise in unemployment.' Discuss this assertion, showing its effects on labour demand, the labour force and job acceptances.
2 How is high unemployment explained by (a) a Keynesian, (b) a classical economist?
3 How do lower taxes affect unemployment (a) when the economy begins at equilibrium unemployment, (b) when initially it also has Keynesian unemployment?
4 Why is unemployment among school leavers higher than that among adults?
5 **Common fallacies** (a) So long as there is unemployment, there is pressure on wages to fall. (b) Unemployment arises only because greedy workers are pricing themselves out of a job.

Answers on pages 278–90

10

Open economy macroeconomics

10-1 Exchange rates and the balance of payments

Learning outcomes

By the end of this section, you should understand:

- The forex market
- Balance of payments accounting
- Internal and external balance
- The effects of devaluation
- What determines floating exchange rates
- Monetary and fiscal policy in open economies

Exports and imports are each about 10 per cent of GDP in the US and Japan, but nearer 30 per cent in the UK and Germany. Having to specialise to trade in the global economies, smaller economies tend to be more open to trade, both in exports and import. Hence, the exchange rate, international competitiveness and the trade deficit are major policy issues. We shall now show how openness to trade and financial flows affects the domestic economy, and assess how monetary and fiscal policies are altered.

The foreign exchange market

> The **foreign exchange (forex) market** exchanges one national currency for another. The **exchange rate** is the price at which two currencies exchange.

An exchange rate of $1.40/£ measures the international value of sterling: how much foreign currency ($) a unit of the domestic currency (£) is worth.

Who supplies dollars to the forex market, wanting pounds in exchange?

Figure 10-1

Exports and imports, 2000 (% of GDP)

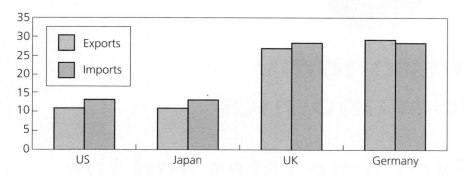

Figure 10-2

The forex market

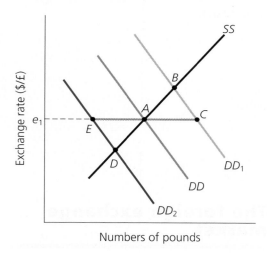

Numbers of pounds

This demand for pounds arises from UK exporters wanting to convert dollars back into pounds, and from US residents wanting to buy UK assets for which they must pay in pounds. Conversely, a supply of pounds to the forex market reflects UK importers wanting dollars to buy US goods, and UK residents wishing to buy US dollar assets.

Figure 10-2 shows the resulting supply SS and demand DD for pounds. The equilibrium exchange rate e_1 equates the quantity of £ supplied and demanded. If the US demand for UK goods or assets rises, the demand for pounds shifts right to DD_1, and the equilibrium $/£ exchange rate rises. A higher $/£ exchange rate means the pound has *appreciated*, because its international value has risen. The dollar has simultaneously *depreciated*, since its international value is lower. A fall in the $/£ exchange rate has the opposite effects.

Exchange rate regimes

An exchange rate regime describes the rules under which governments allow exchange rates to be determined.

> A **fixed exchange rate** means that governments, acting through their central banks, will buy or sell as much of the currency as people want to exchange at the fixed rate.

In Figure 10-2 a fixed exchange rate e_1 is the free market equilibrium rate if the supply and demand for pounds are *SS* and *DD*. The market clears unaided. Suppose the demand for pounds now shifts up to DD_1. Americans, hooked on whisky, need more pounds to import from the UK. In a free market, the equilibrium is now at *B* and the pound appreciates against the dollar.

At the fixed exchange rate e_1 there is an excess demand *AC* for pounds. To meet this, the Bank of England prints *AC* extra pounds and sells them in exchange for ($e_1 \times AC$) of dollars, which are added to the UK foreign exchange reserves.

The **foreign exchange reserves** are the foreign currency holdings of the domestic central bank.

Conversely, if the demand for pounds shifts down to DD_2, few foreigners now want British goods or assets. The free market equilibrium exchange rate is below e_1 unless the central bank intervenes. To defend the fixed exchange rate e_1, at which there would be an excess supply *EA* of pounds, the central bank demands *EA* in pounds, paid for by selling ($EA \times e_1$) of dollars from the foreign exchange reserves. When the central bank is forced to buy or sell pounds to support the fixed exchange rate, it *intervenes* in the forex market.

If the demand for pounds on average is DD_2, the Bank on average is reducing the UK forex reserves to support the pound at e_1. The pound is overvalued. As reserves run out, the government may try to borrow foreign exchange reserves from the International Monetary Fund (IMF), an international body that lends to governments in short-term difficulties. At best this is a temporary solution. Unless the demand for pounds rises in the long

run, it will be necessary to *devalue* the pound.

A **devaluation (revaluation)** is a fall (rise) in the fixed exchange rate.

In November 1967, the UK government, after consultations with other governments, devalued the pound from \$2.80/£ to \$2.40/£. However, the UK has not always pursued a fixed exchange rate.

In a **floating exchange rate** regime, the exchange rate is allowed to find its free market equilibrium without any intervention using the foreign exchange reserves.

Thus, in Figure 10-2 the demand schedule shifts from DD_2 to *DD* to DD_1 would be allowed to move the equilibrium point from *D* to *A* to *B*.

Of course, it is not necessary to adopt the extreme regimes of pure floating or perfectly fixed exchange rates. *Dirty floating* means some intervention in the short run but allowing the exchange rate to find its equilibrium level in the longer run. By understanding the two polar cases – completely fixed and freely floating – we can see how the intermediate regimes would work.

Next, we explain balance of payments accounting and its connection to exchange rate regimes.

The balance of payments

The **balance of payments** records all transactions between a country and the rest of the world.

All international transactions giving rise to an inflow of pounds to the UK are

Box 10-1

Effective exchange rates

Each currency has a bilateral exchange rate against each other currency. For example, we can measure the $/£ or euro/£. Sometimes it is useful to examine the average exchange rate against all countries.

> The **effective exchange rate (eer)** is a weighted average of individual bilateral exchange rates.

Usually, we use the share of trade with each country to decide the weights. Important trading partners get more weight in the effective exchange rate index.

The figure shows *actual* exchange rates of the UK's two main trading partners, the US and the euro zone. The pound has fluctuated against both. However, the pound's *effective* exchange rate against all currencies has been much more stable. The effective exchange rate is an index, whose value we have set at 1.00 in 1990. However, this starting value is arbitrary. We could have started it at 1.50 to emphasise that it is an average of the main bilateral exchange rates with which the UK trades.

The point of the figure is that the effective exchange rate, being an average, fluctuates less than its component parts. Since UK trade with the euro zone greatly exceeds trade with the US, the overall average is closer to the euro/£ than to the $/£.

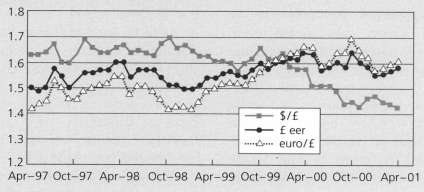

Source: ONS, *Financial Statistics*

credits in the UK balance of payments accounts. Outflows of pounds are debits, entered with a minus sign. Table 10-1 shows the actual UK balance of payments accounts in 2001.

> The **current account** of the balance of payments records international flows of goods, services and transfer payments.

Visible trade is exports and imports of goods (cars, food, steel). *Invisible trade* is exports and imports of services (banking, shipping, tourism). Together, these make up the trade balance or net exports of goods and services. To get the current account, we take the trade balance and add *net* transfer payments from abroad (interest income on net foreign assets, minus foreign aid and net EU budget contribution). The UK current account was £17 billion in deficit in 2001.

> The **capital account** of the balance of payments records net purchases and sales of foreign assets.

Table 10-1 shows a net inflow of £21 billion on the capital account in 2001. Foreigners bought more UK assets than British people bought foreign assets.

The balancing item is a statistical adjustment, which would be zero if all previous items had been correctly measured. It reflects a failure to record all transactions in the official statistics. Adding together the current account (1), the capital account (2) and the balancing item (3) yields the UK *balance of payments* in 2001. As it happens, it was just in balance.

> The **balance of payments** records the net monetary inflow from abroad when households, firms, and the government make their desired transactions.

The final entry in Table 10-1 is *official financing*. This is always of equal magnitude and opposite sign to the balance of payments in the line above, so that the sum of all the entries is *always* zero. Official financing measures the international transactions that the government must take to *accommodate* all the other transactions in the balance of payments accounts.

Floating exchange rates

If the exchange rate is freely floating, with no central bank intervention, the forex reserves are constant, and the exchange rate equates the supply and demand for pounds.

The supply of pounds, by people needing dollars to buy imports or foreign assets, measures outflows or minus items in the UK balance of payments. The demand for pounds, by people selling dollars earned from exports and sales of assets to foreigners, measures inflows

Table 10-1

UK balance of payments, 2001 (£ bn)

(1)	Current account		−17
	Of which	Trade in goods	−33
		Trade in services	−12
		Transfer payments	+4
(2)	Capital Account		+21
(3)	Balancing item		−4
(4)	UK Balance of Payments (1 + 2 + 3)		0
(5)	Official financing		0

Source: ONS, *Financial Trends*, June 2002

or plus items in the UK balance of payments. A freely floating exchange rate equates the quantities of pounds supplied and demanded. Hence inflows equal outflows and the balance of payments is *exactly* zero. There is no intervention in the forex market, and thus no official financing.

With a zero balance of payments, under floating exchange rates a current account surplus is exactly matched by a capital account deficit, or vice versa. A current account surplus (deficit) means a country underspends (overspends) its international income. This saving (dis-saving) adds to (subtracts from) its net international assets. That is precisely what the capital account records.

Fixed exchange rates

With a fixed exchange rate, the balance of payments need not be zero. A payments deficit means that total outflows exceed total inflows on the combined current and capital accounts. The supply of pounds to the forex market, from UK imports or purchases of foreign assets, exceeds the demand for pounds, from UK exports or sales of assets to foreigners. The balance of payments deficit is precisely the excess supply of pounds in the forex market.

To peg the exchange rate, the Bank of England must demand this excess supply of pounds, reducing UK forex reserves by selling dollars to buy pounds. This is 'official financing' in the balance of payments. Hence, with a balance of payments deficit (surplus), forex reserves must be sold (bought).

The current account

UK imports depend in part on the level of UK income. Hence UK exports, which are someone else's imports, depend partly on income in the rest of the world. The second key determinant of net exports is international competitiveness. However, we must distinguish nominal and real variables. International competitiveness depends on the real exchange rate.

> The **real exchange rate** is the relative price of domestic and foreign goods, when measured in a common currency.

Comparing UK and US prices, both in dollars, the real exchange rate is

$$\text{Real exchange rate} = \left(\frac{\text{£ price of UK goods}}{\text{\$ price of US goods}} \right) \times (\text{\$/£ exchange rate})$$

A higher real exchange rate, raising the price of UK goods relative to US goods measured in the same currency, makes the UK less competitive relative to the US. A fall in the UK's real exchange rate makes the UK more competitive in international markets.

The real exchange rate can thus depreciate for three different reasons: a fall in the actual or nominal \$/£ exchange rate; a rise in the price of US goods; or a fall in the price of UK goods. The arithmetic does not care which it is.

Thus, if the UK annual inflation is 10 per cent and US inflation is zero, the UK's real exchange rate depreciates by 10 per cent a year if the nominal exchange rate is fixed. However, the real exchange rate would appreciate if the nominal exchange rate fell by more than 10 per cent a year.

In summary, higher UK output raises UK imports, reducing UK net exports. Higher output abroad raises demand for UK exports, raising UK net exports. A depreciation of the UK real exchange rate makes the UK more competitive, raising UK net exports.

Other items on the current account include net government transfers to foreigners, which we treat as given. However, a country with large foreign assets has a large net inflow of property income, boosting its current account. Conversely, a country with large foreign debts has a large outflow of net property income, making its current account balance smaller than its trade balance.

The capital account

Purchases and sales of foreign assets are increasingly important. Computers and telecommunications make it as easy for a UK resident to transact in the financial markets of New York, and Tokyo, as it is in London. Moreover, the elaborate system of controls restricting capital flows has gradually been dismantled. There is now a global financial market in which footloose funds flow freely from one

Box 10-2

Calculating real exchange rates

Each row in the table below shows a different combination of the nominal exchange rate, the price of domestic goods and the price of foreign goods. In the first row, UK shirts cost £6 and US shirts $10. At a nominal exchange rate of $2/£, a UK shirt costs $12 and is 1.2 times as expensive as a US shirt when measured in dollars. Since a $10 US shirt costs £5 at an exchange rate of $2/£, £6 UK shirts are also 1.2 as expensive as US shirts if we measure them both in pounds. It never matters which currency we use for the comparison, but we must use the same currency for both.

In the second row, the nominal exchange rate falls by 25 per cent from $2/£ to $1.5/£, and the table shows that, other things equal, the real exchange rate also falls by 25 per cent. Nominal devaluation of the $/£ has made the UK more competitive and the US less competitive.

The third and fourth rows show that the same change in the real exchange rate can be achieved by a fall in UK prices, or a rise in US prices, without any change in the nominal exchange rate. Real exchange rates can therefore change in a monetary union even though nominal exchange rates are fixed for ever.

Nominal exchange rate ($/£)	UK shirt price (£)	UK shirt price ($)	US shirt price ($)	Real exchange rate
2.0	6	12	10	1.2
1.5	6	9	10	0.9
2.0	4.5	9	10	0.9
2.0	6	12	13.3	0.9

country to another in search of the highest expected return.

Huge one-way capital account flows would swamp the typical flows of imports and exports on the current account. Forex market equilibrium requires that expected returns adjust until assets in different currencies offer the *same* expected return, *removing* the incentive for vast, one-way capital flows.

The return on any asset is the interest rate plus the capital gain you make while the asset is held. Exchange rate changes lead to capital gains or losses while you temporarily hold assets abroad. You have £100 to invest for a year. UK interest rates are 10 per cent, but US interest rates are zero. Keeping your funds in pounds, you have £110 by the end of the year. What if you lend abroad for a year?

At an initial exchange rate of $2/£, your £100 buys $200. At a zero interest rate, you have $200 at the end of the year. But if the pound falls 10 per cent in the year to $1.80/£, your $200 converts back to £110. You made 10 per cent less interest in dollars but earned an extra 10 per cent capital gain while the dollar rose against the pound and the pound fell against the dollar

If the $/£ exchange rate falls by more than 10 per cent during the year, you do better by lending in dollars, since the capital gain outweighs the interest foregone. When international capital mobility is high, massive capital flows are avoided only if the interest parity condition holds.

Perfect capital mobility means expected total returns on assets in different currencies must be equal if huge capital flows are to be avoided. A positive interest differential must be offset by an expected exchange rate fall of equal magnitude. This is the **interest parity condition**.

Internal and external balance

Internal balance means aggregate demand equals potential output.
External balance means that the current account of the balance of payments is zero. Long-run equilibrium requires both.

Chapter 9 explained how a closed economy eventually returns to potential output and internal balance. External balance must also hold in the long run. The current account shows a country's flow of income from abroad minus its flow of spending on foreign goods, services and transfer payments. With a permanent current account deficit, a country goes bankrupt by overspending its foreign income indefinitely. With a permanent current account surplus, the country is saving and adding to net foreign assets for ever. This makes no sense since the country could afford to import more foreign goods.

We can use internal and external balance to analyse a country's equilibrium real exchange rate in the long run. Internal balance means each country's output is at potential output. Taking this as given, the main determinant of the current account is the real exchange rate. A higher real exchange rate makes the country less competitive, reducing its net exports.

In Figure 10-3 the current account schedule *CA* shows how a higher real exchange rate reduces the current account balance by making the country less competitive. Only the real exchange rate *R* will achieve external balance in the long run. With a higher real exchange rate, competitiveness is too low and there would be a current account deficit for ever. A real exchange rate below *R* makes the country too competitive and it would have a permanent current account surplus.

Suppose the UK discovers North Sea oil. It now has a larger current account surplus at any real exchange rate since it no longer has to import oil. The current account schedule shifts right from *CA* to *CA*$_1$. Only an appreciation of the real exchange rate to *R*$_1$ can restore external balance. Manufacturers complain that they are doing badly at the less competitive exchange rate, but the brutal reality is that if the UK exports more oil, it must export less of something else.

Forget North Sea oil, now think of net foreign assets. A country that has previously stockpiled a lot of foreign assets now has a big current account inflow from interest, profit and dividends. Again, its *CA* schedule shifts right to *CA*$_1$. Again, this induces a rise in the long-run real exchange rate. With more current account inflows from net asset income, net exports must fall if the overall current account is to remain in balance. Getting uncompetitive is what makes this happen.

Thus countries with large foreign debts, on which they pay flows of interest on the current account, face a schedule *CA*$_2$ in Figure 10-3. However, a suitably low real exchange rate makes them competitive enough to have net export surpluses large enough to finance the outflow of interest payments on the current account.

Macroeconomic policy under fixed exchange rates

Perfect capital mobility means international lenders must get the same expected return in all currencies. Pegging the exchange rate prevents capital gains or losses on the exchange rate while holding foreign assets. Capital mobility and pegged exchange rates can be reconciled only by setting the same interest rate in both countries. For at least one country, this represents a loss of monetary sovereignty. It can no longer set the interest rates that it wants. Fixed exchange rates take away monetary independence.

Fiscal policy, on the other hand, is more powerful under pegged exchange rates. In a closed economy, a fiscal expansion may prompt the central bank to react by

Figure 10-3

External balance

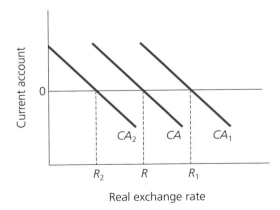

Box 10-3

Capital account flows

Capital account flows may be short-term, such as putting money in a foreign bank account, or may be long-term, such as taking a permanent stake in a foreign company.

Foreign direct investment (FDI) is the purchase of foreign firms or the establishment of foreign subsidiaries.

Has globalisation made capital flows bigger recently? The figure shows the scale of average annual capital flows, relative to GDP, for 12 OECD economies in peacetime years since 1870. Capital flows dried up in the 1930s, in the Great Depression, but today we forget that the late nineteenth century was also an age of foreign investment.

Such figures need to be interpreted with care. Since official financing is usually small, our balance of payments arithmetic implies that the sum of the current and capital account must be near zero, especially if averaged over many years. If countries cannot run large current account deficits, they cannot have large capital inflows either.

Looking at the *size* of capital flows does not itself tell us about capital mobility, which relates to the *sensitivity* of capital flows to profit opportunities. If exchange rates adjust to *prevent* massive capital flows, we never see huge flows in the data whatever the degree of capital mobility.

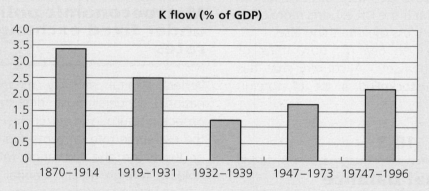

K flow (% of GDP)

Source: M. Obstfeld, 'The global capital market: benefactor or menace?', *Journal of Economic Perspectives, 1999*

raising interest rates in order still to meet its inflation target. Crowding out of private spending dampens the effect of fiscal expansion. In an open economy with a pegged exchange rate, the interest rate cannot rise and hence fiscal expansion delivers a bigger kick to aggregate demand.

What would happen if the central bank then tried to raise interest rates? With a pegged exchange rate, there would be a massive capital inflow to take advantage of the high interest rate. This balance of payments surplus and excess demand for pounds forces the Bank of England to print more pounds, with which it buys foreign exchange reserves. However, the rise in the UK money supply, or stock of circulating pounds, bids down UK interest rates. The attempt to raise interest rates is thwarted by the capital inflow then induced.

Adjusting to shocks

Suppose export demand falls. Interest rates cannot respond. Suppose fiscal policy is also unchanged. Hence, the fall in aggregate demand causes a fall in output and a rise in unemployment. Eventually, this bids down wages and prices. With a given nominal exchange rate, the real exchange rate falls and the country gets more competitive. This eventually restores net exports to their former level. Internal and external balances are then restored

Devaluation

If wage and price adjustment is slow to react to the recession, it may be better to devalue the nominal exchange rate peg, thereby speeding up the change in the real exchange rate described above.

When prices and wages adjust slowly, devaluation immediately raises competitiveness. Resources are drawn into export industries and into domestic industries that compete with imports. However, there are two points to note.

First, the initial quantity response may be quite slow. Demand may change slowly if there were some long-term contracts made at the old exchange rate. Supply may change slowly if it takes time to expand new production. Devaluation may not improve the trade balance in the short run. The trade balance refers to value not volume. With low initial quantity responses, cutting the dollar price of UK goods may initially yield less revenue not more. However, in the longer run, quantities are more responsive and net trade revenues increase.[1]

In the medium run, the country will regain internal balance at which potential output equals aggregate demand $[(C + I + G) + (X - Z)]$. For a given level of potential output, net exports can respond more to devaluation the lower is the level of domestic absorption $(C + I + G)$.

If the economy returns to internal balance before net exports have increased by the desired amount, further increases in net exports raise aggregate demand above potential output. This causes inflation, reducing competitiveness at the fixed nominal exchange rate and undoing all the good work that devaluation has accomplished. Sometimes it is necessary to tighten *fiscal* policy, thereby reducing domestic absorption, to make sure that there are enough spare resources to produce the extra net exports required.

Taking an even longer view, in the very long run real variables determine other real variables. Changing the nominal exchange rate will not accomplish anything that adjustments of domestic wages and prices could also have accomplished. The case for devaluation is that it may speed up the process when wage and price adjustment is sluggish.

---

1 Since devaluation leads first to a fall in the value of net exports, but then to an increase, this response is called a J-curve. As time elapses, the current account falls down to the bottom of the J but then rises to *above* its initial position.

Box 10-4

The 1992 sterling devaluation

During the period 1990–92 the UK belonged to the exchange rate mechanism (ERM) of the European Monetary System, an arrangement to peg exchange rates between member states but jointly float against other currencies. In 1990 German unification led to huge fiscal subsidies to East Germany and a big boost to aggregate demand in Germany, prompting a large rise in interest rates to stop German inflation getting out of control. High interest rates caused misery for Germany's partners in the EMS. In 1992 the UK and Italy left the ERM and floated their exchange rates in order to be able then to reduce interest rates and end their recessions.

This immediately led to sharply lower exchange rates for Britain and Italy. The figures below, showing the path of the UK's nominal and real exchange rate against its trading partners during 1992–95 and corresponding changes in the current account of the balance of payments, contain three lessons. First, the sharp fall in the nominal exchange rate was initially accompanied by a sharp fall in the real exchange rate and hence an immediate rise in competitiveness. Second, this still took a couple of years to have its full effect on the current account of the balance of payments, which improved from a deficit of £10 billion in 1992 to a deficit of only £1 billion in 1994.

Third, by 1995 all the gain in competitiveness had been lost despite the nominal exchange rate remaining well below its level of 1992. As an export boom dragged the UK out of recession, domestic wages and prices began to rise, thus offsetting the competitive edge created by the nominal devaluation.

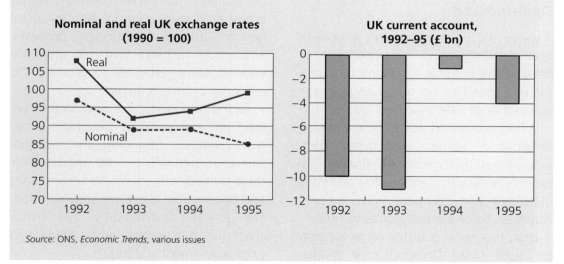

Source: ONS, *Economic Trends*, various issues

Putting this differently, devaluation, which raises the cost of imports, is eventually passed on in higher wages and prices, making no real difference.

Most computer models of the UK economy, based on past data, conclude that the effects of a nominal devaluation are offset by a rise in domestic prices and wages by the end of five years.

Floating exchange rates

With a floating exchange rate, domestic monetary policy can set any interest rate it wishes. Monetary sovereignty is restored, and may use an inflation target to decide how to set interest rates.

Figure 10-2 showed how the long-run real exchange rate is determined. If the nominal exchange rate is fixed, domestic prices and wages must eventually adjust to get the appropriate real exchange rate. Under a floating exchange rate, knowing the inflation targets at home and abroad, people can work out what path the nominal exchange rate must eventually reach to deliver the appropriate equilibrium real exchange rate in the long run. The higher a country's price level has become, relative to its competitors, the lower must be its nominal exchange rate to achieve the correct real exchange rate.

Countries cannot depart from external balance in the long run, and the current account is all important. But in the short run, the role of the current account is dwarfed by the *threat* of massive capital movements. The forex market cannot cope with massive one-way capital flows, and must keep adjusting the exchange rate to prevent them. This implies setting the exchange at a level from which interest parity is expected to hold *from now on*. In the short run, the capital account can drive the exchange rate a long way away from the path that balances the current account.

In the long run, countries with high inflation rates also have higher nominal interest rates. Their long-run equilibrium exchange rate is falling steadily to preserve the right real exchange rate. This does not stimulate big capital flows because the capital losses on the depreciating exchange rate are just off-setting the high nominal interest rates earned by lending in that currency.

However, when a country has higher interest rates in the short run than it is expected to have in the long run, the currency looks temporarily attractive to financial investors. To stop them all piling in, the currency must appreciate rapidly and significantly to such a level that from now on the only way is down. The prospect of capital losses from holding the currency from now on is what offsets the attraction of high interest rates in the short run.

The upward jump in the exchange rate takes the market by surprise. Had they seen it coming, they would already have piled into the currency to get the capital gain. The exchange rate jumps up to make it credible that the foreseeable direction will be down from now on. Conversely, a temporary cut in domestic interest rates makes the exchange rate jump down, so that from now on it can offer capital gains to offset the low interest rate.

Monetary and fiscal policy under floating exchange rates

Under fixed exchange rates, domestic monetary policy was powerless but fiscal policy was more powerful than in a closed economy. Under floating exchange rates, the converse is true.

A given rise in domestic interest rates not merely depresses domestic demand, it also makes the exchange rate jump up, which reduces net export demand substantially if wages and prices are sluggish and cannot respond quickly. Hence, monetary policy has a strong effect in the short run under floating exchange rates.

Fiscal policy is correspondingly weaker. A fiscal expansion adds to aggregate demand, but the central bank must raise interest rates to keep meeting its inflation target. Higher interest rates lead to an upward jump in the nominal exchange rate to choke off a capital inflow. Fiscal expansion crowds out private spending not merely through the direct effect of the higher interest rates that are induced, but also because nominal exchange rate appreciation causes a loss in competitiveness if wage and price adjustment is slow.

The pound since 1980

Figure 10-4 shows the behaviour of the UK's nominal and real effective exchange rates against a basket of the currencies most important for the UK's international trade. The UK's real exchange rate had appreciated substantially during 1977–80 for two reasons. First, real interest rates had been raised to fight inflation. Second, the UK had found North Sea oil.

After 1981, competitiveness gradually improved as the real exchange rate fell. The boom of the mid-1980s was partly built on rising competitiveness. However, domestic tax cuts and reductions in interest rates eventually caused the economy to overheat in the Lawson boom. To get inflation under control at the end of the 1980s required another

upward hike in interest rates, causing another sharp exchange rate appreciation to stave off a speculative inflow. The late 1980s were partly a rerun of the late 1970s.

As explained in Box 10-4, in 1990 the UK joined the Exchange Rate Mechanism, but was unable to live with high interest rates within the ERM after German unification. A speculative capital outflow forced the UK out of the ERM in September 1992. The UK left the ERM, the pound floated sharply downwards, and the UK government happily then cut interest rates.

Not only did the nominal depreciation fail to reduce the real exchange rate for long, after 1996 the nominal exchange rate itself was appreciating sharply again.

This brief examination of the evolution of nominal and real UK exchange rates indicates three main lessons. First, nominal devaluation does change the real

Figure 10-4

The exchange rates (1990 = 100)

Sources: IMF, *International Financial Statistics*

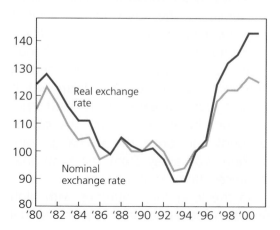

exchange rate. Second, the competitive advantage may not last for long. Third, monetary and fiscal policies affect what interest rates are needed, and thus the exchange rate needed to prevent large capital flows.

Recap

- The exchange rate is the relative price of two currencies in the forex market.
- The demand for domestic currency arises from exports and from sales of domestic assets to foreigners; the supply of domestic currency arises from imports and purchases of foreign assets. Floating exchange rates equate supply and demand when there is no government intervention in the forex market.
- Under fixed exchange rates, the Bank of England intervenes to buy any excess supply of pounds, thus reducing its forex reserves. The Bank creates and supplies pounds to meet any excess demand for pounds, thus raising its forex reserves.
- The balance of payments records monetary inflows as credits and monetary outflows as debits. The current account is the trade balance plus net transfer payments from abroad, which mainly reflect income on net foreign assets. The capital account shows net sales of foreign assets. The balance of payments is the sum of the current and capital account balances.
- Under floating exchange rates, the balance of payments is zero. Under fixed exchange rates, a payments surplus (deficit) is offset by official financing, raising (lowering) the domestic money supply.
- The real exchange rate adjusts the nominal exchange rate for prices at home and abroad. It is the relative price of domestic to foreign goods, when measured in a common currency. A higher real exchange rate reduces competitiveness.
- Higher domestic (foreign) income raises the demand for imports (exports). A higher real exchange rate reduces the demand for net exports.
- Perfect international capital mobility implies a vast capital account flow if the expected return differs across countries. To prevent this, any interest differential between domestic and foreign assets must be offset by a matching expected capital gain or loss on the exchange rate while temporarily holding foreign assets.

- At internal balance, aggregate demand equals potential output. At external balance, the current account is zero. Both are needed for long-run equilibrium.

- Discovery of a natural resource, or higher net foreign assets, raise the long-run equilibrium real exchange rate.

- With perfect capital mobility, monetary policy is powerless under pegged exchange rates. Domestic interest rates must match foreign interest rates. However, fiscal expansion no longer bids up domestic interest rates.

- A devaluation lowers the fixed exchange rate. With sluggish price adjustment, it raises competitiveness and aggregate demand. With spare resources, output increases. Without spare resources, higher demand bids up prices, reducing competitiveness again.

- In the long run, devaluing the nominal exchange rate has little real effect. But it adjusts competitiveness quickly in the short run.

- Under floating exchange rates, domestic and foreign monetary policies determine domestic and foreign prices. Together with the real exchange rate required for external balance, this determines the eventual nominal exchange. However, in the short run the exchange rate moves around to prevent massive one-way capital flows. Temporarily, the exchange rate can deviate a lot from the level that achieves current account balance.

- Floating exchange rates magnify the effect of interest rate changes on aggregate demand, by inducing short-run changes in the exchange rate and competitiveness.

- Fiscal policy is then less powerful in the short run. Fiscal expansion (contraction) induces the central bank to raise (cut) interest rates, causing an exchange rate appreciation (depreciation) that further dampens the effect of fiscal policy on aggregate demand.

Review questions

1 A country has a current account surplus of £6 billion but a capital account deficit of £4 billion. (a) Is its balance of payments in deficit or surplus? (b) Are the country's foreign exchange reserves rising or falling? (c) Is the central bank buying or selling domestic currency?

2 For over 20 years, Japan has run a current account surplus. (a) How is this compatible with the statement that countries must eventually get back to external balance? (b) Would it be so easy to run a persistent current account deficit?

3 Rank the following according to the ability of monetary policy to affect real output in the short run: (a) a closed economy; (b) an open economy with fixed exchange rates; (c) an open economy with floating exchange rates. Explain.

4 Newsreaders say that 'the pound had a good day' if the UK exchange rate rises. (a) When is an appreciation of the exchange rate desirable? (b) Undesirable?

5 *Common fallacies* Why are these statements wrong? (a) If global speculators have more money than central banks, central banks can no longer defend fixed exchange rates. (b) Floating exchange rates are volatile because imports and exports fluctuate a lot.

Answers on pages 278–90

10-2 The economics of the euro zone

Learning outcomes

By the end of this section, you should understand:
- Why small open economies in Europe opted for monetary union
- The economics of monetary union
- UK reluctance to join

In comparison with the US or Japan, European countries are small. Firms within a large country can produce on a large scale for the domestic market. In small countries, scale and specialisation require access to foreign markets. Hence, small countries are more open to trade than large countries. Being more open, they care more about competitiveness and the real exchange rate.

Small open European countries mainly trade with each other. Hence, European policy makers came under great pressure to prevent sharp changes in competitiveness with their European trading partners. This led to a quest for exchange rate stability in Europe.

Greater openness and closer European integration also reflected deliberate policy. The EU has abolished tariff and other barriers within Europe to create a unified 'domestic' market rivalling that enjoyed by Americans. The more integrated Europe became, the more it wanted to stabilise exchange rates within Europe. As an offshore island, the UK is semi-detached from Western Europe, but the gap is relentlessly closing. Figure 10-5 confirms that the EU has replaced the Commonwealth as the UK's main trading partner.

An early attempt at exchange rate stability in Europe was the Exchange Rate Mechanism of the European Monetary System. The ERM created exchange rate bands between member countries, within which mutual exchange rates

Figure 10-5

UK trade 1972–2000 (% of exports)

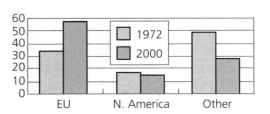

were supposed to be contained, while the whole system floated against the rest of the world.

After years of exchange rate stability in the late 1980s, which encouraged the UK to join in 1990, the system was blown apart by speculative capital flows in 1992. Spain, Portugal and Ireland had to devalue. Italy and the UK suspended membership, letting their currencies float downwards. Those who remained, especially France and Germany, protested about extra competitiveness that their neighbours had thereby gained.

These exchange rates had neither been permanently fixed nor fully flexible, but somewhere uncomfortably in between. Giving up all controls on capital flows made things too easy for speculators. Floating exchange rates, and further swings in competitiveness, was not an option if continental Europe was to consolidate its single market and preserve a level playing field across member states. There seemed no alternative to monetary union.

> A **monetary union** has permanently fixed exchange rates within the union, an integrated financial market and a single central bank setting the single interest rate.

The Treaty of Maastricht in 1991 set out the conditions that countries would have to satisfy to join the European monetary union. They had to have low inflation, and hence low nominal interest rates (showing that financial markets agreed that inflation expectations were low). They had to have sound government finances, showing that fiscal policy was under control. Budget deficits had to be less than 3 per cent of GDP, and national debt had to be less than 60 per cent, or at least heading in that direction. Finally, entrants were not allowed to have devalued during the two preceding years, in order to prevent countries trying to grab a competitive advantage just before joining monetary union.

UK reluctance to join

North Sea oil used to make the UK behave differently from its continental cousins. A rise in world oil prices would make the pound appreciate, but cause depreciation of the currencies of oil importers, such as France and Germany. As UK oil production wound down, this stopped being a serious obstacle to UK entry.

More generally, whereas the core countries of Europe are now very integrated with one another, offshore UK is less integrated with the rest of Europe. An interest rate suiting the needs of the majority may not always suit the UK. However, as the UK's integration with other EU continues to grow, this objection is also gradually receding.

Finally, Black Wednesday (16 September 1992), when speculators forced sterling to abandon the ERM, makes it hard for UK politicians to favour monetary union. UK voters remember the UK flirtation with a single European interest rate as an unhappy experience.

The economics of monetary union

In 1999, Bob Mundell won the Nobel Prize for Economics, in part for his

Box 10-5

The ERM: a quick history lesson

The 1923 hyperinflation changed German history. Now Germans hate inflation. The German central bank, the Bundesbank (Buba), thus had a constitution making stable prices its key objective.

In 1979 several Western European countries created the Exchange Rate Mechanism, in which exchange rates were pegged to each other, but jointly floated against the rest of the world. The pegged exchange rates were initially changed about every six months, but remained fixed during 1987–92.

With mobile capital, pegging the exchange rate means the same interest rate in both countries. The issue is who sets the single interest rate. Initially, capital account controls prevented capital mobility, and the ERM could duck the issue of monetary sovereignty.

By the mid-1980s, capital account controls had largely gone and the Deutschemark became the linchpin of the ERM. The Buba set interest rates for purely German reasons, and other countries then followed suit. Germany felt safe, and other countries enjoyed rapid falls in inflation expectations now the Buba was seen to be in charge. The UK joined the ERM in 1990.

The Buba had always had a private understanding with the German government that it would not defend the exchange rate of weaker currencies if this meant printing too much money and threatened inflation in Germany. In mid-1992, several exchange rates appeared overvalued. Germany proposed a general realignment which other countries declined. The Buba intervened massively to help the lira and sterling, but both were forced out of the ERM by speculators, and depreciated substantially. The peseta, escudo and punt were devalued but stayed in the ERM.

ERM devaluations, 1990–98

Date	Punt	Peseta	Escudo	Lira	Pound
9/92		−5		Left ERM	Left ERM
11/92		−6	−6		
2/93	−10				
5/93		−8	−6.5		
3/95		−7			
12/96				Rejoined ERM	

pioneering work on optimal currency areas.

An **optimal currency area** is a group of countries better off with a common currency than keeping separate national currencies.

Mundell, and the economists who came after him, identified three attributes that might make countries suitable for a currency area. First, countries that trade a lot with each other are tempted to devalue to gain a short-run competitive advantage, even though induced changes in wages and prices undo this effect again. A fixed exchange rate rules out such behaviour, allowing gains from trade to be enjoyed.

Second, the more similar the economic and industrial structure of potential partners, the more likely it is they face common shocks, which can be dealt with by a common monetary policy. Only country-specific shocks pose difficulties for a single monetary policy.

Third, the more flexible are the labour markets within the currency area, the more easily any necessary changes in competitiveness and real exchange rates can be accomplished by (different) changes in the price level in different member countries.

Conversely, countries gain most by keeping their monetary sovereignty when they are not so closely integrated with potential partners, have a different structure and hence face different shocks, and cannot rely on domestic wage and price flexibility as a substitute for exchange rate changes.

To these purely economic arguments, we should add an important political argument. Currency areas are more likely to work when countries within the area are prepared to make at least some fiscal transfers to partner countries. In practice, this cultural and political identity may be at least as important as any narrow economic criteria for success.

Is Europe an optimal currency area?

Empirical research suggests that Europe is quite, but not very, integrated. It has a clear inner core of countries – France, Germany, Austria, and the Benelux countries – more closely integrated than the rest. However, these correlations are not set in stone. The act of joining a monetary union will *change* the degree of integration, possibly quite substantially. The segmentation into national markets is greatly reduced. There is also evidence that countries that belong to currency unions tend historically to trade much more with each other than can be explained simply by the fact that their exchange rates are fixed.[2]

Hence, it may be possible to start a currency union before the microeconomic pre-conditions are fully in place. The act of starting speeds up the process.

The Stability Pact

The Stability Pact, ratified by the Treaty of Amsterdam in 1997, confirmed that members of the euro zone have to maintain budget deficits below 3 per cent of GDP. Countries with sound government finances would not need to pressure the European Central Bank to create inflation just to reduce the real value of their outstanding nominal debt.

Governments exceeding the 3 per cent limit on budget deficits may be fined unless their economy is in evident recession. Thus, countries may have to wait for output to fall before they are allowed to expand fiscal policy.

If all countries are hit by the same shock, the single monetary policy can take care of it. What is needed by one country is needed by the others. That is why it is desirable that members of the euro zone be highly correlated with one

2 A. Rose, 'One money, one market', *Economic Policy*, 2000.

another. However, when a shock hits one country alone, it can expect no help from the single interest rate, set to reflect aggregate conditions in the euro zone. Nor can the country change its exchange rate against its monetary union partners. If the Stability Pact also limits the ability of individual countries to use fiscal policy to offset country-specific shocks, how can they ensure that aggregate demand remains close to potential output?

First, understanding the problem, national governments may decide to operate close to budget balance over the cycle. In booms, they will have a budget surplus because tax revenue rises when output rises. In slumps, they automatically lose tax revenue since output falls. Provided their average budget position is sufficiently healthy, they can allow the automatic stabilisers to loosen fiscal policy in a recession without going beyond the deficit limit set by the Pact.

Second, since wage and price flexibility is a substitute for active demand management, an alternative solution is to pursue institutional reform of labour markets to encourage greater wage flexibility. However, as yet, there is little sign of this happening within the euro zone.

The European Central Bank

The single monetary policy is now set in Frankfurt by the European Central Bank (ECB). National central banks have not been abolished, but the board of the ECB sets the interest rate on the euro.

The ECB mandate says its first duty is to ensure price stability, but it can take other aims into account provided price stability is not in doubt. In press conferences, officials of the ECB have emphasised that their interest rate decisions aim to keep the annual growth of the Harmonised Index of Consumer Prices (HICP) in the range of 0 to 2 per cent. In practice, ECB interest rate decisions appear to be influenced also by whether output is above or below potential output in the euro area.

The ECB has not adopted the inflation targeting that has become so popular with other central banks in the last decade. Rather it has two 'pillars' or leading indicators to guide the setting of interest rates. The first pillar is a monetary target, the growth rate of the M3 measure of nominal money. The second pillar is expected inflation. The ECB insists that it takes both pillars into account in setting interest rates in the euro area.

Figure 10-6 shows interest rate decisions of the ECB, the evolution of inflation and the rate of nominal money growth. The rise and fall of inflation is closely correlated with the ECB's interest rate decisions. When actual and expected inflation were higher, interest rates were raised, as one would expect. However, it is hard to see any connection between ECB interest rate decisions and the growth of nominal money.

Swings in the demand for *holding* money have made money an unreliable indicator of spending on goods, and hence likely inflation. Most central banks have abandoned monetary targeting in favour of inflation targets. The ECB wanted to emphasise its similarity to the German Bundesbank, which had used monetary targets. However, as the ECB establishes it own track record, it may gradually abandon the emphasis on the monetary pillar.

Figure 10-6

Annual M3 growth, HICP inflation and ECB interest rate decisions

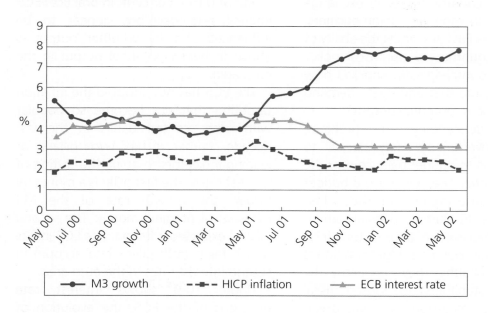

Macroeconomic policy in the euro zone

Each individual country must take as given the interest rates set by the ECB in Frankfurt, and has a permanently fixed exchange rate against trading partners in the euro zone. Suppose a country begins at internal and external balance but then faces a fall in demand for its exports. Suppose too that the country cannot use fiscal expansion because that will infringe the deficit ceiling set by the Stability Pact.

Initially, the country experiences a recession since export demand has fallen. This gradually bids down wages and prices. At the fixed nominal exchange rate against its partners, this makes the country more competitive, raising demand for net exports again. If wage and price flexibility is high enough, there may be no need for fiscal policy. However, given that many European labour markets are quite sluggish, sensible use of fiscal policy may speed up the process. That is why countries may be driven to run 'precautionary' budget surpluses, so that they have plenty of room for fiscal expansion should the need arise.

Recap

- A monetary union means permanently fixed exchange rates, free capital movements and a common monetary policy setting the single interest rate. The euro zone began in January 1999.

- The Maastricht criteria say that entrants must already have shown that they can achieve low inflation and sound fiscal policy. The Stability Pact says that ceilings on budget deficits apply even after joining the euro zone. A country wanting to be able to loosen fiscal policy during recession will therefore have to impose a tighter fiscal policy the rest of the time.

- The Stability Pact is intended to reinforce the independence of the European Central Bank, whose constitution already makes it independent of political control, and commits it to the pursuit of price stability as its overriding objective. Inflation must be kept between 0 and 2 per cent a year.

- The ECB's interest rate decisions are guided by two pillars, nominal money growth and other predictors of inflation. There is little evidence that nominal money growth is a good predictor of inflation. In practice, ECB decisions cannot be explained by nominal money growth, but clearly respond to actual and expected inflation

- A shock hitting all euro countries will induce a change in interest rates, but a country-specific shock will not. Unless the country can use its own fiscal policy, it must then rely on domestic wage and price adjustment to offset the shock. Recessions (booms) reduce (raise) wages, making the country more (less) competitive against euro zone partners.

- Hence, an optimal currency area has three criteria: openness and similarity of industrial structure, which together induce high correlation of shocks across member countries; and wage and price flexibility, which is a substitute for nominal exchange rate changes. However, the act of joining a monetary union is likely to improve all three attributes.

Review questions

1 Suppose two countries fix their exchange rate, but have capital account controls preventing private sector capital account flows between them. Is this a monetary union? If not, why not?

2 What are the arguments for and against UK membership of the euro zone?

3 'Fixing the nominal exchange rate makes sense only when this does not fix the real exchange rate'. Explain.

4 If countries in the euro zone grow steadily, what is likely to happen to the ratio of government debt to GDP? How is this affected by the Stability Pact? Does this imply that the Pact may eventually become redundant?

5 *Common fallacies* Why are these statements wrong? (a) Monetary union is doomed because countries are prevented from adjusting to shocks. (b) No country should join until its economy has converged to the behaviour of the average behaviour of euro zone countries.

Answers on pages 278–90

11

Growth and cycles

11-1 Economic growth

Learning outcomes

By the end of this section, you should understand:
- Determinants of economic growth
- Why economics was called the dismal science
- Evidence about growth rates
- The costs of growth

During 1870–2000 UK real GDP grew ten-fold and real income per person five-fold. We are richer than our grandparents, but less rich than our grandchildren will be. Table 11-1 shows that sustaining a slightly higher growth rate for a long time makes a huge difference. What is long-run economic growth? What causes it?

In 1798 Thomas Malthus's *First Essay on Population* predicted that output growth would be far outstripped by population growth, causing starvation that would end population growth. Some countries are still stuck in a Malthusian trap. Others broke through to sustained growth and prosperity. To see how they did it, we study the theory of economic growth and compare it with the facts. Finally, we discuss whether the costs of growth might make it better to grow more slowly.

Economic growth is the rate of change of real income or real output.

Had we been growing for thousands of years, we would be even richer now than we are. It is only in the last 250 years that real GDP per person has been persistently increasing.

Potential output is the level of GDP when all markets are in equilibrium.

Short-run shifts in demand or supply can lead to a temporary period in which output differs from potential output. However, in the long run, changes in output caused by any fluctuations around potential output are swamped by the effect of persistent growth of potential output itself.

Potential output grows either because the quantity of inputs grows, or because a given quantity of inputs makes more output. The main inputs are labour, capital and land (the environment). How much output a given bundle of inputs produces depends on the productivity of these inputs.

Like us, our grandparents had a 24-hour day, but were probably fitter since they got more exercise. Why can we make more output than they could? We must have accumulated lasting advantages in the meantime. These cumulated advantages are physical capital, skills that we call human capital, or technical ideas that we call technology.

> **Technology** is the current stock of ideas about how to make output.
> **Technical progress** or better technology needs both **invention**, the discovery of new ideas, and **innovation** to incorporate them into actual production techniques.

Major inventions lead to spectacular gains in knowledge. The wheel, the steam engine and the modern computer changed the world. Industrialised societies began only when productivity improvements in agriculture allowed some of the workforce to be freed for industrial production. Before then, almost everyone had to work the land merely to get enough food for survival.

Embodiment of knowledge in capital

To introduce new ideas to production, innovation usually needs investment in new machines. Without investment, bullocks cannot be transformed into tractors even when a blueprint for tractors exists. Major inventions lead to waves of investment and innovation to put these ideas into practice. The mid-nineteenth century was the age of the train. We are now in the age of the microchip.

Learning by doing

Human capital matters also matters. With practice, workers get better at a

Table 11-1

Long-run growth, 1870–2000

	Real GDP		Real GDP per person	
	Ratio of 2000 to 1870	Annual growth (%)	Ratio of 2000 to 1870	Annual growth (%)
Japan	100	3.7	27	2.7
US	66	3.4	10	1.8
Australia	45	3.1	4	1.2
France	15	2.2	10	1.9
UK	10	1.9	5	1.3

Source: Angus Maddison, 'Phases of Capitalist Development', in R. C. O. Matthews (ed.), *Economic Growth and Resources*, Macmillan, 1979; updated from IMF, *International Financial Statistics*

Box 11-1

The road to riches

For centuries, growth in income per person was tiny. Most people were near starvation. Now we take growth for granted. After 1750 industrialisation changed everything. Capital and knowledge, accumulated by one generation, were inherited and augmented by the next generation.

Why 1750? Partly because mathematical and scientific ideas reached a critical mass, allowing an explosion of practical spinoffs. Yet many pioneers of the Industrial Revolution were common-sense artisans with little scientific training. Conversely, the ancient Greece of Pythagoras and Archimedes achieved scientific learning but not economic prosperity.

By the start of the fifteenth century, China understood hydraulic engineering, artificial fertilisers and veterinary medicine. It had blast furnaces in 200 BC, 1500 years before Europe. It had paper 1000 years before Europe, and invented printing 400 years before Gutenberg. Yet in 1600 China was overtaken by Western Europe, and by 1800 had been left far behind.

Economic historians continue to debate the root causes of progress, but three ingredients seem crucial: values, politics and economic institutions. Growth entails a willingness to embrace change. China's rulers liked social order, stability and isolation from foreign ideas, fine attitudes when progress was slow and domestic but a disaster when the world experienced a profusion of new technologies and applications.

Powerful Chinese rulers could enforce bans and block change in their huge empire. When individual European rules did the same, competition between small European states undermined this sovereignty and offered opportunities for growth and change. Economic competition helped separate markets from political control. Rights of merchants led to laws of contracts, patent, company law, and property. Competition between forms of institution allowed more effective solutions to emerge and evolve. Arbitrary intervention by heads of state was reduced. Opportunities for business, trade, invention and innovation flourished.

The making of Western Europe

Year	Income per person (1990 prices)	Inventions
1000	400	Watermills
1100	430	Padded horse collar
1200	480	Windmills
1300	510	Compass
1400	600	Blast furnace
1500	660	Gutenberg printing press
1600	780	Telescope
1700	880	Pendulum clock, canals
1800	1280	Steam engine, spinning and weaving machines, cast iron, electric battery
1900	3400	Telegraph, telephone, electric light, wireless
2000	17400	Steel, cars, planes, computers, nuclear energy

Source: The Economist, 31 December 1999

particular job. Difficult skills take years to master, whether the skill is bending it like Beckham, using computer software or diagnosing and fixing a mechanical failure. Sometimes productivity and output rise even without more physical capital or new technology. However, eventually we master even difficult tasks. Further output growth then requires the use of more inputs or the application of newer technology

Growth and accumulation

Thomas Malthus, an early doomster, lived in an agricultural age. Adding more and more workers to a fixed supply of land reduces labour productivity and thus living standards. Malthus predicted that population growth would drive down living standards to the starvation level. Population growth would halt and the economy would stagnate. Permanent growth in living standards was thus impossible, a dire prediction branding economics as 'the dismal science'.

Some of the poorest countries today face this *Malthusian trap*. Agricultural productivity is so low that everyone must work the land to produce food. As population grows but agricultural output fails to keep pace, famine sets in and people die. If better fertilisers or irrigation raise agricultural output, population quickly rises as nutrition improves and people are driven back to starvation.

Today's rich countries broke out of the Malthusian trap. How did they manage it? First, by raising agricultural productivity (*without* an immediate rise in population), some workers could be shifted to industrial production. The capital goods then made included better ploughs, machinery to pump water and drain fields, and transport to distribute food more effectively. With more capital input, productivity rose further in agriculture, releasing more workers for industry to make yet more capital.

Second, rapid technical progress in agricultural production caused steady growth in productivity, reinforcing the effect of more capital input. Living standards improved steadily. Hence, even with land in fixed supply, sustained growth is possible. Accumulated capital can grow, substituting for fixed land, and technical progress keeps output growing even when inputs do not increase.

Capital accumulation

By 1960 Nobel Prize winner Robert Solow had worked out the neoclassical theory of growth used in empirical work ever since. It is *neoclassical* because it simply assumes that actual output always equals potential output, rather than worrying also about how this happens in the short run.

In the long run, output, labour and capital all grow. Since they cannot be constant, the idea of equilibrium must be applied not to levels but rather to growth rates and ratios.

> Along the **steady-state path**, output, capital and labour grow at the same rate. Hence output per worker y and capital per worker k are constant.

For simplicity, consider a closed economy isolated from the rest of the world. Suppose population growth raises labour input at a constant rate n. Assume too that a constant fraction s of income is saved; the rest is consumed. Aggregate investment (public plus private) is the part of output not consumed by either the public or private sector.

> In a growing economy, **capital widening** gives each new worker as much capital as that used by existing workers. **Capital deepening** raises capital per worker for all workers.

Capital widening needs more investment per person (a) the faster is population growth n (more new workers for whom new capital is needed) and (b) the more capital per person k that new workers need to match that of existing workers. Figure 11-1 plots the line nk along which capital per person is constant.

Adding more and more capital per worker k increases output per worker y, but with diminishing returns. Hence the curve y in Figure 11-1 gets flatter as we move to the right.

Figure 11-1

Neoclassical growth

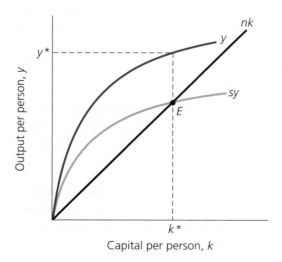

If a constant fraction s of output is saved, sy is saving per person. Since saving and investment are equal, the curve sy also shows investment per person. In the steady state, the capital per person k is constant. Hence investment per person sy must equal nk, the investment per person needed to keep k constant by making capital grow as fast as labour. Here k^* is the steady-state capital per person, and y^* the steady-state output per person. Capital and output grow at the same rate n as labour along this steady-state path.

Figure 11-1 also shows what happens away from the steady state. If capital per worker is low, the economy begins to the left of the steady state. Per capita saving and investment sy exceeds nk, the per capita investment that makes capital grow in line with labour. Hence, capital per person rises and we move to the right. Conversely, to the right of the steady state, sy lies below nk, capital per person falls, and we move to the left. Figure 11-1 says that, from whatever k the economy begins, it gradually converges on the (unique) steady state.

In that steady state, labour is growing at the rate n as it always does. Hence capital and output are growing at the rate n, keeping k^* and y^* constant.

A higher savings rate

Suppose people permanently increase the fraction of income saved, from s to s'. We get more saving and more investment, but *not* permanently faster growth! Figure 11-2 explains why not. There is no change in the production function, which relates output to inputs. At the original saving rate s, the steady state is at *E* as before. At the higher savings rate, *s'y* now shows savings and investment per person. At *F* it equals *nk*, the per capita investment needed to stop *k* rising or falling. Thus *F* is the new steady state. Output per person is *y***.

F has more capital per worker *k* than does *E*. Productivity and output per worker are higher. That is the permanent effect of a higher saving rate. It is an effect on levels, not on growth rates. In *any* steady state, *L*, *K* and *Y* all grow at the same rate, and that rate is determined 'outside the model': it is the rate of growth of labour and population. We return to this issue shortly.

To make the transition from *E* to *F*, there is a *temporary* period in which capital grows faster than labour; raising capital per worker as required. But a higher saving rate, even if successfully translated into higher investment to keep the economy at full employment, does not cause permanently higher output growth. Once capital per worker rises sufficiently, higher rates of saving and investment go entirely in capital widening, which is now more demanding than before. Further capital deepening, the basis of productivity growth, cannot continue without bound.

Growth through technical progress

So far, the theory says that output, labour and capital all grow at rate *n*. Although it is true that capital and output grow at the same rate, in practice both grow more rapidly than labour. That is why we are better off than our great grandparents.

The answer may lie in technical progress, which we ignored in trying to explain output growth entirely through growth in factor supplies (population growth, capital accumulation). Imagine that new knowledge at the rate *t* lets each worker do the work of (1 + *t*) previous workers.

Labour-augmenting technical progress increases the effective labour supply.

Effective labour input grows at rate (*t* + *n*) because of technical progress and population growth. In Figure 11-3, we draw a line (*t* + *n*)*k* instead of the previous *nk*. To make this valid, we have to redefine *k* and *y* as capital and output not per actual worker but per worker-equivalent. Worker-equivalents are created by population growth or technical progress. Otherwise the diagram is identical to before.

In the steady state is at *E*, output per worker-equivalent and capital per

Figure 11-2

A higher savings rate

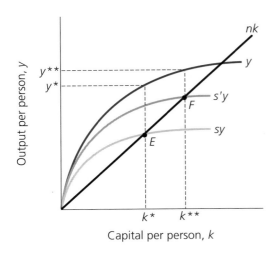

Capital per person, *k*

worker-equivalent are constant. Since worker-equivalents grow at rate $(t + n)$, so do capital and output. But actual workers increase at rate n through population growth. Hence, output and capital per actual worker each *grow* steadily at the rate t. Now our growth theory fits all the facts.

Figure 11-3

Population growth and technical progress

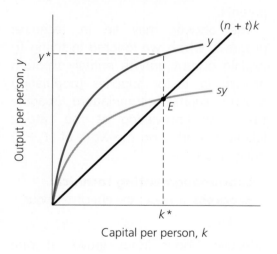

Capital per person, k

Evidence about growth

The Organisation for Economic Cooperation and Development (OECD) is a club of the world's richest countries, from industrial giants like the US and Germany to smaller economies like New Zealand, Ireland, and Turkey. Table 11-2 shows the growth of OECD countries since 1950. The table shows the sharp productivity slowdown after 1973 in all OECD countries.

Why did productivity growth slow down? 1973 was also the year of the first OPEC oil price shock, when real oil prices quadrupled. This had two effects. First, it diverted R&D towards very long-term efforts to find alternative energy-saving technologies. These efforts may take decades to pay off and show up in improvements in actual productivity. Second, the higher energy prices made much of the capital stock useless. Energy-guzzling factories, too expensive to operate, were scrapped. The world lost part of its capital stock, reducing output per head.

The second reason was that, increasing regulation and pollution control, although socially desirable, raised production costs and reduced *measured*

Table 11-2

Average annual growth in real output per worker (%)

	OECD	Japan	Germany	France	UK	US
1950–73	3.6	8.9	5.6	4.5	3.6	2.2
1973–2000	1.4	2.3	2.7	2.0	1.7	0.7

Source: S. Dowrick and D. Nguyen, 'OECD Comparative Economic Growth 1950–85', *American Economic Review*, 1989; OECD, *Economic Outlook*

output and hence *measured* productivity. We return shortly to the mismeasurement of output and hence of output growth.

Having discussed differences in growth across sub-periods, we now discuss differences across countries. The fact that OECD countries move together across sub-periods shows that many aspects of growth are not within a country's control. Technical progress spreads quickly wherever it originates. Countries are increasingly dependent on the same global economy.

The convergence hypothesis

Figures 11-2 and 11-3 have a unique steady state, to which a country converges whatever its initial level of capital per worker. When capital per worker is low, it takes little investment to equip new workers (capital-widening), so the rest of investment raises capital per worker (capital-deepening). Conversely, when capital per worker is already high, saving and investment are insufficient to give new workers the old level of capital per worker, which therefore falls.

> The **convergence hypothesis** says poor countries should grow quickly but rich countries should grow slowly.

Since this seems plausible, why is sub-Saharan Africa not growing really quickly? Basically, for two reasons. First, Figure 11-1 assumed that a constant fraction of income is saved. But people with low living standards may have to consume *all* their income. With no saving, they then have no resources to invest at all.

Second, many of these countries continue to have civil wars or corrupt governments that appropriate the country's meagre wealth for the ruling elite. This reminds us that economic success depends on a flourishing civil society, good governance and other attributes that cannot narrowly be explained by economics alone.

The costs of growth

Some people believe that the benefits of economic growth are outweighed by its costs. Pollution, congestion and a hectic life-style are too high a price to pay for a rising output of cars, washing machines and video games.

Since GDP is an imperfect measure of the net economic value of output made by the economy, there is no presumption that we should aim to maximise the growth of measured GDP. We discussed issues such as pollution in Chapter 6. Without government intervention, a free market economy is likely to produce too much pollution.

However, zero pollution is also wasteful. Eliminating the last little bit of pollution cost a lot and has only a little benefit. Rather society should reduce pollution until the marginal benefit of more pollution reduction equals its marginal cost.

This is the most sensible and direct way in which to approach the problem. In contrast, the 'zero-growth' solution tackles the problem only indirectly.

> The **zero-growth proposal** argues that, because higher output has adverse side effects such as pollution and congestion, we should therefore aim for zero growth of measured output.

Box 11-2

Standards of living and the convergence hypothesis

The table below shows estimates of per capita income in 1997 and of its annual real growth 1980–97. Three points stand out. First, the East Asian economies grew very quickly. Even India is now growing steadily. Second, convergence cannot be a powerful force in the world or the very poorest countries would grow more rapidly. Poor countries stay poor and sometimes even decline. Third, within the rich OECD countries, convergence is much more reliable. The richest OECD countries tend to grow less quickly than the poorer OECD countries.

Why did the East Asian countries grow so quickly in the post-war period? Professor Alwyn Young has shown that there is little mystery. These economies managed rapid growth in measured inputs – labour (via higher in participation rates), capital (via high saving and investment rates) and human capital (via substantial expenditure on education). Allowing for rapid growth of these inputs, Young showed that the growth of output in the tigers was not very different from what standard estimates, based on OECD and Latin American countries, would have led us to expect. (See A. Young: 'The tyranny of numbers: Confronting the statistics realities of the East Asian growth experience', *Quarterly Journal of Economics*, 1995.)

Per capita GNP in 1997 and annual GDP growth 1980–97

Poor and middle income	1997 GNP $000	1980–97 annual growth (%)	OECD countries	1997 GNP $000	1980–97 annual growth (%)
Mozambique	0.1	−1.2	Portugal	10.5	2.9
Bangladesh	0.3	2.3	Spain	14.5	2.0
Nigeria	0.3	−1.2	Ireland	18.3	4.2
China	0.8	11.0	Italy	20.1	1.4
Indonesia	1.1	5.5	UK	20.7	2.0
Philippines	1.2	1.1	France	26.5	2.0
Turkey	3.1	1.7	US	28.7	1.7
Korea	10.5	7.8	Switzerland	44.3	1.6

Source: World Bank, *World Development Report*

The zero-growth approach does not distinguish between outputs that have adverse side effects and those that do not. It does not provide the right incentives. When society believes that there is too much pollution, congestion, environmental damage, or stress, the best solution is to provide incentives that directly reduce these activities. Restricting growth in measured output is a very crude alternative that is distinctly second best.

Some of these difficulties might be removed if economists and statisticians could devise a more comprehensive measure of GDP that included all the 'quality of life' activities (clean air, environmental beauty, serenity) that yield consumption benefits but at present are omitted from measured GDP. Inevitably voters and commentators assess government performance according to published, measurable statistics. A better measure of GDP might remove some of the conflicts that governments feel between measured output and the quality of life.

Recap

- Economic growth is the percentage annual rise in real GDP or real GDP per head. It is an imperfect measure of the growth in economic well-being.

- Output rises because of larger quantities of inputs of land, labour and capital, or because technical progress raises the output produced by given input quantities.

- In the steady state, all variables grow at the same rate. Without technical progress, capital, output and labour grow at the same rate. Whatever its initial level of capital, an economy tends to converge on this steady-state path. With a growing population, this theory can explain output growth but not productivity growth.

- Adding technical progress to this model explains which labour productivity and living standards can grow for ever.

- Growth rates should converge because capital-deepening is easier when capital per worker is low than when it is high. In practice, some poor countries miss out on growth either because they cannot save or because conflict, corruption and mistrust undermine it.

Review questions

1 'Britain produces too many scientists but too few engineers.' What kind of evidence might help you decide if this is true? Will a free market lead people to choose the career that most benefits society?

2 Name two economic bads. Can they be measured? Are they included in GNP? *Could* they be?

3 'Because we know Malthus got it wrong, we take a more relaxed view about the fact that some minerals are in finite supply.' Is there a connection? Explain.

4 Use a diagram like Figure 11-1 to compare two economies with different rates of population growth. Which has the higher living standards in the long run? Why?

5 *Common fallacies* Why are these statements wrong? (a) Since the earth's resources are limited, growth cannot continue for ever. (d) If we save more, we would definitely grow faster.

Answers on pages 278–90

11-2 The business cycle

Learning outcomes

By the end of this section, you should understand:
- Trend growth and cycles around this path
- Why business cycles occur
- Whether national cycles are becoming more correlated
- Recent UK business cycles

Is there a business cycle? We know output fluctuates a lot in the short run, but a cycle also requires a degree of regularity. Can we see it in the data? If so, how do we explain it? Is there now an international dimension? Can a single country display cycles that are out of phase with those in its trading partners?

Trend and cycle: statistics or economics?

In practice, aggregate output and productivity do not grow smoothly. In some years they grow a lot, but in other years they actually fall.

> The **business cycle** is short-term fluctuation of output around its trend path.

Figure 11-4 shows a business cycle. The smooth curve is the steady growth in trend output over time. Actual output follows the wavy curve. Point *A* is a

slump, the bottom of a business cycle. At *B* the economy enters the *recovery* phase of the cycle. As recovery proceeds, output climbs above its trend path, reaching *C*, which we call a *boom*. Then it enters a *recession* in which output is growing less quickly than trend output, and may even

Figure 11-4

The business cycle

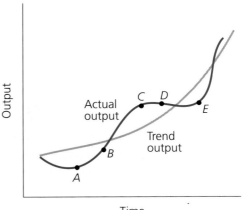

Figure 11-5

UK cycles in output and productivity

Source: ONS, *Economic Trends*

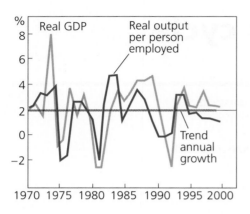

be falling. Point *E* shows a *slump*, after which the cycle starts again.

Figure 11-5 shows the annual growth of real GDP and of real output per worker in the UK during 1970–2001. Output and productivity grew rapidly in 1964, 1968, 1973, and 1986–88 but stagnated in 1974–75, 1980–82, and 1990–92. The figure makes two points. First, short-run cycles are important. Second, in the short-run there is a close relation between changes in output and changes in output per worker. These are the facts that we need to explain.

Any series of points may be decomposed statistically into a trend and fluctuations around the trend. We begin by assuming that potential output grows smoothly. Later we discuss whether potential output itself can fluctuate in the short run. For the moment, we assume that deviations of output from trend

reflect departures of aggregate demand from potential output.

One could argue that aggregate demand just happens to fluctuate cyclically in the short run. But why would it do so? One possibility is a *political business cycle*. Suppose voters have short memories and are heavily influenced by how the economy is doing just before the election. To get re-elected, the government manipulates the economy into a slump, then mops up this spare capacity by loosening policies as the election approaches, achieving a temporary period of impressive looking growth. The voters think that the government has got things under control and votes them in for another term of office.

> A **political business cycle** is caused by cycles in policy between general elections.

This theory explains why each cycle might last around five years, the period between successive elections in many countries. The theory contains a grain of truth, but it supposes that voters are pretty naive. In 1997 the Major government lost the UK election even though output was growing strongly. Voters thought Labour could do even better. Moreover, the Bank of England has now been made independent of political control precisely to take the politics out of monetary policy decisions.

The multiplier–accelerator model

The multiplier–accelerator model distinguishes the causes and effects of a change in investment spending. In the simplest Keynesian model, the effect of higher investment is higher output in the short run. Higher investment adds directly to aggregate demand but the induced rise in income then adds further to consumption demand. In Chapter 7 we called this process the multiplier.

What about the cause of a change in investment spending? Firms invest when their existing capital stock is smaller than the capital stock they would like to hold. The desired capital stock depends partly on the interest rate and hence the opportunity cost of the funds tied up in the capital goods. However, *real* interest rates do not change very much in practice.

Changes in expectations about future profits are usually a more important determinant of investment decisions. If real interest rates and real wages change only slowly, the main reason to invest in more capital capacity is because demand and output are expected to grow.

The **accelerator** model of investment assumes that firms guess future output and profits by extrapolating past output growth.

Constant output growth leads to a constant level of investment. It takes accelerating output growth to increase the desired level of investment. The accelerator model is only a simplification. Nevertheless, many empirical studies confirm that it is useful in explaining movements in investment.

We now show how a simple version of the multiplier–accelerator model can lead to a business cycle. Table 11-3 makes two specific assumptions, although the argument holds much more generally. First, we assume that the multiplier is 2. A unit of extra investment raises income and output by 2 units. Second, we assume that if last period's income grew by 2 units,

Table 11-3

The multiplier–accelerator model of the business cycle

Period t	Change in last period's output $Y_{t-1} - Y_{t-2}$	Investment I_t	Output Y_1
$t + 1$	0	10	100
$t + 2$	0	10	120
$t + 3$	20	20	140
$t + 4$	20	20	140
$t + 5$	0	10	120
$t + 6$	220	0	100
$t + 7$	220	0	100
$t + 8$	0	10	120
$t + 9$	20	20	140

firms now increase current investment by 1 unit.

The economy begins in equilibrium with output Y_t equal to 100. Since output is constant, the last period's output change was zero. Investment I_t is 10, which we can think of as the amount of investment required to offset depreciation and maintain the capital stock intact.

Suppose in period 2 that some component of aggregate demand increases by 20 units. Output increases from 100 to 120. Since we have assumed that a growth of 2 units in the previous period's output leads to a unit increase in current investment, the table shows that in period 3 there is a 10-unit increase in investment in response to the 20-unit output increase during the previous period. Since the assumed value of the multiplier is 2, the 10-unit *increase* in investment in period 3 leads to a further increase of 20 units in output, which increases from 120 to 140.

In period 4 investment remains at 20 since the output growth in the previous period was 20. Thus output in period 4 remains at 140. But in period 5 investment reverts to its original level of 10, since there was no output growth in the previous period. This fall of 10 units in investment leads to a multiplied fall of 20 units in output in period 5. In turn this induces a further fall of 10 units of investment in period 6 and a further fall of 20 units in output. But since the rate of output change is not accelerating, investment in period 7 remains at its level of period 6. Hence output is stabilised at the level of 100 in period 7. With no output change in the previous period, investment in period 8 returns to 10 units

again and the multiplier implies that output increases to 120. In period 9 the 20-unit increase in output in the previous period increases investment from 10 to 20 units and the cycle begins all over again.

The **multiplier–accelerator model** explains business cycles by the dynamic interaction of consumption and investment demand.

The insight of the multiplier–accelerator model is that it takes an *accelerating* output growth to keep increasing investment. But this does not happen in Table 11-3. Once output growth settles down to a constant level of 20, investment settles down to a constant rate of 20 per period. Then in the following period, the level of investment must *fall*, since output growth has been reduced. The economy moves into a period of recession, but once the rate of output fall stops accelerating, investment starts to pick up again.

This simple model should not be regarded as the definitive model of the business cycle. If output keeps cycling, surely firms will stop extrapolating past output growth to form assessments of future profits? Firms, like economists, will begin to recognise that there is a business cycle. The less firms' investment decisions respond to the most recent change in past output, the less pronounced will be the cycle. Even so, this simple model drives home a simple result which can be derived in more realistic models. When the economy reacts sluggishly, its behaviour is likely to resemble that of a large oil tanker at sea: it takes a long time to get it moving and a long time to slow it down again. Unless the brakes are applied well before the desired level of the capital stock is reached, it is quite likely that the economy will overshoot its desired position. It will have to turn round and come back again.

Ceilings and floors

The multiplier–accelerator model can generate cycles even without any physical limits on the extent of fluctuations. Cycles are even more likely when we recognise the limits imposed by supply and demand. Aggregate supply provides a *ceiling* in practice. Although it is possible temporarily to meet high aggregate demand by working overtime and running down stocks of finished goods, output cannot expand indefinitely. In itself this tends to slow down growth as the economy reaches a boom. Having overstretched itself, the economy is likely to bounce back off the ceiling and begin a downturn. Conversely, there is a *floor*, or a limit to the extent to which aggregate demand is likely to fall. Gross investment (including replacement investment) cannot actually become negative unless, for the economy as a whole, machines are being unbolted and sold to foreigners. Thus although falling investment may be an important component of a downswing, investment cannot fall indefinitely, whatever our model of investment behaviour.

Fluctuations in stockbuilding

Thus far we have emphasised investment in fixed capital. Now we consider inventory investment in working capital. Firms hold stocks of goods despite the cost in interest cost foregone on the funds tied up in making goods for which no revenue has yet been received. The corresponding benefit of holding stocks is to avoid temporary but costly changes in production. Output expansion entails overtime payments and costs of recruiting new workers. Cutting output involves redundancy payments. Holding stocks lets firms meet short-run fluctuations in demand without incurring the expense of short-run fluctuations in output.

If aggregate demand falls, in the short run firms build up stocks of unsold output. If aggregate demand remains low, firms gradually cut output rather than stockpile goods indefinitely. Once aggregate demand recovers again, firms are still holding all the extra stocks built up during the recession. Only by increasing output *more slowly* than the rise in aggregate demand can firms eventually sell off these stocks and get back to long-run equilibrium levels of stocks.

Thus, the evolution of stocks helps explain why output adjustment is so sluggish. Output changes more slowly than aggregate demand. This helps explain the behaviour of productivity in Figure 11-4. Output per worker rises in a boom and falls in a slump. This is because output adjusts more quickly than employment, the most costly thing to adjust.

A fall in demand is met initially both by cutting hours and increasing stocks. With a shorter work week, output per worker falls. If the recession intensifies, firms undertake the costlier process of sacking workers and restoring hours to their normal level. Conversely, a boom is the time when output and overtime are high, and productivity per worker peaks.

Real business cycles

The above account of the business cycle is completely consistent with the earlier analysis of sluggish wage adjustment in the short run. The principal source of output fluctuations is thus swings in aggregate demand that lead to output fluctuations around potential output.

However, there is a second possibility, that output fluctuations reflect cycles in potential output itself.

> **Real business cycles** are output fluctuations caused by fluctuations in potential output itself.

In the Keynesian world of sluggish nominal adjustment, changes in the nominal money supply have real effects in the short run because they change the real money supply and hence the interest rate needed for money market equilibrium. In the Classical world, changes in money simply induce changes in other nominal variables, leaving output at potential output. Hence, real business cycles refer to cycles that occur in the Classical model without relying on Keynesian explanations.

One important source of shocks in real business cycle theories is shocks to technology, which affect potential output by affecting productivity. The age of the train, the car and the microchip have required huge waves of investment, affecting aggregate demand, but have also affected potential output.

Some economists have been sceptical of this approach for two reasons. First, changes in aggregate supply may occur more slowly than changes in aggregate demand. Second, to provide a theory of cycles, the economy would also need to experience some periods in which productivity *fell* because technology deteriorated. Can we really forget today what we knew how to do yesterday?

The bust of the internet boom in 2001 had many features of a real business cycle. It was not that actual productivity fell. Rather, people were unsure about how rapidly the new technologies would increase future productivity. Initially, everyone was optimistic that growth rates would be very high indeed. Investment was very high, anticipating rapid future growth.

As evidence accumulated that productivity growth was going to be a little slower than first imagined, suddenly everybody realised that there had already been far too much investment in some new economy sectors. Share prices collapsed and further investment dried up. This reflected both a downgrading of ideas about the future level of potential output and a fall in current aggregate demand since investment then fell.

Policy implications

Research on real business cycles is still relatively recent, but it does have one vital message for macroeconomic policy. It may no longer be appropriate to try to stabilise output over the business cycle. When output falls *because* potential output has fallen, there is no longer any output gap between actual and potential output that needs to be closed.

Empirical research has found some evidence that technology shocks do move actual output. But demand shocks matter a lot as well. When wage and price adjustment is sluggish, it is appropriate to change aggregate demand, whether one cares about output or inflation. The task for stabilisation policy – the headache that the Bank of England confronts once a month – is to decide whether visible changes in output have been accompanied by invisible changes in potential output, or whether the output gap has altered. Nobody said their job was easy.

Recap

- The trend path of output is the long-run path after short-run fluctuations are ironed out. The business cycle describes fluctuations in output around this trend. Cycles last about five years but are not perfectly regular.
- The political business cycle argues that the government manipulates the economy to make things look good just before an election.
- The multiplier–accelerator model highlights the dependence of investment on expected future profits and assumes that expectations reflect past output growth. This model delivers a cycle but assumes that firms are pretty stupid.
- Full capacity and the impossibility of negative gross investment provide ceilings and floors, limiting the extent to which output can fluctuate.
- Fluctuations in stockbuilding add to the business cycle and reflect costs of adjusting output.
- Real business cycles assume that cycles reflect fluctuations in potential output. Technology shocks can have this effect.
- Thus, both demand and supply shocks contribute to the business cycle, however stabilisation policy is appropriate only to offset demand shocks that create a gap between actual and potential output.

Review questions

1 Recompute Table 11-3 when a 1-unit rise in I_t induces a 1-unit rise in Y_t and a 1-unit rise in the $[Y_{t-1} - Y_{t-2}]$ induces a 1-unit rise in I_t. The economy again begins at $Y_t = 100$, and the initial shock is a rise in I_t from 0 to 10.

2 'If firms could forecast future output and profits accurately, there could not be a business cycle.' Is this true?

3 Would it be more helpful for the world economy if all the largest countries elected governments on the same day? Why, or why not?

4 What is 'real' about a real business cycle?

5 *Common fallacies* Why are these statements wrong? (a) Closer integration of national economies will abolish business cycles. (b) The more we expect cycles, the more we get them.

Answers on pages 278–90

12

Trade, development and globalisation

12-1 International trade

Learning outcomes

By the end of this section, you should understand:
- Patterns of international trade
- Comparative advantage
- Two-way trade in the same product
- The gains from trade
- When trade restrictions are beneficial

This final chapter looks at the world economy as a trading system. Why does international trade occur? Why have some countries been left behind while others prosper as never before? And what can we say about globalisation, so frequently a source of fear and concern in the public debate? Is globalisation a threat or an opportunity?

International trade is part of daily life. Britons drink French wine, Americans drive Japanese cars, and Russians eat American wheat. Through *exchange* and *specialisation*, countries supply the world economy with things that they produce relatively cheaply, receiving in exchange things made relatively more cheaply elsewhere.

These gains from trade are reinforced by scale economies in production. Instead of each country having many small producers, different countries specialise in different things so that all countries benefit from the cost reductions that ensue. Because foreign competition may make life difficult for some voters, governments are often under pressure to restrict imports. We end the section by discussing trade policy and whether it is ever a good idea to restrict imports.

World exports are now 20 per cent of world GDP. World trade has grown by 7.5 per cent a year since 1950, as transport costs and other barriers to trade keep falling. Countries are becoming

Figure 12-1

Exports (% of GDP)

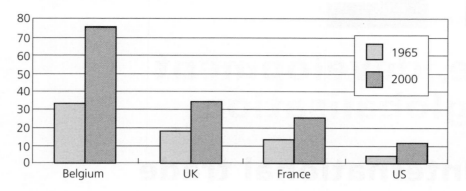

steadily more open to trade, as Figure 12-1 confirms. Events in other countries affect our daily lives much more than they did 20 years ago. Smaller countries are of course more open; when New York trades with California it does not count as *international* trade.

Table 12-1 shows that half of world trade is trade between the rich industrial countries, and only 14 per cent of trade does not involve these countries at all. World trade and world income are organised around the rich industrial countries.

Services are around 70 per cent of GDP in rich countries, but a much smaller share of their trade. Trade in goods (merchandise trade) remains important because many countries import goods, add a little value, and then re-export them. The value added makes a small contribution to GDP but gross flows of imports and exports of goods are large.

Table 12-2 distinguishes between *primary products* (agricultural commodities, minerals, and fuels) and

Table 12-1

Trade patterns, 2000
(% of world exports)

	Origin country	
	Rich	*Others*
Destination country		
Rich	49	19
Others	18	14

Source: GATT, *Directions of Trade*

manufactured commodities. Although the EU is chiefly an exporter of manufactures, primary commodities account for one-fifth of exports. And although the EU has to import many raw materials, imports of wholly or partly finished manufactures account for three-quarters of EU imports. US trade exhibits the same general pattern.

Having discussed trade patterns, we now examine the reasons why trade takes place at all.

Table 12-2

Trade patterns, late-1990s

	EU	N. America	Asia
% of exports			
Primary products	19	21	16
Manufactures	79	73	83
% of imports			
Primary products	25	18	28
Manufactures	73	79	69

Source: GATT, International Trade

Table 12-3

Relative costs and comparative advantage

		ULR (hours)	Hourly wage	ULC (cost)	OC (sacrifice)
US	Cars	30	$6	£180	6 shirts
	Shirts	5	$6	$30	1/6 car
UK	Cars	60	£2	$120	10 shirts
	Shirts	6	£2	£12	1/10 car

Gains from trade

Comparative advantage

Trade is mutually beneficial when there are cross-country differences in the *relative* cost of making goods.

> The **law of comparative advantage** says that countries specialise in producing and exporting the goods that they produce at a lower relative cost than other countries.

One reason why relative costs may differ is differences in technology across countries. Suppose labour is the only production and there are constant returns to scale. Table 12-3 assumes that it takes 30 hours of American labour to make a car and 5 hours to make a shirt. UK labour is less productive. It takes 60 hours of UK labour to make a car and 6 hours to make a shirt.

Suppose US workers earn $6 an hour, and British workers £2 an hour. Table 12-3 shows the *unit labour requirement (ULR)* or hours of work to make a unit of each good. US labour is *absolutely* more productive than UK labour in making either good. However, US labour is *relatively* more productive in cars than in shirts. UK labour takes twice as long to make a car, but only 6/5 as long as US labour to make a shirt. Different relative productivity makes trade mutually beneficial.

The *opportunity cost OC* of making a unit of one good is the quantity of the other good that must be given up to create the extra production resources. Table 12-3 shows these opportunity costs *OC* in each country prior to trade. Because of different relative productivity, the opportunity cost of a car is 6 shirts in the US but 10 shirts in the UK, whereas the opportunity cost of a shirt is 1/6 of a car in the US but only 1/10 of a car in the UK.

If the UK makes 60 more shirts, giving up 6 cars, the US makes these 6 cars for the loss of only 36 shirts. International trade and specialisation let the world economy have 24 more shirts with no loss of cars. Similarly, if the US makes 10 more cars, giving up 60 shirts, the UK makes these extra shirts for the loss of only 6 cars, giving the world 4 more cars but no fewer shirts.

> The **gains from trade** are additional output of some goods with no loss of other goods.

The market also gets the world economy to the right answer. Table 12-3 also shows the *unit labour cost ULC* of making each good. We assume that the hourly wage is $6 in the US and £2 in the UK. If labour is the only input, the unit labour cost is the average total cost of a good, and the price for which it is sold in a competitive market.

Since the US and UK use different currencies, a foreign exchange market is set up and an equilibrium exchange rate established. Suppose the $/£ exchange rate is high. This makes all UK goods, initially produced in pounds, cost a lot of dollars. The UK is uncompetitive in both goods. Now consider lower and lower values of $/£. When the exchange rate is low enough, the UK can compete by exporting one good. Which one? The one it is relatively better at making.

For example, in Table 12-3 if the exchange rate is $2/£, then UK cars can be sold for $240 and UK shirts for £24. The UK can undercut the US in shirts but not in cars. Similarly, US cars sell for £90 and US shirts for £15. Again, the UK is competitive in shirts but not in cars.

This is why absolute advantage is unimportant. The single exchange rate can adjust to make any country's goods competitive *on average*. But which goods it then imports, and which it then exports, depends on which it makes relatively better or worse than average, which is precisely what the Law of Comparative Advantage promises us.

The Law has many applications in everyday life. Suppose two students share a flat. One is faster both at making the dinner and at vacuuming the carpet. If tasks are allocated according to absolute advantage, one student does nothing. The jobs get done faster if each student does the task at which he or she is *relatively* faster.

Relative factor abundance

One country can eventually learn another country's technology. Technology differences are probably not the main explanation for comparative advantage. The main reason that a country has a relatively low price for a particular output is that it has a relatively low price for the inputs which that output uses. In turn, relatively low input prices are largely explained by having relatively abundant quantities of those inputs available.

If the UK is relatively generously supplied with human capital, it should export university places to foreign students from the Caribbean. If the Caribbean is relatively well endowed with tropical land, it exports bananas and nutmeg to the UK. Differences in relative factor supply are a vital reason for comparative advantage and the pattern of international trade.

Figure 12-2 displays evidence confirming this analysis. Countries with scarce land but abundant skills have high shares of manufactures in their exports;

countries with lots of land but few skills typically export raw materials. As well as dots for individual countries, the figure also shows that the explanation works for groups of countries, represented by diamond shapes.

Thus, comparative advantage reflects initial differences in relative production costs, arising from differences in technology or in relative factor abundance.

Two-way trade

Different relative factor abundance explains why OPEC exports oil and China exports labour intensive goods from toys to trainers. But this approach cannot explain why the UK exports cars (Rover, Jaguar, MG) to Germany but also imports cars (Mercedes, BMW, VW) from Germany. The UK cannot simultaneously be scarce and abundant in the inputs used to make cars.

> **Intra-industry trade** is two-way trade in goods made by the same industry.

Two-way trade *within* the same industry occurs where consumers like a wide choice of brands that are similar but not identical. A Jaguar is not quite a Mercedes, nor is Danish Carlsberg identical to Belgian Stella. Consumers like variety.

However, we also need economies of scale. Instead of each country trying to make small quantities of each brand in each industry, the UK makes Jaguars, Germany makes Mercedes and Sweden makes Volvos, then we swap them around through international trade. We all benefit from low cost and greater variety.

Figure 12-2

Relative factor abundance and export composition

Source: World Bank, *World Development Report, 1995*

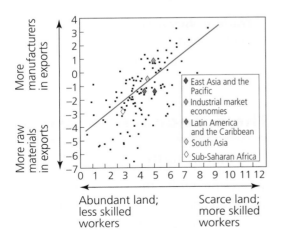

Winners and losers

Table 12-3 confirms that exploiting initial differences in relative costs allows gains from trade. The world gets more output from any given inputs. Similarly, intra-industry trade offers variety and cost reduction through scale economies. But this does not imply that *everybody* gains. Here are two examples of how some people can lose.

Refrigeration

The invention of refrigeration let Argentina supply frozen meat to the world market. Its meat exports, non-existent in 1900, were 400 000 tons a year by 1913. The US, with exports of 150 000 tons in 1900, had virtually stopped exporting beef by 1913.

Who gained and who lost? Argentinian cattle grazers and meat exporters attracted resources. Owners of cattle and land gained; other land users lost out because, with higher demand, land rents increased. Argentine consumers found their steaks got dearer as meat was shipped abroad. Argentina's GNP rose a lot, but the benefits of trade were not equally distributed. Some people in Argentina were worse off. In Europe and the US, cheaper beef made consumers better off. But beef producers lost out because beef prices fell.

As a whole, the world gained. In principle, the gainers could have compensated the losers and still had something left over. In practice, gainers rarely compensate losers. Some people lost out.

The UK car industry

As recently as 1971, UK imports of cars were only 15 per cent of the domestic UK market, while 35 per cent of UK car output was exported. The UK was a net exporter of cars. Imports are now over 60 per cent of the UK market; however, exports recovered in the 1990s as Nissan, Honda and Toyota established UK plants to produce for the EU market.

UK car buyers and foreign producers like VW benefited from the rise in UK imports of cheaper foreign cars. But UK car producers like Rover had a tough time. UK governments faced repeated pressure to protect UK car producers from foreign competition. Restricting imports would help domestic producers but hurt domestic consumers by raising prices to UK car buyers.

Should the government please producers or consumers? More generally, how should we decide whether to restrict imports or have free trade in all goods? In analysing the costs and benefits of tariffs or other trade restrictions, we move from *positive economics*, why trade exists and what form it takes, to *normative economics*, what trade policy the government should adopt.

> **Trade policy** operates through import tariffs, export subsidies and direct quotas on imports and exports.

The economics of tariffs

> An **import tariff** is a tax on imports.

If t is the tariff, the domestic price of imported goods is $(1 + t)$ times the world price of the imported good. By raising the

Figure 12-3

The effect of a tariff

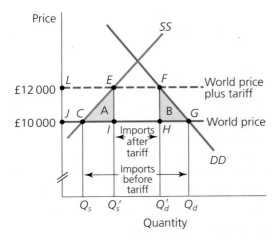

The broken horizontal line at this price shows that importers are willing to sell any number of cars in the domestic market at a price of £12 000. The tariff raises the domestic tariff-inclusive price above the world price.

By raising domestic car prices, the tariff boosts domestic car production from Q_s to Q_s' and offers some protection to domestic producers. In moving up the supply curve from C to E, domestic producers with marginal costs between £10 000 and £12 000 can now survive because the domestic price of imports has been raised by the tariff.

The higher price also moves consumers up their demand curve from G to F. The quantity of cars demanded falls from Q_d to Q_d'. From the consumers' viewpoint, the tariff is like a tax. Consumers pay more for cars.

Imports fall from CG to EF both because domestic production rises *and* because domestic consumption falls. The flatter are the domestic supply and demand schedules, the more a given tariff reduces imports. If both schedules are steep, the tariff-induced rise in the domestic price has much less effect on the quantity of imports.

domestic price of imports, a tariff helps domestic producers but hurts domestic consumers.

Figure 12-3 shows the domestic market for cars. Suppose the UK faces a given world price, £10 000 per car, shown by the solid horizontal line. Schedules *DD* and *SS* are the domestic demand for cars and supply of cars. Suppose brands do not matter. Domestic and foreign cars are then perfect substitutes.

At a price of £10 000, UK consumers wish to purchase Q_d cars, at point G on their demand curve. Domestic firms want to make Q_s cars at this price. *CG* shows imports, the gap between domestic supply Q_s and domestic demand Q_d.

The effect of a tariff

With a 20 per cent tariff on imported cars, car importers must charge £12 000 to cover their costs inclusive of the tariff.

Costs and benefits of a tariff

We need to distinguish *net costs to society* from *transfers* between one part of the economy and another. After the tariff, consumers buy Q_d', which costs them (£2000 × Q_d') *more* than buying this quantity at the world price. Who gets these extra payments, the area *LFHJ* in Figure 12-3?

Some goes to the government, whose revenue from the tariff is the rectangle

$EIHF$, the tariff of £2000 $\times$ $(Q_d' - Q_s')$ imported cars. This transfer $EIHF$ from consumers to the government is *not* a net cost to society. The government may use the tariff revenue to reduce income tax rates.

Some of higher consumer payments go to firms as extra profits. The supply curve shows how much firms need to cover production costs. Hence the area $ECJL$ is the rise in firms' profits, extra revenue from higher prices over and above extra production costs. Thus $ECJL$ is transferred from consumers to the profits of firms, but not a net cost to society as a whole.

The shaded area A is part of the extra consumer payments $LFHJ$ going neither to firms as extra profit nor to government as tariff revenue. It *is* a net cost to society: the cost of supporting inefficient domestic firms.

Society *could* import cars from the rest of the world in unlimited quantities at the world price of £10 000, which is the true marginal cost of cars to the domestic economy. The triangle A is the resources society wastes by producing $(Q_s' - Q_s)$ domestically when it could have been imported at a lower cost. The resources drawn into domestic car production could be used more efficiently elsewhere in the economy, including its export sectors.

There is another net loss to society, the triangle B. If the tariff was abolished, the quantity of cars demanded would rise Q_d. The triangle B is the excess of consumer benefits, as measured by the height of the demand curve showing how much consumers want the last unit demanded, over the marginal costs of expanding from Q_d' to Q_d, the world price at which imports could be purchased. The triangle B shows the net benefit society has lost by consuming too few cars.

To sum up, a tariff leads to a rise in the domestic price, inducing both transfers and pure waste. Money is transferred from consumers to the government and to producers. As a first approximation, the net cost of these transfers to society as a whole is zero, though there are distributional implications. Some individuals win while others lose.

In addition, a tariff involves pure waste, since post-tariff prices exceed the true marginal cost of cars to society, which remains the world price. Hence, consumers buy too few cars, and domestic producers make too many cars. Since zero tariffs avoid this waste, this is the *case for free trade*.

Should a tariff ever be adopted? Table 12-4 lists some of the common arguments for tariffs. The *first-best* argument is a case where a tariff is *the* best way to achieve a given objective. *Second-best* arguments are cases where the policy is beneficial but another policy that would be even better. Non-arguments are partly or completely fallacious.

Table 12-4

Arguments for tariffs

	Example
First-best	Imports bid up world prices
Second-best	Way of life, anti-luxury
	Infant industry, defence, revenue
Fallacious	Cheap foreign labour

The optimal tariff: the first-best argument

The case for free trade requires that an economy's imports have no effect on the world price. For a small economy this is correct. However, a large country may affect the world price of its imports. For society, the marginal cost of the last unit of imports then exceeds the world price. Another import bids up the world price that all other importers must pay, but each small importer in the big country ignores any effect of their actions on world prices. Under free trade the country imports too much.

For the country as a whole, the marginal cost of imports exceeds the price paid by individual importers. A tariff puts this effect back into the price, inducing individual importers to act in the way that is best for society.

> When a country affects the price of its imports, the **optimal tariff** makes individual importers take account of their effect on the price that other importers must pay.

Second-best arguments for tariffs

> The **principle of targeting** says that the best way to meet an aim is to use a policy that affects the activity directly. Policies with side effects are second-best because they distort other activities.

The optimal tariff is an application of the principle of targeting. When the problem lies in the market for imports, a tariff on imports is the most efficient solution. Now we turn to second-best arguments for tariffs where the original problem is not directly to do with trade. The principle of targeting tells us that there are other ways to solve these problems at a lower net social cost.

Suppose society wishes to help inefficient farmers or craft industries to *preserve the old way of life*. Tariffs protect these producers from foreign competition but also hurt domestic consumers through higher prices. A *production subsidy* would still keep farmers in business but, by tackling the problem directly, would not hurt consumers. In Figure 12-3, the cost of triangle A must be incurred to prop up domestic producers so they can make Q'_s not Q_s. But a tariff unnecessarily incurs the cost of triangle B as well.

Some poor countries dislike their few rich citizens enjoying luxury yachts when society needs its resources to stop people starving. To *suppress luxury consumption*, a *consumption tax* is best. Of course, it incurs triangle B in Figure 12-3 since domestic prices rise to consumers, but it avoids triangle A. A tariff on yachts also reduces consumption, but higher domestic prices then provide an incentive for inefficient domestic firms to make yachts, incurring triangle A as well.

In case there is a future war, some countries want to preserve their *defence capability* by protecting domestic industries making food or jet fighters. Again, a production subsidy not an import tariff is the best way to meet this objective.

A common argument for tariffs is to let *infant industries* get started. With initial protection, they learn the business and can eventually meet foreign competitors on equal terms. But if the industry is such a good idea in the long run, why cannot private firms borrow the money to see them through the early period until they can compete? If the problem lies in bank lending to small firms, the principle of targeting says that a better policy is to solve the banking problem directly. Failing this, a production subsidy in the early years is still better than a tariff, which also penalises consumers. And the worst outcome is the imposition of a *permanent* tariff, which lets the industry remain inefficient long after it is supposed to have mastered its trade.

In the eighteenth century, most *tax revenue* came from tariffs, which were administratively easy to collect. This remains in some developing countries. But modern economies can raise taxes through many channels. Administrative simplicity is no longer a pressing concern.

Fallacious arguments for tariffs

Domestic firms often complain about *cheap foreign labour*. However, the whole point of trade is to exploit international differences in the relative prices of different goods. If the domestic economy is relatively well endowed with capital, it benefits from trade because its exports of capital-intensive goods let it buy labour-intensive goods more cheaply from abroad than it could make them at home.

Over time, countries' comparative advantage evolves. Nineteenth-century Britain exported Lancashire textiles all over the world. But textile production is labour-intensive. Once South-East Asian countries got the technology, their relatively abundant labour endowment gave them a comparative advantage in making textiles. The domestic producers who lost their comparative advantage started complaining about competition from imports using cheap foreign labour.

In the long run, the country as a whole benefits from facing facts, recognising that its comparative advantage has changed and transferring production to the industries in which its comparative advantage now lies. Our analysis of comparative advantage promises us that there *must* be some industry in which each country has a comparative advantage. In the long run, trying to use tariffs to prop up industries that have lost their comparative advantage is both futile and expensive.

In the short run the adjustment may be painful and costly. Workers lose their jobs and must start afresh in industries where they do not have years of experience and acquired skills. But the principle of targeting tells us that, if society wants to smooth this transition, some kind of retraining or relocation subsidy is more efficient than a tariff.

Even though anti-capitalist protesters may sympathise with domestic workers who are losing their jobs and having to adjust, freezing the previous structure of employment is not merely undesirable but probably impossible. We now longer have decorators of cave dwellings or handloom weavers.

The World Trade Organisation

In the nineteenth century world trade grew rapidly. The leading country, the UK, pursued a vigorous policy of free trade. US tariffs averaged about 50 per cent, but had fallen to around 30 per cent by

Figure 12-4

World exports (% of US GDP)

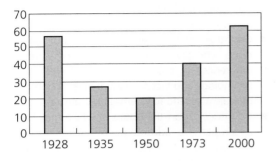

Figure 12-5

Falling transport costs

Sources: World Bank, *World Development Report, 1995*

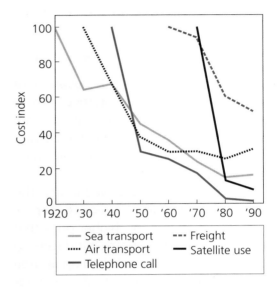

the early 1920s. As the industrial economies went into the Great Depression of the late 1920s and 1930s, there was increasing pressure to protect domestic jobs by keeping out imports. Tariffs in the US returned to around 50 per cent and the UK abandoned the policy of free trade it had pursued for nearly a century. The combination of world recession and increasing tariffs led to a disastrous slump in the volume of world trade. Figure 12-4 shows that it took a long time for world trade to recover.

After the war, there was a collective determination to restore world trade. The International Monetary Fund and the World Bank were set up, and many countries signed the General Agreement on Tariffs and Trade (GATT), a commitment to reduce tariffs successively and dismantle trade restrictions.

Under successive rounds of GATT, tariffs fell steadily. By 1960, US tariffs were only about one-fifth of their level in 1939. By 2000 Europe had completely abolished tariffs and other trade barriers

for trade within the European union, and the US and China had reached agreement to allow Chinese membership of the WTO.

Thus, tariff levels throughout the world are probably as low as they have ever been. And world trade has seen five decades of rapid growth, arising at least in part from tariff reduction. Figure 12-5 shows that lower transport costs have also been important.

Non-tariff barriers to trade

Domestic firms can be protected by their governments in many subtle ways. Build a railway with a different width, favour domestic firms in defence procurement, drive on the other side of the road, create paperwork to ensure major delays at the border. One reason that the European Union is keen to harmonise standards is to reduce segmentation of the European market that shelters inefficient national firms.

A more direct form of protection is a quota on imports.

A **quota** is a ceiling on import quantities.

Although quotas restrict the *quantity* of imports, this does not mean they have no effect on domestic prices of the restricted goods. With a lower supply, the equilibrium domestic price is higher than under free trade.

Thus quotas are rather like tariffs. The domestic price to the consumer is increased, and it is this higher price that allows inefficient domestic producers to produce a higher output than under free trade. Quotas lead to social waste for exactly the same reasons as tariffs.

Because quotas raise the domestic price of the restricted good, the lucky foreign suppliers who manage to sell goods make large profits on these sales. In terms of Figure 12-3, the rectangle *EFHI*, which would have been tariff revenue for the government, now goes in profits to foreign supplies. It is the difference between domestic and world prices of the goods imported, multiplied by the quantity of imports allowed.

If these profits accrue to foreigners this means the social cost of quotas is much bigger than the social cost of the equivalent tariff. Sometimes, however, the government can auction licences to import and thus recoup this revenue. Private importers or foreign suppliers will bid up to this amount to get their hands on a valuable import licence.

Recap

- World trade has grown rapidly in the last 50 years, and is dominated by the developed industrial countries. Primary commodities make up a quarter of world trade; the rest is trade in manufactures.
- Countries trade because they can buy goods more cheaply from abroad. Cross-country differences in costs arise from differences in technology and factor endowments. Economies of scale also lead to international specialisation.
- Countries export the goods in which they have a comparative advantage, or make relatively cheaply. The equilibrium exchange rate offsets average differences in absolute advantage. Every country has a comparative advantage in something.
- By exploiting international differences in opportunity costs, trade leads to a pure gain. Since different people share differently in the gain, some may actually lose.
- Intra-industry trade reflects scale economies plus consumer demand for variety.
- By raising the domestic price, a tariff reduces domestic consumption but raises domestic production. Hence imports fall.
- A tariff has two social costs: overproduction by domestic firms whose marginal cost exceeds the world price, and underconsumption by consumers whose marginal benefit exceeds the world price.
- When a country collectively affects the price of its imports, the optimal tariff induces individual importers to take account of their adverse effect on other importers for whom the import price is bid up.
- Other arguments for tariffs are either second-best solutions – a production subsidy or consumption tax would meet the objective at lower social cost – or are fallacious.
- Tariffs have fallen a lot since 1945, partly in response to the damage high tariffs did in the 1930s. The World Trade Organisation attempts to negotiate further reductions and regulate existing agreements.

Review questions

1 'A country with uniformly low productivity must be hurt by allowing foreign competition.' Is this true? Can you give a counterexample?.

2 'Large countries gain less from world trade than small countries.' True or false? Why?

3 Cars, wine, steel: which of these do you think have high intra-industry trade? Why?

4 To preserve its national heritage, society bans exports of works of art. (a) Is this better than an export tax? (b) Who gains and who loses from the export ban? (c) Will this measure encourage young domestic artists?

5 *Common fallacies* Why are these statements wrong? (a) British producers are becoming uncompetitive in everything. (b) Free trade is always best. (c) Buy British to help Britain.

Answers on pages 278–90

12-2 Less developed countries

Learning outcomes

By the end of this section, you should understand:
- The handicaps with which poor countries begin
- Whether comparative advantage is a secure route to prosperity
- Industrialisation and the export of manufactures
- The international debt crisis
- The importance of aid from rich countries

In Europe or the US a drought is bad for the garden; in poor countries it kills people.

Less developed countries (LDCs) have low levels of per capita output.

Many LDCs feel that the world economy is arranged to benefit the industrial countries and to exploit poor countries. About 41 per cent of the world's people live in poor countries, with an average annual income of about £280 per person. In the rich countries, average annual income is over £18 000 per person. *Most of the world's people live in poverty beyond the imagination of people in rich Western countries*. Table 12-5 shows data on per capita income, life expectancy at birth and adult illiteracy. The low-income countries are badly off on every measure.

Nevertheless, the situation of low-income countries has improved. Table 12-5 shows a marked increase in life expectancy in low-income countries, an indication that the quality of life has improved since 1965. Per capita income grew in all groups of countries yet, in absolute terms, poor countries fell even further behind the rest of the world.

To be so poor, these countries must have grown slowly for a long time. What special problems do they face?

Population growth

In rich countries birth control is widespread; in poor countries much less so. Without state pensions and other benefits, having children is one way people try to provide security against their old age when they can no longer work. With faster population growth, merely to maintain living standards poor countries grow more quickly than rich countries. However, poor countries cannot expand supplies of land, capital and natural resources at the same rate as the labour force. Decreasing returns to labour set in, the Malthusian trap.

Table 12-5

World welfare indicators, 2000

	Country group		
	Poor	Middle	Rich
Per capita GNP (£)	280	1310	18 340
Life expectancy at birth (years)	59	69	78
Adult illiteracy (%)	39	15	1

Source: World Bank, Development Report (various issues)

Resource scarcity

Dubai, generously endowed with oil, has a per capita income above that of the US or Germany. Many poor countries have not been blessed with natural resources that can profitably be exploited. And having resource deposits is not enough: it takes scarce capital resources to extract mineral deposits. Allowing foreign investors to do the job seems to let them keep most of the income too.

Capital

Rich countries have built up large stocks of physical capital which make their workers productive. Poor countries have few spare domestic resources to devote to physical investment. Financial loans and aid let poor countries buy foreign machinery and pay foreign construction firms. However, LDCs frequently complain that financial assistance is inadequate.[1]

1 At the 1996 Food Summit, Jacques Diouf, Director of the Food and Agriculture Organisation, said his annual budget was 'less than what nine developed countries spend on dog and cat food in six days, and less than 5 per cent of what inhabitants of just one developed country spend on slimming products every year'. The Times, 14 November 1996

Human capital

Without resources to devote to investment in health, education and industrial training, workers in poor countries are less productive than workers using the same technology in rich countries. Yet without higher productivity, it is hard to generate enough output (surplus to consumption requirements) to raise investment in people as well as in machinery.

Lack of human capital also makes it more difficult to regulate domestic markets to offset market failures such as monopoly or environmental pollution, and to achieve reliable enforcement of contracts through a transparent legal system.

Social investment in infrastructure

Developed countries achieve economies of scale and high productivity through specialisation, assisted by sophisticated transport and communications. Without investment in power generation, roads, telephones, and urban housing, poor countries must operate in smaller communities, unable to exploit scale economies and specialisation.

Conflict

Some of the poorest regions have been those where colonially imposed boundaries made little sense and where the end of empire left governments without wide domestic support. Both internal and international conflict has followed.

How can the world economy help? Our discussion examines all countries classified as LDCs, from the newly-industrialised nearly-rich to the very poorest countries lagging far behind.

Development through exports of primary products

Section 12-1 analysed the gains from trade when countries specialise in the commodities in which they have a comparative advantage. Relative factor abundance is an important determinant of comparative advantage. In many LDCs, the relatively abundant input is land. This suggests that LDCs can best use the world economy by exporting goods using land relatively intensively.

> **Primary products** are agricultural goods and minerals, whose output relies heavily on the input of land.

These include 'soft' commodities, such as coffee, cotton and sugar, and 'hard' commodities or minerals, such as copper or aluminium. As late as 1960, exports of primary commodities were 84 per cent of all LDC exports. Many LDCs are now sceptical of development through specialisation in production of primary products. Today, less than half of all LDC exports are primary products.

Figure 12-6 shows that, except for petroleum whose supply was curtailed by OPEC, the real price of other primary products has collapsed since 1975. This reflected both greater supply and lower demand. Technical advances, such as

Figure 12-6

Falling prices of primary products (1990 = 100)

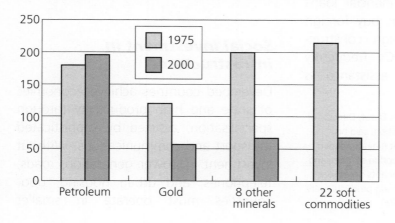

artificial rubber and plastics, reduced the demand for many primary products. Greater supply reflected the very success of LDCs in increasing productivity and output. With better drainage and irrigation, better seeds and more fertiliser, agriculture was transformed by the 'green revolution'. Similarly, mineral producers, often with foreign help, developed more capital-intensive mining methods. Even where each individual LDC was small, their collective effort to raise exports induced a fall in the real price of their export commodities.

This effect has been exacerbated by extensive protection of farmers in rich countries such as the US and those in the EU. Deprived of access to these large markets, LDCs have had to sell their larger supply in smaller markets, thus depressing the price much further than would otherwise have been the case.

Allowing LDC agricultural goods into the markets of the rich countries is probably the policy change that would have the greatest benefit for LDCs as a whole. Their income from exports of primary products would soar, providing a surplus to invest in physical and human capital. Consumers in rich countries would also benefit. A rise in the supply of food would reduce the price of food in London and New York.

A second disadvantage of concentrating on the production of primary products has been the volatility of their real prices. Both supply and demand are price-inelastic in the short run. On the demand side, people need food and industrial raw materials. On the supply side, crops have already been planted and perishable output has to be marketed whatever the price. When both supply and demand curves are very steep, a small shift in one curve leads to a big change in the equilibrium price.

Declining prices and price volatility are especially important when exports of a single crop are a large share of total export revenue. As shown in Figure 12-7, some LDCs are very vulnerable because they depend so heavily on a single export crop.

Development through industrialisation

Many countries have concluded that the route to development lies not through increased specialisation in making primary products but in the expansion of manufacturing industry. This has taken two very different forms.

Import substitution

When world trade collapsed in the 1930s, many LDCs found their export revenues cut in half. Many LDCs resolved never again to be so dependent on the world economy. After the war, they began a policy of import substitution.

> **Import substitution** replaces imports by domestic production under the protection of high tariffs or import quotas.

Import substitution reduces world trade and suppresses the principle of comparative advantage. LDCs used tariffs and quotas to direct domestic resources away from the primary products into industrial manufacturing where initially they had a comparative disadvantage.

Figure 12-7

Single crop as % of export revenue

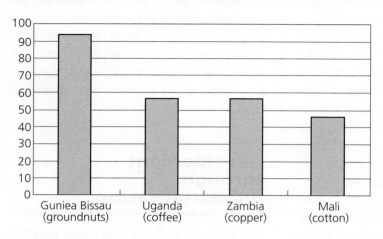

International trade theory suggests that this policy is likely to be wasteful. For example, by closing itself off from the world economy, the communist bloc pursued import substitution on a grand scale, but without eventual success. Import substitution has one great danger and one possible merit.

The danger is that import substitution may be a dead end. Although domestic industry may expand quite rapidly behind tariff barriers while imports are being replaced, once import substitution has been completed economic growth may come to a halt. The country is then specialised in industries in which it has a comparative *disadvantage*, and further expansion can come only from expanding *domestic* demand.

The possible merit is that comparative advantage is dynamic not static. A tariff may help an infant industry, even though production subsidies would achieve the same outcome at lower social cost. By

developing an industrial sector and learning to use the technology, LDCs may eventually acquire a comparative advantage in some industrial products. Thus import substitution may not be an end in itself, but a prelude to export-led growth.

Export-led growth stresses output and income growth via exports, rather than by displacing imports.

Exports of manufactures

The real success story of the last three decades is the group of countries that have turned the world economy to their advantage by exporting manufactures using their relatively cheap labour. Many of these countries are in South-East Asia. Table 12-6 shows how successful they have been.

LDCs are justifiably frightened that their strategy of economic development

Table 12-6

The Asian tigers

	Annual real growth of per capita GDP (%)		% of manufactures in total exports	
	1965–80	1980–2000	1965	2000
Indonesia	9	5	2	54
Hong Kong	9	4	90	95
Malaysia	7	4	6	80
Singapore	10	6	34	86
S. Korea	10	7	59	91
Thailand	7	5	4	74
China	–	9	47	88

Source: World Bank, World Development Report

through industrialisation and export-led growth through manufactures will also be frustrated by protection that freezes them out of markets in the rich countries. The booming industries of a middle-income country are often the declining industries of the rich countries, where a further loss of market share causes problems as workers have to be reallocated elsewhere. Although the evolution of comparative advantage says that this is efficient, politicians still have to respond to the short-run difficulties, and may be tempted to try to postpone adjustment for a little longer.

Development through borrowing

A third route to economic development is by external borrowing, and a third complaint of LDCs about the way the world economy works is that borrowing terms are too tough. LDCs have traditionally borrowed in world markets to finance imports of capital goods. Recall the balance of payments arithmetic:

Current
account = trade deficit + debt interest
deficit
        = increase in net foreign debt

The first line shows the sources of the current account deficit; the second reminds us that it has to be financed by selling domestic assets to foreigners or by new foreign borrowing. Table 12-7 shows debt/GDP ratios for some of the most indebted countries.

The *burden* of the debt depends not merely on the size of debt relative to GDP, but also on the interest rate that debtors must pay. When world interest rates rise, indebted countries suffer even more. Had these loans all been successfully invested

Table 12-7

Major debtors, 1999
(foreign debt as % of GDP)

Sub-Saharan Africa		Latin America	
Angola	344	Nicaragua	278
Zaire	307	Argentina	56
Zambia	175	Brazil	48
Mauritania	168	Colombia	40
Sierra Leone	136	Mexico	37
Ivory Coast	117	Venezuela	37

Source: World Bank, *World Development Report*

Box 12-1

Debt forgiveness

Bob Geldorf and other famous personalities have long been campaigning for rich countries to write off the debts of the world's poorest nations. It is a laudable aim, but we have to do it correctly. One difficulty is to do so without encouraging the belief that all future debtors will be bailed out. Another problem is that the big winners could be Western banks not impoverished borrowers.

Suppose a country owes £100 million a year, but can only pay £50 million a year. Every creditor is only getting half what they should get. Now benevolent European governments write off the £50 million owed to them. But the country still owes £50 million to private banks in London and New York. Since the country can still afford to pay £50 million, these banks now demand to be paid in full. The country gets no relief. Rather, European taxpayers bailed out European and American banks, that now get £50 million a year instead of having to split this with other creditors.

Helping rich banks was not the intention. The message? Debt forgiveness must write off *more than* the amount the borrower was failing to pay. Remaining creditors are paid in full, but there is some left over to reduce total payments by the borrower.

---

in productive projects, output might now be sufficiently large to meet the interest payments with ease. Part of the problem is usually that the rate of return on large investment projects has been disappointing. Countries are then left with the cost of the debt without a corresponding benefit.

Aid

Aid is an international transfer payment from rich countries to poor countries.

Poor countries often argue that they should get more aid from rich countries. Many of the rich countries are also failing to honour their previous promises about the amount of aid that they will give.

Aid can take many forms: subsidised loans, gifts of food or machinery, or technical help and free advice. How much aid rich countries should give is of course a moral or value judgement. However, many of the poorest countries feel that Northern prosperity was built during a colonial period when the resources of the South were exploited. Aid seems at least partial compensation. The Northern countries do not share this interpretation of history.

As we indicated earlier, many LDCs believe the best contribution rich countries can make is to provide free access for the LDCs to markets of the developed countries. 'Trade, not aid' is the slogan. Just as it is better for the government to retrain a domestic worker who has become unemployed than to provide a lifetime of welfare support, LDCs want useful market access, not another culture of dependency.

The quickest way to equalise world income distribution would be to permit free migration between countries. Residents of poor countries could go elsewhere in search of higher incomes. And in emigrating, they would increase capital and land per worker for those who stayed behind.

The massive movements of population from Europe to the Americas and the colonies in the nineteenth and early twentieth centuries were an income-equalising movement of this sort. Since 1945 migrations have been much smaller. If the gap between rich and poor widens further, rich countries may find it harder and harder to keep out economic migrants.

In this respect, one trend will eventually operate in favour of LDCs. The richest countries are getting top-heavy with old people, and have fewer and fewer young workers to pay the taxes and finance the pensions. Eventually, young labour will be in high demand, and it may have to be imported. At some future date, immigrants may be shown the red carpet not the cold shoulder.

Recap

World income and wealth are very unequally divided. LDSs complain that they are denied access to Northern markets, exacerbating falls in the prices of primary and industrial products that they export, that borrowing is too expensive, and that aid is insufficient.

- In the poorest countries, population and labour are growing faster than other production inputs, driving down living standards and removing surplus resources to invest in sustainable growth.

- Falling real prices, price volatility and concentration in a single commodity have made LDCs reluctant to pursue development by exporting primary products.

- LDCs' exports of labour-intensive manufactures are growing rapidly. Potential gains from trade suggest that rich countries should not respond by protecting their manufacturers.

- Many LDCs have large external debts without having the corresponding fruits of these investments. High interest rates raise the burden of debt. Token debt relief will probably benefit Western creditors not LDC borrowers. To be successful, debt relief will have to be substantial.

- Market access and trade may help the LDCs more effectively than aid, though more aid would also help. Migration would also reduce income disparities.

Review questions

1 Discuss two forces tending to reduce the real price of food in the long run.
2 Why were LDCs so successful in exporting textiles, clothing and leather footwear?
3 A country pays 8 per cent interest on its foreign debt, but its GDP grows by 8 per cent a year. What happens to its debt/GDP ratio if it meets all existing interest payments by new borrowing? What happens if its output growth then slows?
4 Prior to their full membership of the European Union, countries in Eastern Europe have been given associate membership, which includes free trade in many products but with some notable exceptions. (a) Guess the products on which the EU still applies big tariffs. (b) Are these likely to be goods in which Eastern Europe has a comparative advantage?
5 **Common fallacies** Why are these statements wrong? (a) Aid is all the help LDCs need. (b) Europe needs tariffs to protect it from cheap labour in the LDCs.

Answers on pages 278–90

12-3 Globalisation

Global brands, such as Coca Cola and McDonalds, are highly visible symbols of the increasing integration of world markets. Lower transport costs, better communications, new information technology, and deliberate policies to reduce trade barriers have all enhanced the size of the relevant economic market.

This starts to erode the sovereignty of national governments, by undermining the ability of an individual government to raise taxes, constrain firms and regulate markets. Too much intervention and the business migrates to an easier location elsewhere. In turn, perceiving the erosion of the power of their national governments to influence events, voters become apathetic and lose interest in national politics. Multinational corporations (MNCs) sometimes seem to have become more powerful than governments.

> **Globalisation** is the increase in cross-border trade and influence on the economic and social behaviour of nation states

Section 12-1 discussed how international trade can benefit everyone, but may also create losers if the winners claim all the spoils for themselves. Section 12-2 identified the disadvantages with which poor countries begin, and why some countries have yet to share in world prosperity.

Have the benefits of globalisation been outweighed by its costs? Should globalisation now be resisted? The next time a hamburger outlet is being trashed by anti-globalisation protesters, should you be leading the charge or explaining that there is a better way to meet their concerns? To help you make up your mind, we now discuss some of the most frequent criticisms of globalisation.

Is globalisation new

Actually, since communications and transport have been steadily increasing for centuries, globalisation is also centuries old. By many measures of trade, migration and capital flows across borders, the period 1870–1913 was comparable to the globalisation of the last few decades.

Globalisation is thus neither new nor irreversible. Globalisation during 1870–1913 created many winners but also some powerful losers. Cheaper grain from the US drove down grain prices and land rents in Europe, prompting agricultural protection in the 1920s. Massive migration to the US drove down wages there, leading to the introduction of immigration controls in the interwar period. History warns us that sustaining the momentum for globalisation requires sufficient redistribution to ensure that powerful groups of losers do not emerge to create a backlash.

Does globalisation increase inequality?

A few facts are helpful. Table 12-8 summarises the last 200 years. Globalisation *did* cause a big increase in inequality during 1820–1950, when the income share of the richest 10 per cent of the world population rose from 43 per cent to 51 per cent while the income share of the poorest 10 per cent of people fell from 5 per cent to 2 per cent. However, since 1950 it is *not* true that the income share of the poor has kept falling, nor has the income share of the rich risen much.

Global inequality is acute, but not getting worse.

Inequality is about relative incomes. We can also ask what is happening to the absolute incomes of the poor. Table 12-8 shows that the number of people earning less than a dollar a day (inflation adjusted, at 1990 prices) has fallen since 1950, *despite* the doubling of world population in the same period. Most of us would feel happier if the conditions of the poor were improving more rapidly. But they are improving slowly, whether measured by income, as in Table 12-8, or by life expectancy or literacy (see Table 12-5 in the previous section).

Why then do people make the connection between globalisation and poverty? Nowadays, we see it on the news, on documentaries and on charity appeals. Previously, it was there, and was worse, but we were less aware of it. Similarly, people living in poor countries are much better informed about how rich the rich countries have become. Globalisation of information has increased dissatisfaction about what always existed.

Table 12-8

World welfare indicators 1820–1992

	1820	1910	1950	1992
Average income/person (1990 $000s)	0.7	1.5	2.1	5.0
World population (billion)	1.1	1.7	2.5	5.5
Income share: richest 10% of people	43	51	51	53
poorest 10% of people	5	4	2	2
Billion people earning <$1/day	0.9	1.1	1.4	1.3

Source: CEPR (2002) Making Sense of Globalization, Centre for Economic Policy Research, London

Do multinational firms exploit workers and LDC governments?

Local workers employed by MNCs, whether mining minerals or producing clothes and trainers, seem to us to work for pitifully low wages and in conditions that workers in rich countries would not tolerate. However, their wages are usually higher than those earned by their compatriots in domestic industries, and working conditions in MNCs are often better than those in domestic factories, not least because MNCs care about their global image.

If workers in poor countries began with much larger quantities of physical and human capital, they would be richer and more productive. In principle, rich countries could vote for a massive transfer of aid to purchase these valuable inputs for poor countries. But they never have and the reality is that they probably never will. Without these advantages, the equilibrium wage of the disadvantaged is low but allowing them access to the world economy lets them gradually accumulate more of the valuable inputs that eventually enhance their own prosperity.

Well-meaning attempts to force 'improvements' in their wages and working conditions simply price them out of world markets and reduce their eventual prosperity. For an example closer to home, think of German unification in 1990. West German trade unions raised wages in Eastern Germany. But East Germans were not initially as productive as West Germans. The result was a decade of high unemployment and discontent in East Germany. So who gained? West German workers, protected from competition from cheap labour in East Germany!

What poor countries need is not less globalisation but more. Here, rich countries can help a lot, principally by opening up their market in agriculture and textiles, industries in which poor countries have a natural comparative advantage. By removing tariffs, this would reduce prices in the rich countries but raise prices received by LDC exporters. Current estimates are that a 40 per cent reduction in agricultural tariffs would generate gains of $70 billion a year. Incidentally, it would also reduce the food bill of each EU citizen by £200 a year.[2] Since the losers would be farmers in rich countries, the challenge for policy makers is to find a way to buy off these losers sufficiently.

What about the claim that MNCs play off one LDC against another? The trainers that you wear may have an American logo, but they were probably made in China or the Dominican Republic. MNCs effectively get each country to bid for hosting inward investment in a new factory. Does competition between countries ensure that the investment goes to the country with the lowest wages and lightest regulation?

Actually it does not. MNCs like low wages, but they also like workers with education and skills, good transport infrastructure and predictable legal environments. Foreign investment has flooded into Singapore not Senegal.

Moreover, competition between countries is one disciplining force on corruption in national bureaucracies that

2 *Source*: as in Table 12-8.

would otherwise be sheltered monopolies. The price of abuse is the failure to attract valuable inward investment. Globalisation on balance is probably a force that fosters democracy, transparency and good governance. One problem with Sub-Saharan Africa is that it has been too little exposed to the global economy, not too much.

Does globalisation destroy the environment?

Rainforests are cut down to rear beef cows for hamburgers, oil production wipes out wildlife and mining scars the landscape. All true. And all exacerbated by globalisation. However, we need to remember the principle of targeting.

If the environment is wrongly priced, encouraging overexploitation because producers do not pay the full social cost of what they do, the best solution is to encourage better pricing of the environment. Trying to suppress trade is a second-best solution.

Though logically correct, this is a counsel of perfection. Even countries rich in human capital have yet to implement sophisticated schemes that price and regulate use of the environment adequately. It is unrealistic to imagine that countries with fewer enforcement resources will do better.

Global measures, such as a carbon tax that applies everywhere, may be a reasonable compromise. Not only could this protect the environment, it would be a useful source of tax revenue for poor countries. However, the failure of the US to sign up to the Kyoto Agreement indicates a current unwillingness to play a role in such agreements. History suggests that it is wrong for the winners to believe that there is no need to heed the grievances of the losers, as the collapse of globalisation in the interwar period attests. If globalisation is not harnessed through better political management of the process, it may eventually be undone by conflict.

Recap

- Globalisation, the rise of foreign influence on domestic economic and social behaviour, is neither new nor irreversible. It is caused by cheaper transport, better communications and policies to reduce trade protection. In the absence of other distortions, this yields gains from trade and net benefits for the global economy. However, some groups may lose out.

- In the last half century, global inequality has not increased and the number of people in absolute poverty has fallen, despite rapid population growth. Trade is usually the route to prosperity and no country has ever got rich without international trade. However, better global information has made everyone aware of the extent of poverty that still exists in the world.

- Liberalising agriculture and textile markets in rich countries would hugely benefit not only their own citizens but also potential exporters in poor countries. The gains would easily allow the losers (rich farmers) to be bought off.

- Globalisation exacerbates existing distortions, for example the overexploitation of the environment or inadequate financial regulation in poor countries. The ideal solution is to improve these by domestic policy reform, not to curtail trade. Foreign aid could usefully be channelled into these areas.

- Failing this, there is a greater role for international agencies to devise rules that offset existing market failures and allow the benefits of globalisation to be enjoyed without incurring these additional costs. Taxing pollution and environmental depreciation would also generate useful tax revenue, in both poor and rich countries.

- Allowing powerful groups of uncompensated losers to arise is the most likely way in which globalisation may eventually be arrested or even reversed. This increases the case for redistribution to allow the benefits of globalisation to continue to help raise living standards in poor countries. Aid alone will never be enough.

Review questions

1 Could it be justified to protect the local film industry from 'cultural imperialism' from Hollywood? If so, what would be the best way in which to do this?

2 Absolute poverty refers to the real amount of income or consumption that a person enjoys. Relative poverty refers to their income relative to the national or global average. (a) Can relative poverty ever be eliminated? (b) What would increase the amount of relative poverty?

3 Drugs companies say that much R&D leads to failure, so it is only the prospect of large profits when they succeed that keeps them in the industry. Poor countries in Sub-Saharan Africa say they should not have to pay high prices for drugs that combat AIDS. Can an economist offer any advice?

4 Countries mainly interact with their near neighbours. There is a lot of evidence that physical distance reduces trade flows and thus acts as a protective barrier. The following table shows much activity falls as distance increases.

% of volume that occurs in countries 1000 kilometres apart

Kilometres apart	Trade	Technology
2000	42	65
4000	18	28
8000	7	5

Do you expect New Zealand or Austria to have more scope for independent national decisions in economy policy? Explain.

5 *Common fallacies* Why are these statements wrong? (a) Globalisation has now led to cross-border migration on an unprecedented scale. (b) Globalisation has made the poor poorer. (c) Aid is all they need.

Answers on pages 278–90

Answers to questions

Section 1-1

1 Sometimes by hierarchy or command (no, you can't have the car tonight!), sometimes by negotiation (I'll do the dishes if you let me go to the cinema), and sometimes using money and prices (you may get pocket money or an allowance, and have some discretion about what you spend it on).

2 All scarce except (b).

3 (a) 20 cakes, (b) 15 shirts, (c) 1.33 cakes.

4 (a), (c) and (e) are positive; (b) and (d) are normative.

5 Wages fall in jobs that students then want to do (beer tasting, modelling, sports commentating!). With lower wages, firms in these industries can cut their prices, raising the quantity sold and hence the demand for workers in doing these jobs.

6 (a) The hypotheses in positive economics *can* be tested against evidence. Support for different political parties may reflect differing normative value judgements. (b) Beginning from an inefficient point, moving to an efficient point yields more of some things and no less of others, a free lunch. Only at an efficient point is no further free lunch available.

Section 1-2

1 (a) Scatter shows that consumption and income tend to rise together. (b) Can fit an upward-sloping straight line through the points, fitting them quite closely. (c) Consumption is a little over 90% of income.

2 (a) Cross-section data (e.g. by county) for crime and unemployment. (b) Collect other data to control for income, police resources and whether urban or rural. Sort counties by these other attributes. Comparing similar countries, examine whether there is a link between more crime and more unemployment. Even if there is, discuss which causes which.

3 Many sciences (e.g. astronomy) cannot conduct laboratory experiments. What matters is the formulation of testable hypotheses and careful examination of whatever relevant data can be collected.

4 Up-sloping line. Rise by 1 in RPI associated with extra £1300 in house prices; time series.

5 (a) 1960 = 100, 1980 = 200, 2000 = 500. (b) 1960 = 20, 1980 = 40, 2000 = 100.

6 (a) Theory organises facts by providing a simple framework in which to interpret them. (b) Molecules are individually random but collectively predictable. People's individual whims cancel out in larger groups.

Section 1-3

1 Equilibrium price £17, quantity 6.5.

2 (a) Excess demand = 5, and price rises. (b) Excess supply = 3, and price falls.

3 Demand curve for toasters shifts down. Equilibrium price and quantity of toasters fall.

4 Supply curve shifts up, so equilibrium price rises but equilibrium quantity falls.

5 Drought, disease, wild dogs all shift supply curve up. Price falls move farmers down *given* supply curve, not a fall in supply.

6 (a) A low enough price can fill any stadium. (b) It shows the effect of a price floor for farm goods that creates excess supply.

Section 2-1

1 (a) Vertical supply, down-sloping demand. (b) To sell 10% fewer baskets, raise the price 20% to £1.20. Vertical supply curve, now at 90 baskets.
2 (a) Inelastic. (b) More elastic. (c) More elastic still.
3 Vegetables: inelastic, necessity. Catering: elastic, luxury.
4 These data are for nominal not real spending on bread, which fell as real income rose.
5 In the short run, people may still be bound by previous contracts and by habit. It takes time to decide to do something different. In the long run, people can adapt to changes in prices more easily.
6 (a) At high enough prices, demand may be price elastic, even for tobacco. If so, raising taxes and the price of cigarettes may so reduce the quantity demanded that tax revenue then falls. When we talk about demand for particular goods being elastic or inelastic, we mean 'in the range of prices normally experienced'. Outside this range, things could be different. (b) If bad weather hits all farmers, it raises prices and helps incomes: 'good' weather needs insurance! (c) Not when they make inferior goods.

Section 2-2

1 (a) False. Luxury good is a statement about the income elasticity, elastic refers to the price elasticity. (b) True. (c) False. Inferior refers to the fall in demand when income changes, not price.
2 First statement is the substitution effect, second statement is the income effect. Since they go in opposite directions, either outcome is possible when both effects operate together.
3 (a) Both effects reduce demand. (b) Demand curve shifts down: equilibrium price and quantity fall.

4 My utility reflects the quantity of bananas, fish and sunshine that I consume. However, in a confined space with my friend, my utility may be affected by the quantity of cigarettes, baked beans and deodorant that my friend consumes. Compassionate people may also care about the amount that their poor neighbours are able to consume.
5 However large the marginal utility of the first beer or first steak, if you had 10 of each within a couple of hours you'd get sick. Long before then, your marginal utility would have become negative. When we assume marginal utility is usually positive, we mean for typical quantities of consumption.
6 (a) Since both nominal income and prices rise, the previous quantities of goods are still affordable and still best of the affordable bundles. (b) There is also an income effect – since tax cuts make people richer, they demand more leisure and hence work less hard.

Section 2-3

1 Knowing that partners can lose all their personal wealth may encourage trust in the activities of the firm.
2 Loss of green fields, of water purity in lakes and of clean air are all examples of depreciation of the stock of environmental capital. To value this depreciation each year would require an annual estimate of the value of environmental capital, which would be expensive to undertake.
3 At the top of each hill, the slope is zero, but one of these is higher than all the others and is the point of maximum height. A firm will maximise profit by choosing an output at which a marginal change in output has no effect on profit (otherwise it could change output to do better), which implies that marginal cost equals marginal revenue. This is the top of one hill. The other hill that it must check out is the hill corresponding to zero output.

4 Some activities that subtract from short-run profits may be viewed as investing in raising long-run profits. Examples may include advertising, starting new products, research and development. However, a private jet for the chief executive's weekend golf in Florida may simply be extravagance.

5 Only the factory is a stock, the rest are all flows.

6 (a) An accounting profit may not cover the opportunity cost of the time and money tied up in the business. (b) A managerial genius may get to the right answer intuitively, but the laws of arithmetic guarantee that marginal cost will equal marginal revenue if profit maximisation is achieved. (c) Sales revenue is maximised when marginal revenue is zero. Since marginal cost is usually above zero, maximising sales revenue means an output that is too high to maximise profits.

Section 3-1

1 A production function relates output to minimum quantities of inputs required. You still need to know input prices and the demand curve for output to calculate profit-maximising output.

2 Scale economies reflect opportunities to spread fixed costs in the short run and to adopt large-scale production methods in the long run. (b) Choose methods 1, 3 and 5 rather than 2, 4 and 6. Average cost thus falls from 8.25 to 8 to 7.25 as output expands. Scale economies are present.

	Methods					
Units of	1	2	3	4	5	6
Labour input	5	6	10	12	15	16
Capital input	4	2	7	4	11	8
Output	4	4	8	8	12	12
Total cost	33	34	64	68	87	96
Average cost	8.25	8.5	8	8.5	7.25	8

3 Methods 1 and 3 still dominate methods 2 and 4, but now method 5 has total cost of 96 and method 6 has total cost of 94, so if demand conditions make the firm want to produce 12 units, it will now use method 6 not 5. However, total cost (and average cost) are higher at each output when any input price is higher.

4

Output	0	1	2	3	4	5	6	7	8
Total cost	12	25	40	51	60	70	84	105	128
Marginal cost		13	15	11	9	10	14	21	23
Average cost		25	20	17	15	14	14	15	16

These are short-run costs. In the long run, the cost of producing zero output is zero.

5 If $MC < AC$, another unit can be produced more cheaply than the average for existing units, dragging down the average. Hence, to the left of minimum average cost, MC is below AC but AC is falling. Conversely, if $MC > AC$, making another unit increases average costs since the extra unit costs more than the existing average cost. Now MC lies above AC and AC is rising. Hence MC must cross AC at the point of minimum average cost.

6 (a) Given time to adjust it may be possible to reduce costs sufficiently to stop losing money. (b) If diseconomies of scale exist, larger output raises average cost and big firms are undercut by smaller firms. (c) If scale economies exist, a firm can reduce average cost by expanding output, thus undercutting its smaller competitors.

Section 3-2

1 Yes, because firm must take the price as given.

2 In the short run, the cost curves of each firm shift down. By shifting down their marginal cost curves, this shifts down their supply curves. Industry output rises and the price falls a bit, but by less than the downward shift in supply. Existing firms are making profits. In the long run, more firms enter until economic profit is driven down to zero. Hence, the price falls further and quantity expands further.

3 When the market is not in equilibrium, either buyers or sellers are frustrated. This creates temporary market power to change the price. For example, with excess demand, a firm raising its price will not lose all its market share to competitors, who do not have the capacity to take advantage of their relatively lower price.

4 Although each firm in both industries has a U-shaped average cost curve, it is much easier in the long run to expand the supply of new hairdressing firms than to discover new coal-fields. Hairdressing has more elastic long-run supply.

5 Ford cars and Vauxhall cars are subtly different and thus not perfect substitutes for one another. Each firm has some scope to vary its price without losing all its market share to the other. Moreover, since each firm is large, each will try to anticipate the effect of its actions on the other firm. They are not price takers and not perfectly competitive.

6 (a) The opportunity cost of everything is being covered when a firm makes only normal profits, so all resources employed are earning the return they need. (b) Each firm's supply curves shift up, and the induced shift in industry supply changes the equilibrium price and quantity.

Section 4-1

1 Q	1	2	3	4	5	6
P	8	7	6	5	4	3
TR	8	14	18	20	20	18
MR	8	6	4	2	0	−2

The monopolist has $Q = 2$, $P = 7$, competitive industry $Q = 4$, $P = 5$. The monopolist's output is lower because marginal revenue is below price. With lower output, it takes a higher price to equate supply and demand.

2 No effect. MC and MR are unaltered, and profits still positive.

3 (a) No effect on profit-maximising output. Maximising pre-tax profit is still the best way to maximise post-tax profits. (b) Marginal profit is zero on the last unit produced since $MC = MR$. (c) This is why decision about the last unit is independent of the rate of profits tax. With zero profit on the last unit, the tax rate is irrelevant at that point.

4 A golf club faces two separate demand curves, from peak users who really want to play then and do not mind paying for it, and off-peak users who can more easily decide when to play. The club wants to equate marginal revenue across the two groups (otherwise it can make more by having more of one group and less of the other). The more inelastic the demand curve, the more price exceeds marginal revenue. Hence the group with the more inelastic demand curve (peak users) pays more.

5 Because raising its price above marginal cost might lead to new entry, either from new firms or in the form of competition from imports. If the threat of competition prevents a single producer raising prices, that firm is not a monopolist.

6 (a) If scale economies are large, breaking up a large firm into smaller units means that each firm then produces at higher cost. This disadvantage could outweigh the benefits of more competition between the firms. (b) Raising its price above marginal cost might lead to new entry, either from new firms or in the form of competition from imports. If the threat of competition prevents a single producer raising prices, that firm is not a monopolist.

Section 4-2

1 (a) $Q = 4$, $P = 7$. (b) Same again. (c) Because each firm has $MC = 3$, but will face $MR > 3$ if it alone expands: price will not fall so much since the other firm is not expanding too.

2

Q	1	2	3	4	5	6	7
P	8	7	6	5	4	3	2
TR	8	14	18	20	20	18	14
MR	8	6	4	2	0	−2	−4

Z makes $Q = 3$, whereas in Question 1(b) dividing the market in half, Z made $Q = 2$.

3 Certification by a reputable agency saves customers the cost of checking themselves. For mechanics, after a bad experience, you can go elsewhere. Reputation helps solve the information problem. For doctors, you might be dead after a bad experience.

4 *Encyclopaedia Britannica* was forced out of the book business and fired its door-to-door sales reps. Instead, it produced a CD of its own and began advertising to computer users, trying to make use of its reputation for producing the definitive high-quality information product.

5 One device is to invest in building a reputation. Much as the parent dislikes punishing the child the first time, the cost of not punishing is a loss of credibility that makes the future tougher for the parent. Recognising this, the parent is more likely to do what was promised. Another device is to reach agreement on parenting with the other parent or with grandparents (who are usually unreliable allies in this!). Then the cost to the parent of not honouring commitments is loss of reputation with several people. Third, do not promise what you know you will not be able subsequently to deliver.

6 (a) You cannot police cheating on the collective agreement. More importantly, new firms then enter, raising output and driving the price down again. (b) If advertising raises the fixed costs of being in the industry, it deters entry and raises profits on existing output.

Section 5-1

1 A firm simultaneously chooses what output to supply and what inputs therefore to demand. The only purpose of hiring inputs is to use them to make output.

2 (a) By assumption other inputs are fixed, so eventually adding more workers means that each worker is handicapped by having fewer other inputs with which to work. This may not happen initially because there may be too many other inputs for a few workers to use effectively. (b) The downward-sloping labour demand curve shifts up. The vertical axis shows the real wage, the horizontal axis shows the level of employment.

3 (a) The substitution effect means work more, but income effect means work less since leisure is a normal good. (b) More people join labour force and extra bodies may compensate for fewer hours per person.

4 The only reason that film studios pay high salaries is because there is high demand for film output in which these stars appear.

5 When the industry is small relative to the whole economy and is a price taker for workers whose wages are determined in the national labour market.

6 (a) Demand is high; and nobody else can supply it. (b) Only via the substitution effect. The income effect means want more leisure.

Section 5-2

1 Screening lets you get a better paid job on leaving university since firms believe they have discovered a talented worker. It would not matter what you study if all degrees are equally difficult. If economics graduates earn more this means (i) that the degree is tougher than others and screens more effectively, or (ii) that human capital in the form of an economics training is a valuable asset.

2 Lose £30 000 while training. Future salary of £23 000 for 30 years repays this.

3 With fewer economists, their scarcity would raise wages by restricting supply. To restrict entry into economics, the union could have tough exams and early morning lectures that are compulsory. Destroy all copies of *Foundations of Economics*, making study more difficult.

4 If it screens out the good doctors of the future, maybe currently disgruntled doctors should recognise that they will get big future salaries as compensation. A second explanation is that young doctors are implicitly paying for their training, a valuable investment in human capital from which they can recoup high future incomes. A third explanation is that it acts as an entry deterrent, maintaining scarcity of future consultants and keeping their incomes high.

5 Unions raising wages in a single competitive firm simply force it out of business, whereas in a monopoly unions that raise wages simply reduce the firm's profit. Although unions could organise the whole of a competitive industry, free entry makes this extremely difficult. So does globalisation and competition from foreign firms. Hence union power is likely to decline further.

6 (a) Neglects the opportunity cost of wages forgone while in education. (b) Not if the unskilled are disproportionately represented in unions in the first place. They might have got even lower wages without unions.

Section 5-3

1 Only (b) is a flow, the rest are stocks.

2 Demand for capital input depends on demand for the firm's output, on quantities of other inputs with which capital co-operates, and on technology. Higher tax on output reduces the demand for all inputs, including capital. The demand curve for capital shifts down for both firm and industry.

3 Required rental falls, so quantity of capital goods demanded increases. Overnight, the capital stock is given, but higher investment gradually raises capital stock. In new long-run equilibrium, with permanently higher capital stock, there is more replacement investment to keep pace with depreciation. Hence the price of capital goods is higher to induce capital goods suppliers to provide this replacement investment. This restores the required rental to its equilibrium level.

4 The land demand is a derived demand. If supply is fixed, only a rise in demand for land can bid up land prices. Tenant farmers face higher rentals but extra income from their crops is what started the process. However, farmers lose out if land prices and rentals bid up by higher demand for housing.

5 People can affect land supply via fertilisers, reclaiming it from the sea, altering the level of land pollution, and many other channels. Nevertheless, the total supply of land is much harder to change than the supply of capital or labour.

6 (a) It also makes future nominal income rise, raising labour demand. (b) Competition between users is what bids up the price to ration the scarce land supply.

Section 5-4

1 A progressive income tax, excise duties on cars (a luxury good) and inheritance tax. However, taxation of tobacco is regressive, since tobacco is an inferior good.

2 With a vertical supply curve for land, upward shifts in the demand for land raise land prices and land rentals. Since richer countries have increasing demand for land, there is no reason why land rentals should not keep pace with the other incomes.

3 Greater dispersion in educational opportunities means that there are many workers earning low wages, whereas in European countries education is more equally distributed. Nor does Brazil have high inheritance taxes as in Europe. And Brazil's welfare state provision is less generous than in Europe.

Section 6-1

1 (a) Efficient, not equitable. (b) Neither efficient nor equitable. (c) Both efficient and equitable. (d) Not efficient nor very equitable. (e) Efficient not equitable. Equitable asks 'How fair is this distribution?'

2 Yes. Taxing (charging) for rush-hour road use would make drivers pay the true social cost. Since rural roads are not congested, nor are urban roads at 5 a.m., a fuel tax is a blunt instrument – it may reduce rush-hour traffic but also wrongly reduces other valuable road usage.

3 Probably, since in deciding whether to fasten your seatbelt you ignore several spillovers onto others. In the event of an accident, you may not pay the full cost of treatment. You may also cause psychological damage on others if you are killed in an accident that need not have been fatal.

4 The first two are public goods, since either everybody enjoys them or nobody does. A post office network has public good aspects, though individual transactions are private goods.

5 (a) For further pollution reduction, marginal cost exceeds marginal benefit once pollution is already low. (b) The same applies to achieving the last little bit of safety: 100% safe is too safe. (c) Monopoly, externalities, etc. are important market failures.

Section 6-2

1 All except (d).

2 All are progressive except tax on beer, which is a larger share of poor people's income.

3 18, 24, 28.8%. It is progressive, and more so the higher the exemption level. With an exemption of £1 million, the tax would only hit the rich!

4 No change in labour supplied, so no distortion triangle. (b) Big triangle, and firms now bear most of the tax. (c) Draw a supply curve and two demand curves of different slope. For a given vertical tax wedge, the gross-of-tax wage rises more when labour demand is steeper.

5 (a) Some taxes offset externalities. (b) Existence of marginal taxes still induces people to change the quantities that they supply and demand.

Section 6-3

1 Competitive price is £5. Under monopoly, the social cost triangle has height of £3 (the amount by which price exceeds £5), and length of 200 000 (the output fall). Hence cost is £300 000.

2 The triangle now has height £1 and length less than 200 000 since quantity demanded will lie between 800 000 and 1 million. So the social cost is less than £200 000. A price ceiling of £5 will achieve the efficient outcome, since monopolist will regard £5 as marginal revenue and produce as under perfect competition.

3 *MC* lies below *MC* while *AC* is still falling. Although efficient point is where *MC* crosses demand curve, setting that price as a price ceiling would entail losses since *MC* < *AC*. A private monopolist would rather quit.

4 Generally, the need for merger control is less when the market is larger. However, creation of a global monopoly would be worrying, for example if Boeing merged with Airbus, or if all the mobile phone companies merged.

5 (a) Profit may just reflect monopoly power. (b) Private benefit of mergers may include monopoly profits, which are a social cost.

Section 7-1

1 (a) Adding the value addeds: 670 + 190 + 50 + 50 = 960.

2 GDP = 303, national income = 267.

3 GDP falls initially but the country is potentially better off since labour can now be diverted to making other things.

4 (a) Leisure is lost but investment in human capital occurs. (b) No – just a transfer payment. (c) Yes. (d) Pollution should ideally be subtracted from GNP.

5 (a) Just a transfer payment, not real output. (b) Only because people compare nominal receipts. In real terms, *Gone With The Wind* wins by a mile!

Section 7-2

1 (a) Upsloping line with slope 0.7 and intercept 45. At $Y = 100$, $AD = 70 + 45 = 115$. Excess demand and unplanned destocking, so output then rises. Equilibrium output $= I/(1 - c) = 45/0.3 = 450/3 = 150$.

2 (a) Falls from 500 to 300. (b) Since $S = I$, the ratio S/Y rises from 150/500 to 150/300.

3 The first diagram has a horizontal investment line but the upward-sloping desired saving line shifts left, reducing equilibrium output. The second diagram has an upward-sloping AD line with intercept at 150. When desired saving increases, desired consumption falls, and AD rotates flatter as slope falls from 0.7 to 0.5, thus reducing equilibrium output.

4 (a) Equilibrium $Y = 400/0.2 = 2000$. (b) Equilibrium $Y = (400 + 100)/[0.3] = 1667$.

5 (a) There is no causal link between rise in desire to save and change in desired investment. (b) Provided the marginal propensity to consume is smaller than 1, each fall in output induces a smaller fall in AD, so AD and Y eventually converge to new lower level, as the multiplier formula promises.

Section 7-3

1 (a) $Y = 1000$, $C = 800$, $I = 80$, so $G = 120$. (b) When I rises by 50, equilibrium output must rise by 250, so C rises by 200. (c) Yes. (d) $C = 0.8 \times 1200 = 960$, $I = 80$. Hence $G = 160$.

2 Desired injections must equal desired leakages in equilibrium. Desired saving and investment are equal only if the other parts of desired leakages and injections equal one another.

3 Debt would spiral, implying very high future tax payments and perhaps even bankruptcy. Long before this people would choose to stop lending to the government.

4 Multiplier $= 1/[1 + MPZ - (1 - t)MPS] = 1/(1 + 0.4 - 0.04) = 1/(1.36)$. Hence when investment demand rises 136, equilibrium output rises by 100. (b) Equilibrium again rises by 100. Hence desired imports rise by 40. Since exports rise by 136, trade balance improves by 96.

5 (a) A balanced budget multiplier implies aggregate demand will rise. (b) When domestic output falls, import demand will fall and the trade balance will improve.

Section 8-1

1 (a) No. It cannot be used directly to finance subsequent transactions. (b) Watch which is then retraded, not swallowed.

2 By simultaneously creating loans and deposits to match, without requiring a new deposit as part of the transaction. If the reserve requirement is 100% banks are unable to do this, and can no longer create money.

3 (a) They have a once-off use as money but are not subsequently retraded repeatedly. (b) No. (c) They reduce your demand for money, but do not affect supply: credit card stubs cannot be reused to purchase other goods.

4 M0 $= 12 + 2 = 14$, M4 $= 12 + 30 + 60 + 20 = 122$.

5 (a) Most of the money supply is bank deposits, a liability of banks. By simultaneously expanding both sides of their balance sheet, banks increase the money supply. (b) If people put less cash in banks, banks are less able to multiply up reserves into deposits.

Section 8-2

1 The money multiplier $= 1$.

2 They would need less money for precautionary purposes.

3 The opportunity cost of holding money is unaffected by change in interest rates.

4 Data must come out before the data on the variable one is really interested in, and must be reliably correlated with that subsequent data.

5 (a) With more cash in the banks and less with the public, banks can multiply up into more bank deposits. (b) If inflation is negative, the real value of cash is rising at the same rate at which prices are falling.

Section 8-3

1 Initially, the consumption function shifts up (and desired saving falls), since people want to spend more at any income level. Eventually, since people having to pay interest on this new debt, income available for buying goods and services falls and the consumption function shifts down.

2 It makes consumption demand more sensitive to changes in interest rates.

3 UK aggregate demand is reduced. If the government wants to maintain the original level of UK demand, it should loosen fiscal policy. Even without a change in policy, automatic stabilisers will act partly in this direction.

4 Investment rises in advance to get new capacity in place. This raises current output, forcing monetary policy to raise interest rates in order to keep inflation on track. Higher interest rates have most effect on long-term investment.

5 (a) It could be rational if either (i) interest rates have fallen or (ii) people have raised their estimates of expected future income. (b) This is true if people can lend and borrow as much as they want at the going interest rate. However, if lenders require collateral people may be unable to borrow as much as they wish. The quantity of lending will then be important.

Section 9-1

1 Long-run aggregate supply and potential output increase. Eventually, monetary policy will accommodate this supply shock in full, allowing aggregate demand to rise by the same amount. Interest rates will be lower. In the short run, the first effect of more workers may be more unemployment. Eventually, this induces existing workers to reduce wage inflation, shifting the short-run supply curve downwards. Monetary policy will begin cutting interest rates since inflation is now below target and output is now below its new level of potential output. Eventually, demand and output are higher and inflation is unaltered.

2 See the preceding answer.

3 Not if real money demand is changing because of changes in output or changes in the cost of holding money.

4 Aggregate demand rises so the Bank raises interest rates. Hence investment may fall if the interest rate effect outweighs the benefit of higher output. Since aggregate demand exceeds potential output (otherwise there is no reason to have raised interest rates), tax revenue is higher via the automatic stabilisers.

5 (a) Firms' prices rise too. (b) Consumer incomes rise too.

Section 9-2

1 We say that the real interest rate is 2% in both cases. Although on average the same over the life of the contract, the two scenarios are not identical. With zero inflation, your real income and real interest payments are the same year after year. Because lenders (stupidly) insist on constant annual payments even during inflation, when inflation is 100% the initial payments are very high in real terms, but after a few years this constant nominal repayment has shrunk in real terms to a tiny value. If lenders wanted to make you pay a constant annual stream of payments in real terms, then in a world of inflation they would have to arrange loan contracts so that you pay higher nominal payments later in the contract.

2 There is only a weak short-run correlation between money growth and inflation. Different changes in output in different countries are one possible explanation. With stock markets doing badly, large money growth in Japan and the US may also have reflected higher asset demand for money as people baled out of the stock market.

3 Supply shocks should lead inflation and unemployment to move in the same direction, whereas demand shocks should make inflation and unemployment move in opposite directions to one another.

4 Surprise inflation hits people with fixed nominal incomes (lenders, holders of cash, pensioners). Bonds and pensions could have adjusted their nominal payout had inflation been correctly foreseen, but the zero nominal return on cash cannot be adjusted even when inflation is foreseen.

5 (a) Not if nominal interest rates have risen to protect real interest rates. (b) Firms' revenues will also rise in nominal terms. (c) Menu and shoeleather costs cannot be avoided.

Section 9-3

1 Reduced demand for some types of labour, raised demand for others. There is a temporary mismatch, but eventually skills and wages adjust. Millennia of technical progress would have driven unemployment to 100% if there were any permanent relationship between technical progress and unemployment.

2 (a) Deficient demand in the economy. (b) The real wage is too high, for example because of union power or generous welfare benefits.

3 (a) By reducing distortions, it may raise equilibrium output. Also initially it raises aggregate demand. The latter effect is faster and probably larger, so the boom and monetary policy raises interest rates to keep inflation on track. (b) The main effect is a boost to aggregate demand, helping restore output to potential output.

4 Teenagers need training from scratch – they lack skills and job experience; teenage wages are not low enough to compensate.

5 (a) Not if it is equilibrium unemployment. (b) Not if it is Keynesian unemployment.

Section 10-1

1 (a) BoP surplus £2 bn. (b) Reserves rising. (c) Selling domestic currency to buy reserves.

2 Deficit countries are likely to be forced by their creditors into more rapid adjustment. Surplus countries can adjust more slowly if they wish. There is no limit to the foreign assets that a country can build up; it is simply that it is not optimal to save for ever if the purpose of saving is eventually to finance additional consumption.

3 The largest effect is (c) then (a) then (b). No effect in (b) since the interest rate is fixed. In (c) change in interest rates not only affects domestic consumption and investment but induces a change in the floating exchange rate that alters net exports in the same direction.

4 If the initial exchange rate is too low (high), an appreciation is good (bad).

5 (a) They can still change interest rates thus (partly) manipulating the incentives of speculators. (b) Exchange rate volatility chiefly reflects changes in the demand for assets by speculators.

Section 10-2

1 No, because national money markets are still segmented.

2 *For*: Eliminating exchange rate fluctuations with main trading partners will enhance integration with that large market; enhance competition; enhance price transparency; reduce transaction costs of business and tourists; make inward investment to UK more likely (e.g. by Asian firms wanting a foothold in the Eurozone market); raise influence in the EU. *Against*: Loss of monetary sovereignty and ability to set its own interest rate; correlation with Eurozone countries high but not very high; possible restrictions on fiscal policy are implied by the Stability Pact; fear of further European integration.

3 Changes in industries and products over the entire future are bound to require some changes in relative prices. Preventing this would be misguided and ultimately impossible. However, real exchange rates can alter even when nominal exchange rates are pegged. The more flexible are domestic prices and wages, the more easily this is accomplished.

4 With large budget deficits outlawed by the Stability Pact, debt/GDP ratios will probably fall in the long run if GDP grows steadily. If the Pact was devised to reduce concerns about debt (as distinct from deficits) it may thus eventually become unnecessary in the tight form in which it presently exists.

5 (a) If the shocks are common to member states, the single interest rate can achieve adjustment for all. For country-specific shocks, there is some scope for using fiscal policy, especially prudent governments that were not too close to the 3% deficit ceiling before the shock occurred. (b) There is quite a lot of empirical evidence that act of joining is likely to raise correlations above previous levels.

Section 11-1

1 Compare with other countries to see if it is factually true that we are different. For different countries, correlate long-run growth with usual explanations (labour input, capital input, etc.) and see if there is an extra role for the fraction of the population who are scientists or engineers. Private and social benefits differ if there are externalities (some skills make it easier for people with other skills). Subsidies to education also imply discrepancy between private and social cost.

2 Pollution and congestion. We can quantify and value some (e.g. how much house prices are lower under airport flight path). As information technology lets us record data better, it will get easier to include them in GNP.

3 Land input has increased much less than labour, without big diminishing returns to labour. We accumulated other factors (human and physical capital) as substitutes for land, and technical progress invented ways to economise on land. The same is already happening for other scarce inputs.

4 In terms of Figure 11.1, country with higher population growth has steeper nk line, which therefore intersects the sy curve further to the left. This implies a lower level k of capital per person, and hence a lower level y of output per person.

5 (a) Same answer as in Question 3 above. (b) A higher saving rate makes the sy curve intersect the nk line further to the right. This raises capital per person and output per person. However, output, capital and labour all grow at the rate n, which is independent of the saving rate s. If technical progress is also present, output and capital grow at the rate $(t + n)$, and labour grows at n, but again changes in the saving rate have no effect.

Section 11-2

1 Beginning with output of 100, a rise in investment from 0 to 10 has the following effects:

Period	Change in last period's output $Y_{t-1} - Y_{t-2}$	Investment I_t	Output Y_t
$t + 1$	0	10	100
$t + 2$	0	10	120
$t + 3$	20	20	140
$t + 4$	20	20	140
$t + 5$	0	10	120
$t + 6$	220	0	100
$t + 7$	220	0	100
$t + 8$	0	10	120
$t + 9$	20	20	140

2 Forecasting future cycles would kill the multiplier–accelerator model, which depends on mechanical extrapolation of past trends and hence depends on having expectations that are systematically in error.

3 It might accentuate a global political business cycle. With elections at different dates, pre-election booms are more diffuse, occurring at different dates in different countries, which may help stabilise the global economy.

4 The cause lies not in fluctuations in nominal money, or monetary policy, but rather in real shocks such as views about future technology and productivity growth. More generally, the theory tries to explain cycles without nominal rigidities and constraints on adjustment speeds. Persistence is optimal because of intertemporal substitution.

5 (a) Closer integration accentuates international transmission mechanism of booms and slumps, e.g. US high-tech bust of 2001 quickly spread to Europe. (b) The multiplier–accelerator model relies on *failure* to forecast future output correctly. If we anticipated a future slowdown this would already help reduce the current boom.

Section 12-1

1 No. The equilibrium exchange rate can be low enough to offset any absolute disadvantage. To enjoy efficiency gains from comparative advantage, it should allow trade. The UK gains by importing cheap trainers made in China and the Dominican Republic.

2 Small countries cannot enjoy scale economies without international trade, and for this reason rely on it more and benefit more. Additionally, trade by large countries also bids the world price in an adverse direction from their viewpoint.

3 Wine and cars have high two-way trade based on choice and differentiation, steel is based more on comparative advantage and one way.

4 (a) No. Government may as well have the tax revenue too. (b) Domestic art buyers gain since prices fall. Domestic artists lose out, so too foreign art buyers. (c) Probably not.

5 (a) Changes in the exchange rate cope with the changes in the average level of absolute advantage, and every country then has a comparative advantage in something. (b) Not always. The optimal tariff is an example in which a large country gains by a departure from free trade. (c) Fails to exploit comparative advantage and the gains from trade.

Section 12-2

1 Technical progress in agriculture (e.g. winter wheat). Application of machinery and fertiliser to raise land productivity. Both augmented supply a lot, driving down the equilibrium price.

2 They require intensive but low-skilled labour, which LDCs have in relative abundance, but do not need very sophisticated technology and shipping of the finished products is cheap and easy.

3 The debt/GDP ratio stays constant. If output growth then stagnates, the debt/GDP ratio starts to grow because of cumulative interest so eventually the country must run a trade surplus to earn foreign exchange to pay interest to foreign creditors.

4 (a) Declining industries in Western Europe, such as shipbuilding, crude steel and agriculture, cause political difficulties when imports flow in. (b) These are precisely the industries in which Central and Eastern Europe was likely initially to have a comparative advantage.

5 (a) LDCs often argue that aid encourages dependence. They want foreign investment, less protection by rich countries, technology transfer, and debt relief to wipe out mistakes of the past. (b) Europe would make a net gain from greater exploitation of comparative advantage, even though vociferous particular losers have so far blocked the process.

Section 12-3

1 Consumers like variety, but if this is the only argument they should be prepared to pay the appropriately higher price to get it. A cultural heritage may be more like a public good, however, in which case some subsidy may be appropriate. If so, it should take the form of production subsidies not tariffs (the principle of targeting again).

2 (a) Suppose relative poverty is defined as x% of the average income. By definition, there are always some people in this category, and it cannot be eliminated simply by economic growth for everyone. (b) The number in relative poverty would increase (i) if the definition was tightened (e.g. changed from those below 10% of average income to those below 20% of average income) or if the dispersion of incomes increased (in which case the average is unaltered but there are more people in the very rich and very poor groups).

3 When the market is small, it takes a high profit rate to compensate drug companies for the risks they have taken. In principle, with a larger market it now takes a smaller profit per sale to offer the same total reward. Hence, if anything, globalisation eases the conflict between the need to provide adequate rewards for risky research and the need to keep the price down so that the poor can afford key drugs. More-over, if companies making AIDS drugs had *already* been rewarded by their sales in rich markets, there may be no economic case for having them charge such high prices in new LDC markets.

4 Austria is very close to its major trading partners (particularly Germany) and thus faces extensive competition in deciding tax rates, interest rates and regulations; this is why Austria was quite happy to join the EU and adopt the euro. In contrast, New Zealand is shielded by distance from both the US and the EU, and effectively has more scope to make national decisions.

5 (a) The really big migrations (to the US and Australia) took place in the nineteenth century. (b) Absolute poverty has declined and there is quite a lot of evidence that international trade helps economic growth, which is the main solution to national poverty. (c) Trade liberalis-ation would almost certainly be more important than any level of aid that rich countries are likely to offer.

Glossary

Chapter 1

Section 1-1

Page 1

Economics is the study of how society decides what, how and for whom to produce.

Page 3

For a scarce resource, the quantity demanded at a zero price would exceed the available supply.

The opportunity cost of a good is the quantity of *other* goods sacrificed to get another unit of *this* good.

Page 4

A market uses prices to reconcile decisions about consumption and production.

In a command economy government planners decide what, how and for whom goods and services are made. Households, firms and workers are then told what to do.

In a free market economy, prices adjust to reconcile desires and scarcity.

Page 5

In a mixed economy, the government and private sector interact in solving economic problems.

Positive economics deals with scientific explanation of how the economy works. Normative economics offers recommendations based on personal value judgements.

Page 6

Microeconomics makes a detailed study of individual decisions about particular commodities.

Macroeconomics analyses interactions in the economy as a whole.

Section 1-2

Page 8

A model or theory makes assumptions from which it deduces how people behave. It deliberately simplifies reality.

Data are pieces of evidence about economic behaviour.

Page 9

Nominal values are measured in the prices at the time of measurement. Real values adjust nominal values for changes in the general price level.

An index number expresses data relative to a given base value.

Page 10

A scatter diagram plots pairs of values simultaneously observed for two different variables.

Page 11

Other things equal is a device for looking at the relation between two variables, but remembering other variables also matter.

Section 1-3

Page 14

Demand is the quantity buyers wish to purchase at each conceivable price.

Supply is the quantity sellers wish to sell at each conceivable price.

Page 15

The equilibrium price clears the market for chocolate. It is the price at which the quantity supplied equals the quantity demanded.

Page 16

A rise in the price of one good raises the demand for substitutes for this good, but reduces the demand for complements to the good.

Page 16

For a normal good demand rises when incomes rise. For an inferior good demand falls when incomes rise.

Page 19

A price control is a government regulation to fix the price.

Chapter 2

Section 2-1

Page 22

Price elasticity of demand = (% change in Q_D) / (% change in P)

Page 23

Demand is elastic if the price elasticity is more negative than −1. Demand is inelastic if the price elasticity lies between −1 and 0. If the demand elasticity is exactly −1, demand is unit-elastic

Page 26

The cross-price elasticity of good A with respect to the price of good B is the percentage change in Q_A divided by the percentage change in P_B.

The budget share of a good is the spending on that good as a fraction of total consumer spending.

Page 27

$$\text{Income elasticity of demand} = \frac{\text{percentage change in quantity demanded}}{\text{percentage change in income}}$$

The income elasticity of demand is positive for a normal good, but negative for an inferior good.

A luxury good has an income elasticity above 1. A necessity has an income elasticity below 1.

Section 2-2

Page 30

The substitution effect says that, when the relative price of a good falls, quantity demanded rises.

The income effect says, for a given nominal income, a fall in the price of a good raises real income, affecting the demand for all goods.

Page 31

Saving means not spending all today's income, reducing consumption today to raise consumption later.

Tastes describe the utility a consumer gets from the goods consumed. Utility is happiness or satisfaction.

Page 32

The marginal utility of a good is the *extra* utility from consuming one more unit of the good, holding constant the quantity of other goods consumed.

Tastes display diminishing marginal utility from a good if each extra unit adds successively less to total utility when consumption of other goods remains constant.

Page 34

The market demand curve is the horizontal sum of individual demand curves in that market.

Section 2-3

Page 36

Stocks are measured at a point in time, flows are corresponding measures over a period of time.

A firm's revenue is income from sales during the period, its costs are expenses incurred in production and sales during the period, and its profits are the excess of revenue over costs.

Cash flow is the net amount of money received by a firm during a given period.

Page 37

Opportunity cost is the amount lost by not using resources in their best alternative use.

Normal profit is the accounting profit to break even after all economic costs are paid. Economic (supernormal) profits in excess of normal profit are a signal to switch resources into the industry. Economic losses mean that the resources could earn more elsewhere.

Physical capital is any input to production not used up within the production period. Examples include machinery, equipment and buildings. *Investment* is additions to physical capital.

Depreciation is the cost of using capital during the period.

Assets are what the firm owns. Liabilities are what it owes. Net worth is assets minus liabilities.

Page 40

The total cost curve shows the lowest-cost way to make each output level. Total cost rises as output rises.

Marginal cost is the change in total cost as a result of producing the last unit.

Total revenue is the output price times the quantity made and sold. Marginal revenue is the change in total revenue as a result of making and selling the last unit.

Page 41

The marginal principle says that, if the slope is not zero, moving in one direction must make things better, moving the other way makes things worse. Only at a maximum (or a minimum) is the slope temporarily zero.

Chapter 3

Section 3-1

Page 45

Technical efficiency means no other technique could make the same output with fewer inputs. Technology is all the techniques known today. Technical progress is the discovery of a new technique that makes a given output with fewer inputs than before.

Long-run total cost LTC is the lowest cost of making each output level when a firm can adjust fully. Long-run marginal cost LMC is the rise in LTC if output permanently rises by one unit. Long-run average cost LAC is LTC divided by the level of output.

Page 46

There are economies of scale (or increasing returns to scale) if long-run average cost LAC falls as output rises, constant returns to scale if LAC is constant as output rises, and diseconomies of scale (or decreasing returns to scale) if LAC rises as output rises.

Page 47

The lowest output at which all scale economies are achieved is called minimum efficient scale.

Page 49

A fixed input cannot be varied in the short run. A variable input can be adjusted, even in the short run.

Page 50

Fixed costs do not vary with output levels. Variable costs change with output.

The marginal product of a variable factor (labour) is the extra output from adding 1 unit of the variable factor, holding constant the input of all other factors (capital, land) in the short run.

Page 51

Holding all factors constant except one, the law of diminishing returns says that, beyond some level of the variable input, further rises in the variable input steadily reduce the marginal product of that input.

Short-run marginal cost SMC is the extra cost of making one more unit of output in the short-run while some inputs are fixed.

Short-run average fixed cost is short-run fixed cost divided by output. Short-run average variable cost is short-run variable cost divided by output. Short-run average total cost is short-run total cost divided by output.

Page 52

A firm's short-run supply decision is to make Q_1, the output at which $MR = SMC$, provided the price covers short-run average variable cost $SAVC_1$ at this output. If the price is less than $SAVC_1$ the firm produces zero.

Section 3-2

Page 56

In perfect competition, actions of individual buyers and sellers have no effect on the market price.

Page 57

A competitive firm's short-run supply curve is that part of its short-run marginal cost curve above its shutdown price.

Page 59

A competitive firm's long-run supply curve is that part of its long-run marginal cost above minimum average cost. At any price below P_3 the firm leaves the industry. At the price P_3 the firm makes Q_3 and just breaks even after paying all its economic costs.

Entry is when new firms join an industry. Exit is when existing firms leave.

Chapter 4

Section 4-1

Page 65

A monopolist is the sole supplier or potential supplier of the industry's output.

Page 66

Monopoly power is measured by price *minus* marginal cost.

Page 68

A discriminating monopoly charges different prices to different buyers.

Section 4-2

Page 72

An imperfectly competitive firm recognises that its demand curve slopes down.

An oligopoly is an industry with only a few, interdependent producers. An industry with monopolistic competition has many sellers making products that are close but not perfect substitutes for one another. Each firm then has a limited ability to affect its output price.

Page 73

A natural monopoly enjoys sufficient scale economies to have no fear of entry by others.

Page 75

Collusion is an explicit or implicit agreement between existing firms to avoid competition.

Page 77

A game is a situation in which intelligent decisions are necessarily interdependent.

A strategy is a game plan describing how the player will act or move in each situation.

In Nash equilibrium, each player chooses his best strategy, *given* the strategies chosen by other players.

Page 79

A commitment is an arrangement, entered into voluntarily, that restricts one's future actions.

Page 80

A credible threat is one that, after the fact, it is still optimal to carry out.

A contestable market has free entry and free exit.

Page 81

An innocent entry barrier is one made by nature.

Your strategic move influences the other player's decision, in a manner helpful to you, by affecting the other person's expectations of how you will behave.

Page 82

Strategic entry deterrence is behaviour by incumbent firms to make entry less likely.

Chapter 5

Section 5-1

Page 86

The marginal product of labour MPL is the extra physical output when a worker is added, holding other inputs constant.

The marginal revenue product of labour MRPL is the change in sales revenue when an extra worker's output is sold.

Page 87

A monopsonist must raise the wage to attract extra labour.

Page 89

The labour force is everyone in work or seeking a job.

Page 90

The participation rate is the fraction of people of working age who join the labour force.

The poverty trap means that getting a job makes a person worse off than staying at home.

Section 5-2

Page 96

Human capital is the stock of accumulated expertise that raises a worker's productivity.

Page 98

A closed shop means that all a firm's workers must be members of a trade union.

Section 5-3

Page 101

Physical capital is the stock of produced goods used to make other goods and services. Land is the input that nature supplies.

Gross investment is the production of new capital goods and the improvement of existing capital goods. Net investment is gross investment minus the depreciation of the existing capital stock.

Page 102

A stock is the quantity of an asset at a point in time (e.g. 100 machines on 1 January 2003). A flow is the stream of services that an asset provides in a given period. The cost of using capital services is the rental rate for capital. The asset price is the sum for which the stock can be bought, entitling its owner to the future stream of capital services from that asset.

Page 103

The required rental is the income per period that allows the buyer of a capital asset to break even.

The marginal revenue product of capital MRPK is the extra revenue from selling the extra output that an extra unit of capital allows, holding constant all other inputs.

Section 5-4

Page 109

The functional income distribution is the division of national income between the different production inputs.

Page 110

The personal income distribution shows how national income is divided between people, regardless of the inputs from which these people earn their income.

Chapter 6

Section 6-1

Page 112

Horizontal equity is the identical treatment of identical people. Vertical equity is the different treatment of different people in order to reduce the consequences of these innate differences.

Page 113

For given tastes, inputs and technology, an allocation is efficient if no one can then be made better off without making at least one other person worse off.

Page 114

A distortion or market failure exists if society's marginal cost of making a good does not equal society's marginal benefit from consuming that good.

An externality arises if a production or consumption decision affects the physical production or consumption possibilities of other people.

Page 117

A free rider, knowing he cannot be excluded from consuming a good, has no incentive to buy it.

Page 118

A public good is necessarily consumed in equal amounts by everyone.

Page 119

Moral hazard exploits inside information to take advantage of the other party to the contract.

Adverse selection means individuals use their inside information to accept or reject a contract. Those accepting are no longer an average sample of the population.

Section 6-2

Page 122

If T is the amount paid in tax, and Y is income, then T/Y is the average tax rate. The marginal tax rate shows how total tax T increases as income Y increases.

Page 123

Direct taxes are taxes on income, indirect taxes are taxes on spending.

Page 124

Tax incidence is the final tax burden once we allow for all the induced effects of the tax.

The tax wedge is the gap between the price paid by the buyer and the price received by the seller.

Section 6-3

Page 128

There are two social costs of monopoly power. The first is too little output, the second is wastefully high cost curves.

Page 129

Competition policy promotes efficiency through competition between firms. The Competition Commission examines whether a monopoly, or potential monopoly, is against the public interest.

Page 130

A merger is the union of two companies where they think they will do better by amalgamating.

Page 131

A natural monopoly, having vast scale economies, does not fear entry by smaller competitors.

Chapter 7

Section 7-1

Page 134
Macroeconomics studies the economy as a whole.

Page 135
The circular flow is the flow of inputs, outputs and payments between firms and households.

Page 136
Gross domestic product (GDP) measures an economy's output.

Value added is net output, after deducting goods used up during the production process.

Saving S is the part of income not spent buying output. Investment I is firms' purchases of new capital goods made by other firms.

Saving is a leakage from the circular flow, money paid to households but *not* returned to firms as spending. Investment is an injection to the circular flow, money earned by firms but *not* from sales to households. Leakages always equal injections, as a matter of definition

Page 137
Exports X are made at home but sold abroad. Imports Z are made abroad but bought at home.

Page 138
Gross National Product GNP is the total income of citizens wherever it is earned. It is GDP plus net property income from abroad.

Depreciation is the fall in value of the capital stock during the period through use and obsolescence.

National income is GNP minus depreciation during the period.

Nominal GNP is measured at the prices when income was earned. Real GNP adjusts for inflation by valuing GNP in different years at the prices prevailing at a particular date.

Section 7-2

Page 142
Potential output is national output when all inputs are fully employed. The output gap is the difference between actual output and potential output.

Page 143
Personal disposable income is household income from firms, plus government transfers, minus taxes. It is household income available to be spent or saved.

Page 144
The consumption function relates desired consumption to personal disposable income.

The marginal propensity to consume MPC is the fraction of each extra pound of disposable income that households wish to consume.

Page 145
Aggregate demand is total desired spending at each level of income.

Short-run equilibrium output is where aggregate demand equals actual output.

Page 146
The saving function shows desired saving at each income level. The marginal propensity to save MPS is the fraction of each extra pound of income that households wish to save.

Page 148
The multiplier is the ratio of the change in equilibrium output to the change in demand that caused output to change.

Page 149
The paradox of thrift is that a change in the desire to save changes equilibrium output and income, but not equilibrium saving.

Section 7-3

Page 152
Fiscal policy is the government's decisions about spending and taxes.

Page 153
Automatic stabilisers reduce fluctuations in aggregate demand by reducing the multiplier. All leakages act as automatic stabilisers.

Page 154
The balanced budget multiplier means that a rise in government spending initially matched by higher taxes induces a rise in equilibrium output.

Page 155
The trade balance is the value of net exports. When exports exceed imports, the economy has a trade surplus. When imports exceed exports, it has a trade deficit.

Page 156

The marginal propensity to import (MPZ) is the fraction of each extra pound of national income that domestic residents want to spend on extra imports.

Chapter 8

Section 8-1

Page 159

Money is any generally accepted means of payment for delivery of goods or settlement of debt. It is the medium of exchange

A barter economy has no medium of exchange. Goods are simply swapped for other goods.

Page 160

The unit of account is the unit in which prices are quoted and accounts are kept.

Money is also a store of value, available for future purchases.

A token money has a value as money that greatly exceeds its cost of production or value in consumption.

An IOU money is a medium of exchange based on the debt of a private bank.

Bank reserves are cash in the bank to meet possible withdrawals by depositors. The reserve ratio is the ratio of reserves to deposits.

Page 163

The money supply is money in circulation, namely cash outside the bank vaults, plus bank deposits on which cheques can be written.

Page 164

The monetary base is the supply of cash, whether in private circulation or held in bank reserves. The money multiplier is the ratio of the money supply to the monetary base.

Section 8-2

Page 167

A central bank is responsible for printing money, setting interest rates, and acting as banker to commercial banks and the government.

Page 168

An open market operation is a central bank purchase or sale of securities in the open market in exchange for cash.

The lender of last resort lends to banks when financial panic threatens the financial system.

Page 169

The cost of holding money is the interest given up by holding money rather than bonds.

The demand for money is a demand for *real* money balances *M/P*.

Page 173

The monetary instrument is the variable over which a central bank exercises day-to-day control.

Section 8-3

Page 176

The transmission mechanism of monetary policy is the process by which interest rates affect aggregate demand and output.

The real interest rate, the difference between the nominal interest rate and inflation, is what measures the real cost of borrowing and the real return on lending.

Page 177

Borrowers offer collateral to lenders by handing over legal title to assets that the creditor can seize if the borrower fails to repay the loan.

Page 178

The credit channel of monetary policy is the effect of lower interest rates in boosting aggregate demand by raising the value of collateral and thus the ability to borrow and spend.

The investment demand schedule shows desired investment at each interest rate.

Page 181

Crowding out is a fall in private demand caused by higher government spending that induces the central bank to raise interest rates.

Demand management is the use of monetary and fiscal policy to stabilise output near the level of potential output.

Chapter 9

Section 9-1

Page 184

The classical model of macroeconomics assumes wages and prices are completely flexible.

The aggregate supply schedule shows the output firms wish to supply at each inflation rate.

Page 184

Inflation illusion exists if people confuse nominal and real variables.

Page 185

In the classical model, the aggregate supply schedule is vertical at potential output.

Following an inflation target, a central bank raises real interest rates if it expects inflation to be too high, and cuts real interest rates if it expects inflation to be too low.

Page 186

Monetary policy accommodates a permanent supply change by reducing the average level of real interest rates, thereby raising aggregate demand in line with higher aggregate supply.

Page 187

In the classical model, there is complete crowding out. Higher government spending causes an equivalent reduction in private spending, since total output cannot change.

Page 188

The short-run supply curve *SAS* shows how desired output varies with inflation, for a given inherited growth of nominal wages.

The output gap is actual output minus potential output.

Section 9-2

Page 192

The quantity theory of money says that changes in the quantity of nominal money *M* lead to equivalent changes in prices *P*, but have no effect on real output.

Hyperinflation is high inflation, above 50 per cent *per month*.

Page 193

The Phillips curve shows that higher inflation is accompanied by lower unemployment.

Equilibrium unemployment *U** is the level of unemployment in long-run equilibrium.

The long-run Phillips curve is vertical at equilibrium unemployment.

Each short-run Phillips curve is a negative relation between inflation and unemployment, given the inflation expectations already built into nominal wages.

Page 195

Shoe-leather costs of inflation is shorthand for the extra time and effort in transacting when inflation reduces desired real cash holdings.

Menu costs of inflation are the physical resources used in changing price tags, reprinting catalogues and changing vending machines.

Section 9-3

Page 200

The labour force is everyone who has a job or wants one. The unemployment rate is the fraction of the labour force without a job.

Page 201

Frictional unemployment is the irreducible minimum unemployment in a dynamic society.

Page 202

Structural unemployment reflects a mismatch of skills and job opportunities when the pattern of employment is changing.

Demand-deficient unemployment occurs when output is below full capacity.

Classical unemployment arises when the wage is kept above its long-run equilibrium level.

Page 203

Voluntary unemployment is people looking for work who will not yet take a job at that real wage.

Equilibrium unemployment is unemployment when the labour market is in equilibrium.

Involuntary unemployment means the unemployed would take a job offer at the existing wage.

Chapter 10

Section 10-1

Page 209

The foreign exchange (forex) market exchanges one national currency for another. The exchange rate is the price at which two currencies exchange.

Page 210

A fixed exchange rate means that governments, acting through their central banks, will buy or sell as much of the currency as people want to exchange at the fixed rate.

Page 211

The foreign exchange reserves are the foreign currency holdings of the domestic central bank.

A devaluation (revaluation) is a fall (rise) in the fixed exchange rate.

In a floating exchange rate regime, the exchange rate is allowed to find its free market equilibrium without any intervention using the foreign exchange reserves.

The balance of payments records all transactions between a country and the rest of the world.

Page 212

The current account of the balance of payments records international flows of goods, services and transfer payments.

Page 213

The capital account of the balance of payments records net purchases and sales of foreign assets.

The balance of payments records the net monetary inflow from abroad when households, firms, and the government make their desired transactions.

Page 214

The real exchange rate is the relative price of domestic and foreign goods, when measured in a common currency.

Page 216

Perfect capital mobility means expected total returns on assets in different currencies must be equal if huge capital flows are to be avoided. A positive interest differential must be offset by an expected exchange rate fall of equal magnitude. This is the interest parity condition.

Internal balance means aggregate demand equals potential output. External balance means that the current account of the balance of payments is zero. Long-run equilibrium requires both.

Section 10-2

Page 226

A monetary union has permanently fixed exchange rates within the union, an integrated financial market and a single central bank setting the single interest rate.

Page 227

An optimal currency area is a group of countries better off with a common currency than keeping separate national currencies.

Chapter 11

Section 11-1

Page 232

Economic growth is the rate of change of real income or real output.

Potential output is the level of GDP when all markets are in equilibrium.

Page 233

Technology is the current stock of ideas about how to make output. Technical progress or better technology needs both invention, the discovery of new ideas, and innovation to incorporate them into actual production techniques.

Page 235

Along the steady-state path, output, capital and labour grow at the same rate. Hence output per worker y and capital per worker k are constant.

Page 236

In a growing economy, capital widening gives each new worker as much capital as that used by existing workers. Capital deepening raises capital per worker for all workers.

Page 237

Labour-augmenting technical progress increases the effective labour supply.

Page 239

The convergence hypothesis says poor countries should grow quickly but rich countries should grow slowly.

The zero-growth proposal argues that, because higher output has adverse side effects such as pollution and congestion, we should therefore aim for zero growth of measured output.

Section 11-2

Page 243

The business cycle is short-term fluctuation of output around its trend path.

Page 244

A political business cycle is caused by cycles in policy between general elections.

Page 245

The accelerator model of investment assumes that firms guess future output and profits by extrapolating past output growth.

Page 246
The multiplier–accelerator model explains business cycles by the dynamic interaction of consumption and investment demand.

Page 248
Real business cycles are output fluctuations caused by fluctuations in potential output itself.

Chapter 12

Section 12-1

Page 253
The law of comparative advantage says that countries specialise in producing and exporting the goods that they produce at a lower relative cost than other countries.

Page 254
The gains from trade are additional output of some goods with no loss of other goods.

Page 255
Intra-industry trade is two-way trade in goods made by the same industry.

Page 256
Trade policy operates through import tariffs, export subsidies and direct quotas on imports and exports.
An import tariff is a tax on imports.

Page 259
When a country affects the price of its imports, the optimal tariff makes individual importers take account of their effect on the price that other importers must pay.
The principle of targeting says that the best way to meet an aim is to use a policy that affects the activity directly. Policies with side effects are second-best because they distort other activities.

Page 262
A quota is a ceiling on import quantities.

Section 12-2

Page 264
Less developed countries (LDCs) have low levels of per capita output.

Page 266
Primary products are agricultural goods and minerals, whose output relies heavily on the input of land.

Page 267
Import substitution replaces imports by domestic production under the protection of high tariffs or import quotas.

Page 268
Export-led growth stresses output and income growth via exports, rather than by displacing imports.

Page 270
Aid is an international transfer payment from rich countries to poor countries.

Section 12-3

Page 273
Globalisation is the increase in cross-border trade and influence on the economic and social behaviour of nation states.

Index